The Last Male Bastion

The title of this book is a proper summation of its contents. While women have made great inroads in other areas of power and leadership, for instance politics, they are still almost shut out of the boardroom of public companies in the United States. Those who reach CEO status often find their tenure short and securing another position of equal authority very difficult. This title profiles 21 women CEOs, examines how they got there, and the reasons for their success that may serve as lessons for other women who aspire to powerful positions.

Douglas M. Branson received his B.A. from the University of Notre Dame and his J.D. from Northwestern University. He earned an LL.M. from the University of Virginia, specializing in corporate law and securities regulation. Before joining the faculty at Pittsburgh, Professor Branson taught at Seattle University. He has been a visiting professor at a number of schools, including the University of Alabama as Charles Tweedy Distinguished Visiting Professor, the University of Hong Kong as Paul Hastings Distinguished Visiting Professor, the University of Washington (Seattle) as Condon-Faulknor Distinguished Professor, Cornell University, Arizona State University, Washington University (St. Louis), and universities in Australia, New Zealand, Hong Kong, Malaysia, Indonesia, Belgium, Ireland, France, Germany, Spain, South Africa, and England. He holds a permanent faculty appointment as Senior Fellow at the University of Melbourne, Australia, in its Masters of Law Program.

Also by the Author

Corporate Governance (1993)
Problems in Corporate Governance (1997)
Understanding Corporate Law (with A. Pinto) (1999) (2nd edn. 2004)
  (3rd edn. 2009)
Forensic Social Work (with R. Barker) (1995) (2nd edn. 2000)
Boardroom Chronicles (2002)
Questions and Answers: Business Associations (2004)
*No Seat at the Table—How Corporate Governance and Law Keep Women Out of
  the Boardroom* (2007)
Business Enterprises: Legal Structures, Governance, and Policy
  (with J. Heminway et al.) (2009)

The Last Male Bastion

Gender and the CEO Suite in America's
Public Companies

Douglas M. Branson

Routledge
Taylor & Francis Group

NEW YORK AND LONDON

First published 2010
by Routledge
270 Madison Avenue, New York, NY 10016

Simultaneously published in the UK
by Routledge
2 Park Square, Milton Park, Abingdon, Oxon OX14 4RN

Routledge is an imprint of the Taylor & Francis Group, an informa business

© 2010 Taylor & Francis

Typeset in Garamond by
Swales & Willis Ltd, Exeter, Devon
Printed and bound in the United States of America on acid-free paper by
Sheridan Books, Inc.

Library of Congress Cataloging-in-Publication Data
  Branson, Douglas M.
  The last male bastion : gender and the CEO suite in America's public
companies / Douglas M. Branson.
     p. cm.
  Includes bibliographical references and index.
  1. Women chief executive officers—United States.   2. Glass ceiling
(Employment discrimination)—United States.   I. Title.
  HD6054.4.U6.B728 2010
  338.7082′0973—dc22

                                                          2009024215

ISBN 10: 0–415–87295–2 (hbk)
ISBN 10: 0–415–87296–0 (pbk)
ISBN 10: 0–203–86566–9 (ebk)

ISBN 13: 978–0–415–87295–9 (hbk)
ISBN 13: 978–0–415–87296–6 (pbk)
ISBN 13: 978–0–203–86566–8 (ebk)

To the memory of my parents, Joseph W. and Anne S. Branson

Contents

Preface

Hillary Clinton came very close to being the Democratic nominee for president and is President Obama's secretary of state. Nancy Pelosi is speaker of the house. Barbara Boxer and Dianne Feinstein are the U.S. senators from California. Both senators from Washington State, Patty Murray and Maria Cantwell, as well as both senators from Maine, Olympia Snowe and Susan Collins, are women.[1] Two predecessor secretaries of state, Condoleezza Rice and Madeline Albright, are women.

Angela Merkel is the German chancellor. Women head governments in Argentina and Chile. Among the member states of the Organization for Economic Cooperation and Development (OECD), one half of the 30 member nations, and all of those in Europe or North America, have 20 percent or more female members of parliament, with Scandinavian countries in the ascendancy (Sweden, 47 percent; Norway, Finland and Denmark, 40 percent).[2] In the United States, 17 of the 100 senators are women.[3]

Also in the United States, 23 percent of the presidents and chancellors of colleges and universities are women. Among the most prestigious universities, in the Ivy League, 50 percent of the presidents are women.

In 1980, President Reagan appointed Jean Kirkpatrick as ambassador to the United Nations, and in 1981, Sandra Day O'Connor as the 109th and first female justice of the United States Supreme Court. In 1980, Margaret Thatcher became the United Kingdom's prime minister.

Yet until 1997, not one *Fortune 500* (the largest companies by revenues) U.S. company had a woman CEO. In 1997, Jill Barad at Mattel and Marion Sandler at Golden West Financial, both of whom this book portrays, became the first(s), although the number was again reduced to one, as Golden West Financial dropped out of the *Fortune 500*.

Early in 2000, the Mattel board of directors in effect dismissed Jill Barad, leaving the number of women CEOs in major corporations at two: Carleton Fiorina, whom Hewlett-Packard named CEO in July 1999 (removed from office in 2005), and Andrea Jung, whom Avon Products appointed late in 1999 (still in office). In 2001, with the addition of Cinda Hallman at Spherion Corp. (temporary staffing solutions), which has since fallen out of the *Fortune 500*, as well as the re-entry of Golden West into the *Fortune 500*, with CEO Marion Sandler, the number rose from two to four, or eight-tenths of one percent[4] (see Figure 1).

As of early 2009, there are 15 women CEOs in the *Fortune 500* and 25 in the Fortune 1000,[5] which marks significant progress. From a relative viewpoint, in a decade we have moved from none or one to two, then to four, eight, ten, and then 14, back to 11 and now at 15. On an absolute scale, however, the number seems paltry and lags far behind the expectations.

Figure 2 represents the number of female CEOs after the significant "breakthrough" during 2001–2002, when Anne Mulcahy became CEO at Xerox and Pat Russo moved into the CEO suite at Lucent (Chapter 5).

Women account for slightly over 50 percent of the workforce and 50 percent of the middle managers in U.S. corporations.[6] Women have graduated from law and MBA (graduate business) schools in great numbers since the late 1970s.[7] Today they account for nearly 40 percent of the MBA graduates and 50 percent of the law graduates, up from a not insignificant 30 percent and 40 percent, respectively, in the mid-1980s. Yet women are only 12 percent of the senior managers and 4 percent of the most senior executives, sometimes referred to as the bylaw officers (Secretary, COO, CFO, CMO, CLO, collectively the "C suite").[8] Women hold only 3 percent of CEO positions in the *Fortune 500* and 2.6 percent in the Fortune 1000 (see Figure 3).

This book attempts three things. First, Part I chronicles the careers of 15 women CEOs, as well as the careers of women who have in the past achieved notoriety as CEOs of large business organizations, namely, Jill Barad, Carleton Fiorina, Marion Sandler, Patricia Russo, Meg Whitman, and Paula Rosport Reynolds.[9] The portraits give to those on the floor views of women at the very top of the up escalator. Second, Part II evaluates reasons why women have not achieved in the corporate world anything resembling their successes,

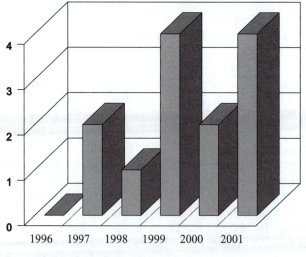

Figure 1 Women CEOs 1996–2001.

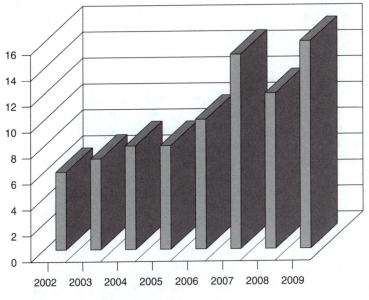

Figure 2 Women CEOs 2002–2009.

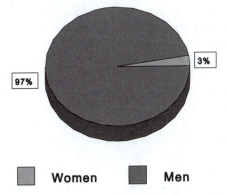

Figure 3 Women vs Men CEOs: January 2009.

say, in the political arena, or what we would predict from the numbers of women matriculating at law and business schools since the mid-1970s. In business, there is a "leaky pipe," with a great flow of women at the intake, but just a trickle at the outfall 20 or so years later. While we might not expect parity, we very well might expect that 12 percent, or 15 percent, or more, not 3 percent, of the corporate CEOs would be women. Why the leaky pipe?

This book is about pathways women have taken to become CEOs of major corporations. It is *not* about what kind of CEO is "right" or "best" once they get there, other than some suggestion as to which kind of CEO model (the "plowhorse" versus the "showhorse") may be more appropriate than others for women to emulate on the way up. This volume does not hold up one model as the paradigm, examining particular women CEOs to see if they fit it. Instead, the analysis proceeds deductively. Let's hold up the careers of 21 women CEOs first, pointing out a few do's and don'ts along the way, then move on in a comprehensive way to see why more have not reached the pinnacle and why those who did succeeded.

Thus, third, Part III bases itself upon what may be gleaned from the careers of women who have risen to the top (Part I), and upon the reasons why greater numbers have not advanced (Part II). This book articulates means whereby aspiring women may rise toward the pool of corporate executives from which a board of directors, or CEO, or both, might chose senior managers or successor CEOs. One salient observation is that, while scores of advice books exist advising women how they might succeed, almost all of them are wrong. Then, now that women have achieved equality in many sectors, a new paradigm is necessary for a new century. While the advice books may have once contained a kernel of truth ("Be Aggressive," "Be Assertive"), they are unidimensional and outmoded.

In 2007, this author published *No Seat at the Table—How Corporate Governance and Law Keep Women Out of the Boardroom*.[10] The studies reported there, of the *Fortune 500*, conclude that, while women have succeeded better at becoming corporate directors than they have in becoming CEOs, the reported numbers do not tell the entire story, and lag behind expectations. For example, as of 2006, 51.2 percent of U.S. corporations had no or only one (out of, say, 10, 11, 13, 14 or 15) female director[11] and, more often than not, the sole woman was a "token." Many corporations who market their products primarily to women, such as Hershey, McDonald's, Nike, had only one, or in rare instances two, women directors.[12] Corporations in information technology were worse: Apple, Microsoft, Micron Technology, Intel, and Oracle, had no women directors.[13]

Reality also lags behind the numbers. Leading organizations over-report the number of women on corporate boards, and preeminent publications, such as the *Wall Street Journal*, accept inflated numbers as gospel.[14] Catalyst, the leading U.S. organization promoting women in business, consistently reports the number of directorships (15.2 percent in 2008, up from 13.6 percent in 2003 and 11.2 percent in 1999)[15] and the number of directors who are female, while the latter is much lower, perhaps less than 11–12 percent.[16] The difference between directorships held by women, and the number of women who are directors, highlights that major corporations chose the same women over and over again. The number of women "trophy directors" (those who hold four or more board seats) climbed from 29 in 2001 to 80 in 2005 while the number of men trophy directors decreased rapidly.[17]

A troubling number of women are super trophy directors. University of Indiana Law Professor Susan Bayh, wife of U.S. Senator Evan Bayh, sits on nine boards; business consultant Bonnie Hill sits on eight; former Renssalaer Polytechnic President Shirley Jackson sits on seven, as does Atlanta-based

Jackie Ward, former CEO of Computer Generation, Inc. Former PepsiCo executive Brenda Barnes—before Sara Lee named her CEO—sat on seven as well.[18] Because of the ubiquity of trophy directors, both among women and persons of color, "[t]here is no real diversity in the diversity of corporate boards."[19]

Prevalence of women trophy directors is important as evidence that the pool of women from which boards of directors might choose CEOs is not growing. That major corporations must repeatedly choose the same women indicates that the pool from which corporations chose senior executives, which overlaps with the pool from which corporations chose directors, is static. Fewer women than could be expected are percolating vertically upwards within corporate organizations.[20]

That said, the women occupying the CEO suite at major corporations as of May 2009, are:

- *Patricia Woertz*, CEO, Archer Daniels Midland Co., Decatur, Illinois (2009 *Fortune 500* rank 27), agricultural and food products processing; born 1953; appointed May 1, 2006; reported annual salary $7.6 million.
- *Angela Braly*, CEO, Wellpoint, Inc., Indianapolis, Indiana (2009 rank 32), health insurance and managed care; born 1962; appointed June 1, 2007; reported annual salary $9.1 million.
- *Indra K. Nooyi*, CEO, Pepsico, Inc., Purchase, New York (rank 52), beverages and snack food products; born 1955; appointed October 1, 2006; reported annual salary $11.8 million.
- *Irene Rosenfeld*, Kraft Foods, Inc., Northfield, Illinois (rank: 53), processed food products; born 1953; appointed June 2006 (spun off by Altria Group, April 2008); salary $11.3 million.
- *Mary F. Sammons*, CEO, Rite Aid, Inc., Camp Hill, Pennsylvania (rank 100), drug and medium box retail chain; born 1946; appointed June 2003; salary $4.3 million.
- *Carol Meyrowitz*, CEO, TJX Co., Framingham, Massachusetts (rank 131), discount retailing; born 1955; appointed January 2007; reported annual salary $7.6 million.
- *Ann Mulcahy*, CEO, Xerox, Inc., Norwalk, Connecticut (rank 147), photocopiers, office products and services; born 1952; appointed January 1, 2002; reported annual salary $13.5 million.
- *Brenda Barnes*, CEO, Sara Lee Corp., Downers Grove, Illinois (rank 199), baking and food products; born 1953; appointed February 2005; reported annual salary $8.7 million.
- *Andrea Jung*, CEO, Avon Products, Inc., New York, New York (rank 255), beauty products and retailing; born 1957; appointed November 1999; reported annual salary $13.7 million.
- *Susan M. Ivey*, CEO, Reynolds American, Inc., Winston Salem, North Carolina (rank 294), tobacco products; born 1957; appointed January 2004; reported annual salary $9.5 million.

- *Christina Gold*, CEO, Western Union, Greenwood Village, Colorado (rank 451), wire and money transfer services; born 1948; appointed September 2006; reported annual salary $9.4 million.[21]

A recent exit is *Patricia F. Russo*, CEO, Alcatel-Lucent Co., Murray Hill, New Jersey and Paris (2008 rank 282), telecommunications hardware; born 1953; appointed January 2002; reported annual salary $3.58 million. CEO Russo resigned in July 2008, effective upon the board appointing a successor, which it did a short time later.

When Ms. Russo resigned, the number of female CEOs declined to 12 in office. Another recent exit was *Paula Rosport Reynolds* who, in September 2008, oversaw the sale of Safeco Insurance (2008 rank 388) to Liberty Mutual Insurance of Boston for $6.2 billion (*Paula Rosport Reynolds*, CEO, Safeco Insurance, Seattle, Washington, home and other casualty insurance; born 1957; appointed January 2006; reported annual salary $6.14 million). With Ms. Reynolds' exit, the number declined to 11, to be followed by a surfeit of appointments over the succeeding months, including:

- *Lynn Laverty Elsenhans*, CEO, Sunoco Inc., Philadelphia, Pennsylvania (rank 41), petroleum refining and distribution; born 1956; appointed August 1, 2008; reported annual salary $1.31 million.
- *Ellen Kullman*, CEO, E.I. DuPont de Nemours, Wilmington, Delaware (rank 75), chemicals and coatings; born 1956; appointed January 1, 2009; salary $4.6 million.
- *Laura Sen*, BJ's Wholesale Club, Inc., Natich, Massachusetts (rank 269), volume discount retailing clubs; born 1957; appointed February 1, 2009; reported annual salary $1.502 million.
- *Carol A. Bartz*, CEO, Yahoo!, Sunnnyvale, California (rank 345), internet websites and search engine; born 1949; appointed January 13, 2009; annual salary unknown.

This book profiles 15 sitting CEOs, as well as the recent exits (Ms. Russo; Ms. Reynolds; and *Meg Whitman*, CEO, Ebay, Inc., San Jose, California (rank 303), online auction services; born 1956; appointed March 1998; reported annual salary $15.74 million (resigned March 1, 2008)). The portraits also include as important historical figures *Jill Barad*, Mattel Toy (resigned January 2000); *Carleton Fiorina*, Hewlett-Packard (resigned February 2002); and *Marion Sandler*, Golden West Financial (sold to Wachovia Bank, April 2007).

On May 22, 2009, Xerox Corp. announced Anne Mulcahy's retirement, effective July 1, 2009. The number of female CEOs remained at 15, however, as Ms. Mulcahy was succeeded by Ursula Burns, who is the first African American woman to head a major U.S. publicly held corporation.[22]

"One could argue that at the top [CEO] level, men and women are held to the same standard."[23] That may be true in most areas but not for salary. Only one woman, ex-CEO Meg Whitman at Ebay, at $15.74 million annually, exceeded the average compensation of CEOs (mostly male) of U.S. large cap public companies, which averaged $13 million in 2007. Among women in business overall, Ms. Whitman suffers by comparison with Safra Catz, CFO of Oracle, Inc., who earned $26.1 million in 2006, and Susan Decker, who while CFO of Yahoo.com earned $24.3 million.[24] Below are the compensation totals for the top five male corporate CEOs in 2007, the last year before the U.S. economy begin slipping into a recession:

- Larry Ellison, Oracle, $192.92 million
- Frederic Poses, Trane, $127.10, million
- Aubrey McClendon, Chesapeake Energy. $116.89 million
- Angelo Mozilo, Countrywide Financial, $102.84
- Howard Schultz, Starbucks, $98.60 million.[25]

By contrast, the totals for the top five female CEOs pale by comparison:

- Meg Whitman, eBay, $15.74 million
- Anne Mulcahy, Xerox, $10.69 million
- Indra Nooyi, Pepsico, $9.37 million
- Andrea Jung, Avon Products, $9.34 million
- Brenda Barnes, Sara Lee Corp., $8.69 million.[26]

The all-time "King" of CEO compensation is Larry Ellison of Oracle, who earned $706 million in 2002, mostly through the exercise of stock options.

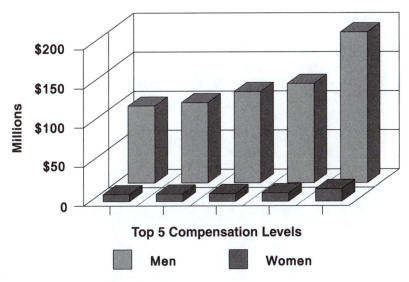

Figure 4 CEO compensation 2007.

The "Crown Prince" is Michael Eisner, who, as CEO of the Walt Disney Company, earned \$576 million in 1998.[27]

Other books exist about CEO compensation.[28] The purpose of this book is to shed some light on how to get there, that is, the CEO suite, where compensation can become an additional issue.

Pittsburgh, Pennsylvania
May 26, 2009

Acknowledgments

I am thankful to the reference librarians at the University of Pittsburgh School of Law, Linda Tashbook, Marc Silverman, Valerie Weiss, and Susanna Leers. With great patience, they tracked down obscure books, facts, and figures for me. I would like to thank my colleague, Professor Richard Delgado, Seattle University School of Law, who read and commented upon the manuscript.

I would also like to thank the students in my Spring, 2008 and Spring, 2009 seminars at the University of Pittsburgh School of Law, "Diversity In Corporate Governance." They supplied me with much of the factual material with which to construct portraits of the newer or lesser known women CEOs.

My editor, John Szilagyi, and his assistant, Sara Werden, at Routledge Press, were patient and understanding.

Last of all, my copy-editor, Janice Baiton, Cambridge, UK, was thoroughly proficient and professional.

Part I

Portraits of Women CEOs

1 The Fall of Jill Barad at Mattel Toy

"Be patient but not passive," advice women in business often receive, is guidance Jill Barad never followed. Showing no patience at all, she brashly demanded progressively better jobs and pay. She showed up on her first day at work wearing purple boots and miniskirt. When she thought it was needed for emphasis, she used profanity. She pushed the pedal to the metal, all the way, for 15 years. It took her to the corner suite, where in 1997 she became the first female CEO in the *Fortune 500*, crashing through the glass ceiling at Mattel, Inc., the Los Angles toy maker.

There was little fanfare when the Mattel board of directors named Barad. There was similarly little fanfare when the board "accepted" her resignation in February 2000. Publicly, Mattel board members stated "they were willing to give her twice as much time to pull it off because of who she was."[1] Privately, many rooted for her to fail.

In the business world, Jill Barad was unconventional. She "looked and acted like a Hollywood star." She wore bright colors, "with accouterments such as fur collars and cuffs,"[2] much like the Barbie doll line she nurtured. *Fortune* named her one of the 50 most powerful women in the United States (6th), *People* one of the "Fifty Most Beautiful People."[3] She reveled in "puff publicity."[4]

As with her appearance, her leadership style was unconventional. Subordinates at Mattel alternatively described her as "nurturing" or "vicious."[5] She had an aggressive "hands on style of management." Less generously, critics alleged her to be of "sharp tongue and combative nature." She "obsessed over the slightest details of 'her' toys" at Mattel.[6]

Despite her high profile, Jill Barad was dismissed, after three years in office. In an 8-hour emergency meeting, the Mattel board of directors fired her. What went wrong?

Early Indeterminacy

Jill Elikann Barad is the Queens, New York daughter of a producer for NBC. As a youth, she longed for a show business career, performing for her family by singing Broadway show tunes. "I'd try to go to sleep, and she'd be standing on her bed, belting out songs from Oklahoma or the Sound of Music," says her sister, Jo-Anne. In her first job, as a teenage cashier at her grandparents' pharmacy, Jill Elikann's exuberance spilled over. She loved "to learn to meet customers, how to sell, how to talk. She took everything in."[7]

After graduating from Queens College, Barad says of herself: "I had no clue what I wanted to do. I just saw jobs as fun. I had no goals." She viewed the life ahead as an opportunity to layer various experiences on top of one another: "[T]he idea of trying everything is important. Somehow all your experiences come together . . . mak[ing] you multidimensional."[8]

She acted on childhood aspirations. Jill Elikann went to Hollywood to pursue an acting career, landing a part playing "Miss Italian America" in a 1974 Dino De Laurentis movie, *Crazy Joe*. To her surprise, the childhood actress found Hollywood to be "silly." She took a job at Coty Cosmetics as an East Coast traveling sales representative.

Managing Coty's brands, she found that retailers hid Coty's cosmetics, giving them limited shelf space. So, on her own, Jill Elikann built a proto-type wall display. She forwarded her design to corporate headquarters. It was a hit. One of her supervisors at Coty recalls that "She knew conceptually what could be done to make products look better . . . [w]e used her display for twenty years."[9]

After meeting movie producer Tom Barad, in 1978 Jill Elikann returned to Los Angeles, where the couple married. Jill Barad quit her job, after finding that she was pregnant with the first of two sons.[10]

Ascent Through the Ranks

Jill Barad re-entered the workforce in 1981, as a $38,000 a year product manager for Mattel, a position she had found through a "headhunter."[11] Her first product at Mattel, called a "Bad Case of Worms," was a flop but Barad's home-made advertising campaign seemed to move some product. After the product flopped, Barad went straight to the CEO, Tom Kalinske. She stormed into his office, asking "What the f . . . do I have to do to get a decent assignment around here?"

Mattel assigned Barad to market an action figure for girls, She-Ra, Princess of Power—an attempt to capitalize on the popularity of Master of the Universe, an action figure for boys. She-Ra ultimately flopped too, but Mattel executives were impressed with Barad. In 1982, they promoted Barad to the position of marketing director for the Barbie doll product line, after she had been at Mattel for a year.[12]

Barad became known as the "woman who saved Barbie." But she did much more. When Barad took charge of the Barbie product line, the average American girl had only one Barbie. By the time Barad moved on from mar-keting the Barbie line, the average American girl had eight Barbies, plus countless outfits of doll clothing and accessories. Barad marketed Barbies to adult collectors. She introduced a Barbie Doll gift voucher system for the holiday season. Barad employed market segmentation and brand proliferation within the Barbie line to increase sales.[13]

At the Management Level

By 1984, Barad was well on the way to creating a Barbie empire within Mattel. In that year, Mattel promoted her to a vice-president title, with the task of creating modern roles for Barbie to convert the product from blonde bombshell into "a doll for the 90s."

While Barad's career was taking off, overall Mattel was in trouble. The video game business had been unable to compete with Nintendo, leaving Mattel on the brink of bankruptcy. Barad's continued success with the Barbie line stood in contrast, suggesting a route out of Mattel's troubles.[14] Yet Barad's quick rise, her success, and her aggression did not sit well with some at Mattel. She recalls, "Many men hated me. I think it can be a tough thing for a man to lose to a woman."[15]

Barad's marketing prowess, though, won over critics. In 1985 she created "Day-to-Night Barbie," the first of many Barbie "theme dolls." She devised a slogan for the new Barbie line: "We girls can do anything!" Each new Barbie was a success in the marketplace. Barad had "executed [her marketing game plan] beyond anyone's wildest dreams."[16]

In 1986, Mattel promoted Barad to executive vice-president. Her business prowess enabled Mattel again to escape bankruptcy in 1987 when the wave it had been riding, action figure toys, crashed. The Barbie line's sterling performance offset the poor performance of Mattel's action figure collection. In 1989, Mattel promoted Barad to president of the girls and activity division. In 1990, she became president of Mattel USA.[17]

Despite her rise in the corporate organization, Barad remained obsessed with Barbie. In the company, she was known for "her overweening attention to detail, monitoring doll designs down to minor details on their faces." She defended her hands-on approach by saying that "[w]hat I do in my job, first and foremost, is protect Barbie."[18] Her obsession was logical, for it had brought great personal success and for Mattel it had averted failure. In the eight years Barad had been involved, Barbie annual sales had gone from $235 million to $1.5 billion.[19]

The Slipper Fits

Within Mattel, Barad complemented her attention to detail with an aggressive approach. One colleague remembers that "[s]he was never afraid to go in and ask for a raise. She would just go in and tell people what she wanted and ask: 'What do I have to do to get it?' " In 1992, she entered Mattel CEO John Amerman's office. She threatened to leave Mattel if Amerman did not assure her that she would succeed him. He would not make that promise: "There was some trepidation on both sides. My retirement was still a long way away." Barad was 20 years younger than Amerman, and a much more "spontaneous and emotional" individual than Amerman, who was "calm" and "distinguished."

Later in 1992, Amerman had a change of heart, prompted by Reebok's courtship of Barad, which culminated in a Barad house hunting trip to Boston, Massachusetts. He called Barad back, assuring her that she would be Amerman's successor as CEO. In 12 years, she had risen from entry level to being the nation's second highest paid female executive. In 1996, Mattel paid her $6.17 million.[20]

On August 22, 1996, the Mattel board of directors named Jill Elikann Barad CEO, effective January 1, 1997. Journalists portrayed her as "the most powerful business woman in the nation."[21]

The Parade of Horribles

It was not an auspicious time to assume the position. Although Mattel had recovered well from its troubles in the 1980s, with seven straight years of double digit sales and profit growth, in July 1996 Mattel reported a flat quarter. Mattel had also failed in its bid to acquire the second largest U.S. toy maker, Hasbro. Barad had been the lead executive on the 1996 attempt. Mattel had to withdraw its $5.2 billion bid after the Department of Justice raised antitrust objections and the controlling Hassenfeld family became skittish. The failed Hasbro bid was seen as a "major public relations blow" to Mattel.[22]

Mattel shareholders had also sued Barad and other Mattel executives in the Delaware Chancery Court, alleging that Mattel executives "inflated sales and disguised profits of its Disney products, allowing management to collect millions of dollars in incentive pay." Mattel's toys based upon Disney's *Hunchback of Notre Dame* performed poorly, resulting in a $40 million earning shortfall.[23]

Barad, though, consistently promised good things to Wall Street. She publicized Mattel's goals of 10 percent increases in sales and 15 percent in profits. Under her leadership, Mattel was to decrease dependence on the U.S. market, from 65 to 50 percent of sales, entering new markets worldwide and strengthening its European presence.[24]

In February 1997, Mattel announced earnings for the fourth quarter 1996. They were flat: 41 cents per share compared to 40 cents in 1995. Mattel also took a one-time $15.1 million charge against earnings to settle the Delaware Disney products litigation.[25]

In March, the Federal Trade Commission gave Mattel the go-ahead ("Hart–Scott–Rodino clearance" based upon information which a prospective acquirer must furnish the government under the Hart–Scott–Rodino antitrust legislation) for Mattel's proposed acquisition of Tyco, the third largest toy maker. Barad hailed the acquisition as an opportunity for Mattel-Tyco to "expand their business into 36 countries." But the $755 million acquisition, as well as other merger activity, would cause Mattel to take a one-time charge of $275 million against earnings for consolidation expense.

Barad then announced that Mattel-Tyco would eliminate 2,700 jobs, nearly 10 percent of their combined workforce, mainly by closing down "noncore" lines of business. About the same time she began pulling back from optimistic projections. Now, due to the Tyco acquisition, Mattel anticipated only 7 percent annual sales growth. European sales were flat. The Fisher Price education toy line was not faring well.[26]

Counterpoint

One bright spot was the Barbie line, to which Barad paid particular attention. Barbie sales rose to $1.7 billion in 1996.[27] Barad announced that Mattel had teamed with Avon Products to launch Barbie in the People's Republic of China, a market of 1.4 billion. The Avon venture arranged for Avon representatives to sell Mattel products in the United States, along with "Barbie cosmetics."[28]

After a spate of bad news, things picked up. Mattel finished 1997 with earnings of $285 million on sales of $4.8 billion. Barad received $10.6 million in overall compensation. Mattel shares had risen from $27 to the mid-thirties.[29]

But Barbie was approaching 40 years of age. Sales of the doll sank 17 percent in the first quarter of 1998. Toy "R" Us, Mattel's largest customer, was encountering difficulties, discontinuing many of Mattel's toy lines. Barad vowed to double Mattel's sales abroad to fill the gap the Toys "R" Us cut back represented and to maintain growth.[30]

During the second quarter of 1998, Mattel's earnings were 20 percent lower than the previous year. Barbie sales had fallen 15 percent during the second quarter when compared to the previous year. The shrinkage in Barbie sales appeared to be taking on permanence. At the time of these announcements, July 1998, the stock held up well, reaching $41.[31]

By September the share price was down to $29.25. Toys "R" Us business would be off as much as $200 million in 1998. Mattel lowered its per share earnings estimate from $1.95 to $1.80.[32]

Then, in December, Mattel stunned Wall Street with drastic revisions. There had been an "unforseen slowdown in shipments following Thanksgiving." For 1998 sales would fall $500 million below projections. The earnings forecast was revised downward again, to $1.20 per share.[33]

The "Big Dumb" Acquisition

Trying to put some positive spin on things, on the same day in December 1998, Mattel and Barad announced that they would expend $3.04 billion to acquire The Learning Company (TLC), maker of Myst and Carmen San Diego ("Where in the U.S. is Carmen San Diego?" "Where in the World is Carmen

San Diego?"), software for highly popular interactive computer games. Through this acquisition, Barad hoped to update the Mattel line, increasing profitability. But, immediately speculation began that Mattel had overpaid drastically.[34]

For 1999, Mattel made conservative projections of 5 to 7 percent growth, "significantly below our typical double digit levels." "We would rather under promise than under deliver," Barad told analysts. Still, the optimist in Barad showed through. She talked of renewed hope for increased Barbie sales due to the doll's upcoming fortieth birthday.[35]

Then TLC began to loom large. In July, Mattel announced that TLC would produce an "expected loss" for the year. At Mattel, sales of Barbie, Disney and Sesame Street merchandise were all falling.

For third quarter 1999, Mattel announced that its results would fall "40 percent to 55 percent short of analysts' estimates." The stock fell to $11.88. To top it all off, Barad discovered that TLC had not informed her of revenue short falls that would now cause a $100 million loss at the TLC unit.[36]

Early in 2000, the stock reached an all-time low of $10.88. There had been a botched acquisition and a bad acquisition. There had been numerous failures to realize on glowing projections. Executives were departing.[37] Wall Street had lost faith in the company's CEO.

The Slipper No Longer Fits

The Mattel board convened a meeting at the New York office of Mattel's investment bankers, Warburg Pincus & Co., whose vice-chairman, John Vogelstein, chaired the Mattel executive committee. After several hours, Vogelstein appeared shoulder-to-shoulder with two other directors—William Rollnick, retired chairman of Genstar Rental Electronics, and Ronald Loeb, vice-president of Williams Sonoma.

Mr. Vogelstein said: "This was a very difficult decision to make from an emotional standpoint. It was a business decision to make. We knew it, she knew it."[38] Privately, an unnamed director expressed a belief that Jill Barad was subjected to unusually close scrutiny: "We can't afford to have such a high profile female chief executive fail."

In her February 3, 2000 press conference, Barad stood tall: "The board of directors and I view the performance of The Learning Company, and its effects on our results, as unacceptable. Therefore, because there must be accountability, the board and I have agreed that I must resign effective today."[39] She slipped out a side door, flying back to Los Angeles.

The Mattel board was generous to its fallen CEO. She would pay $1 for her limousine, office furnishings, and 52-doll Barbie collection. She would receive a $50 million severance, including a $598,000 yearly pension, and forgiveness of a $3 million loan. She exited office with Mattel shares which, even at an all-time low, had a value of $22 million.[40]

Retrospective

What went wrong?

As CEO of Mattel, Jill Barad certainly encountered a "parade of horribles." Every month of her short tenure she, and the company, faced yet another material adverse development that had to be announced to Wall Street and the world. It is difficult to imagine a more unfortunate sequence of events. Of course, other CEOs have weathered protracted spates of adverse developments, one after another but they usually did so by keeping a low profile.[41]

By contrast Barad never lowered her profile. She began her tenure with overly optimistic sales and earnings forecasts. She seemed to have a financial Tourette's syndrome, unable to forestall herself from spewing out glowing projections of revenues and profits. Even when bad news hit she did not shy away. She continued to make forecasts of sales growth. One analyst summed up feelings in the analyst community: "[p]eople feel they were lied to . . . I asked [Mattel executives] hundreds of times . . . and now I am finding that the numbers are not so good. I don't know what to expect from this company."[42] But that is an old lesson—don't promise unless you are certain you can deliver—that most CEOs know and that Jill Barad seemed to be learning but which her false bravado prevented her from implementing.

Did sexism play a role in Wall Street's evaluation of Jill Barad? Ms. Barad was christened repeatedly with sexist and derogatory nicknames: "Toyland's Princess," "The Princess of Power," "The Toy Queen," and "Bossy Barbie."

Was it her obsession with Barbie? Within Mattel a topic of discussion always was "the Jill factor." Underlings criticized her poor grasp of financial matters and her obsession with minute aspects of the Barbie line, at the expense of other business areas. After her departure, one Mattel executive told the press, "When I've seen [Jill Barad] at ad and marketing strategy meetings, everything she says improves the quality or the strategy. But as a long term strategist and as a developer of people . . . No. An ability to accept an alternative point of view? No."[43] Barad puts a more positive spin on her obsession: "Love what you do, do it from your heart of hearts, and do it better than everyone else. Then put yourself in situations where other people can see your passion and its results."[44] She, however, overweighted that otherwise laudable trait, continuing to overweight it after she had become CEO.

Or was it the Big Dumb Acquisition?

Warren Buffet, the "Oracle of Omaha," has had astounding success in investments. He takes share positions in companies such as Gillette (acquired by Proctor & Gamble) or Coca Cola whose brand dominance gives them protection against competition and against new entrants to the business. When asked what he hopes for after he takes a multi-billion dollar position in a stock, Buffet replies: "I just hope that they don't go out and make a big dumb acquisition."[45]

Well, Jill Barad made that "big dumb acquisition." That fact, more than any other, signaled the beginning of the end for her.

Why do CEOs make "big dumb acquisitions," as Barad did? Often the dumb acquisition follows on the heels of a failed one. The failure, as with Mattel's failure to acquire Hasbro, makes the CEO want to prove her mettle even more. We live in an age of deal makers. Pulling off a large acquisition makes a CEO's reputation as a deal maker, a reputation often prized in the business community. Last of all, acquisitions—whether in the form of one large acquisition, or a series—can mask deterioration in a portion of the existing business, thus prolonging the inevitable. The latter was undoubtedly true at Mattel.

Acquisition of The Learning Company made sense because it would bring to Mattel software development capability for educational, entertainment, and multimedia products. But Barad rushed it. Immediately upon completion of the acquisition, financial pundits agreed that Mattel had paid far too much, some calling the price paid "exorbitant."[46] So many surprises followed the TLC acquisition that one has to wonder about the extent of due diligence (pre-closing investigation and examination of the company to be purchased to assure the buyer that all the assets listed exist, the liabilities are not understated, and the earnings not overstated) exercised by Mattel before the acquisition. Proper due diligence eliminates most surprises.

Jill Barad made a "big dumb acquisition." She also may have had talents— marketing brilliance, aggressiveness—more suited to a position as a division head than as CEO of a major public company, who at times must assume statesman-like qualities.

Sequel

New CEO Robert Eckert, former president of Kraft Foods, wasted no time. He closed Mattel's Murray, Kentucky, manufacturing facility. Mattel then would manufacture every toy outside of the United States, in China, Indonesia, Malaysia, Thailand, and Mexico.[47] He quickly put TLC on the sales block, hoping to get as much as one-third of the $3.5 billion Mattel had invested.[48]

The divestiture proved to be as big a debacle as the acquisition. Mattel would sell The Learning Company to Gores Technology Group, a closely held Los Angeles "vulture" group specializing in fallen technology companies. Mattel would receive *no cash*, the purchase price being a share of future TLC earnings, if any. Moreover, Mattel would have to pay off TLC's $500 million in debt, delivering a debt-free asset to Gores Technology. During its brief ownership of TLC, Mattel had absorbed a further $500 million in losses. With the announcement of the sale, Mattel cut its annual dividend from 36 to 5 cents a share, saving $130 million per year.[49]

Analysts agree that Mattel's acquisition of TLC, which cost out of pocket $4.3 billion and resulted in the loss by Mattel of two-thirds of its market capitalization, may have been the biggest "dumb acquisition" of all time.

Tentative Teachings

Below are some lessons learned from Barad's failure (to be elaborated upon later).

Know When and How to Duck

Extreme aggression and assertiveness may or may not help propel a woman upwards but, once in the CEO suite, she must be strategic at times and diplomatic at others. Failed or inaccurate projections become sticks with which analysts and investors will beat the offending CEO, so be wary of all forecasts in the first place.

Resist the Temptation to Make a Reputation as a Deal Maker

The wrong acquisition may unwind the good work that has been done. If times have not been good, an acquisition will only postpone, not mask altogether, a reckoning.

Child Bearing Sooner Rather Than Later?

This book is about getting to the CEO suite, and not necessarily about what to do once there (for example, avoiding improvident acquisitions). One interesting facet of Barad's history is that she had her children first, before commencing her career, contrary to the teachings of the advice books, the admissions practices of MBA schools, and the overwhelming chronology most aspiring women adopt, namely, start a career first and take time out (perhaps) for children later.

Prepare Yourself for the Accounting and Financial Sides of Business

As CEOs, women will have CFOs and comptrollers who deal with such matters on a day-to-day basis. Every CEO, though, must have a working knowledge of managerial accounting, corporate finance, stocks, commodities and the markets, basic economics, and marketing. It is fine to be over-weighted in one area, such as marketing, as was Jill Barad, but not to the exclusion of a facility in all necessary areas, which Barad lacked.

Have a Specialty (The Ying) But don't Overweight It

The yang is that, as a rising executive, with an expertise, whether it be marketing, finance, manufacturing, and the like, don't overweight it and don't rely on it after you have moved on to broader and differing responsibilities.

Balance Your Experiences—Allow Yourself to be Groomed

Some CEO prospects need grooming, either before corporations appoint them or shortly after they get there. Jill Barad certainly did. CEO John Amerman deserves blame. He let Barad's brashness roll over him, with no push back whatsoever. He did not rotate her, however quickly, through some senior management positions, or other departments. Seeing his failure to act, board members should have stepped forward, raising the question of how to give a marketing person some grounding in other fields. In those ways, her predecessor and her board of directors may have set Jill Barad up for failure.

The Aftermath

Seven years after Barad, much remains the same at Mattel. Domestic sales fell 15 percent while overseas sales increased. Early in 2008 the stock stood at $22.[50] Other toy lines have come and gone but Barbie, who in 2009 and amid much fanfare celebrated her fiftieth birthday, remains the flagship.[51] Domestically, Mattel has worked "to leverage the Barbie name into new areas like social networking and fashion." Overseas Barbie sales have increased 13 percent. Mattel has introduced Barbiegirls.com, a free online "play site" for children, and a $60 Barbie digital music player. While children overseas still ask for the doll, domestically children seek accouterments: "[K]ids still care about the brand."

Jill Barad surfaces infrequently. In 2003, the *Wall Street Journal* reported that Ms. Barad had spoken to senior career women at Microsoft about her career path.[52] Otherwise, Barad has dropped from sight, much like a marionette whose strings have been cut.

2 Carleton Fiorina at Hewlett-Packard

Carly Fiorina is truly focused on the success of Carly Fiorina, and of the organization she is leading. Which comes first, I'm not sure.

(Former Lucent Executive)[1]

Pack it in, babe—you stink.

(Financial columnist Christopher Byron in 2001—after Hewlett-Packard failed to meet Fiorina revenue and earnings projections for the fourth successive quarter)[2]

Carly can market the tar out of herself. That's what she's known for.

(Former Hewlett-Packard manager)[3]

Carleton Fiorina is the most celebrated, and controversial, woman CEO of our times. She came to Hewlett-Packard, number 19 on the *Fortune 500* list, as the highest ranking female CEO ever. The media heralded her July 1999 accession as an explosive smash through the glass ceiling.[4] *Fortune* pegged her as the most powerful woman in business for five years running. The HP board removed her from office on February 8, 2005. Only two directors remained in the room to inform her of what the board had done.

Evaluations of her tenure were not mixed. They vary only to the extent of being unfavorable, as opposed to *extremely* unfavorable. The graphic exhortations provided above are not aberrations. At the most favorable, HP employees found her to be as cocksure and judgmental in her opinions assessments as an older sibling would be. Just as often, employees and inves-tors found her to be a raving egomanic, who assiduously fueled "the Carly Buzz Machine" and "All Carly, All of the Time."

A salient exception is Ms. Fiorina's own evaluation of her HP years. Her autobiography *Tough Choices*,[5] has nothing but praise for her abilities. She states at the outset that "I knew we were on the verge of reaping tremendous benefits from all our hard work, and I thought the board knew this too [when they removed me]."[6] In the afterword, she attributes HP's 2006–2009 success "to the massive transformation which had already occurred and which provided a strong and durable foundation" for whoever succeeded her as CEO.[7] But the share price went down and down, and stayed there, while she was CEO, and the revenues and profits never materialized, as she promised.

In 2008, Republican Presidential Nominee John McCain put Carleton Fiorina on his vice-presidential shortlist, despite her shortcomings and the enmity she aroused as CEO. She campaigned extensively on McCain's behalf, both before and after he shortlisted her.

Aside from stagnant share prices and earnings, did Ms. Fiorina do anything to merit invective from news reporters, HP employees, securities analysts, financial reporters, and others—vituperation which exceeds that of any aimed at a corporate CEO in our times? The invectives highlight her failings; they also mask her achievements. The next question is what did she accomplish and how did she achieve it? What were the capabilities and traits which got her there and enabled her to do what she accomplished, or professes to have accomplished, once in office?

Some Highlights

Ms. Fiorina was bold: "a remarkable speaker, an incredibly hard worker, and a top notch salesperson, with relentless drive. Many admire[d] her brilliance, charisma, principled toughness, and kindness."[8] One month after she took office, over a retreat with her managers at Monterey Bay, she achieved reorganization of 87 HP departments into only four components—a task that would take an ordinary mortal years to accomplish. She started the company down the road to reverse what she termed the mentality of "a thousand tribes," or the "silo mentality," in which each of 87 or more work centers acted as its own separate company, rather than as one unified Hewlett-Packard.

Performance did not live up to expectations. Ms. Fiorina consistently ratcheted up forecasts of revenues and earnings, only to have HP fail to reach the projections. The reorganization, which was of her own making, failed to deliver and, despite her claims, has been unwound, at least in part, by successor Mark Hurd.[9]

To emulate IBM, which had great success in consulting, Ms. Fiorina attempted to acquire PricewaterhouseCoopers (PwC) Consulting. The Securities and Exchange Commission (SEC) had forced accounting firms to separate their auditing functions from consulting, the lucrative fees from which compromised auditors' "independence." Sensing the opportunity the divestiture presented, Ms. Fiorina and PwC arrived at a price of $17.5 billion, only to see the "deal crater" when she tried to re-negotiate the price, angering PwC enough that it walked away from the deal.

Then, as has so often been the case when CEOs with outsized egos fail in one acquisition, Ms. Fiorina bound Hewlett-Packard to another—a stock for stock acquisition of Compaq Computer, valued as high as $24.5 billion.[10] The proposed transaction made no sense to anyone other than Ms. Fiorina and HP board members Jay Keyworth and Dick Hackborn, who had suggested it. HP had gone from a proposed "high end" acquisition of consulting capacity to an acquisition in the "junky" part of the high tech business, personal computers (PCs), where economies of scale had become minuscule and margins razor thin. "The visual I see is a slow-motion collision of two garbage trucks," said Sun Microsystems CEO Scott McNealy.[11] The HP Compaq merger seemed to be "the big dumb acquisition" legendary investor Warren Buffett feared.[12]

A final business failing was HP's inability to achieve consistent quarter-to-quarter growth. In her last quarters as CEO, Fiorina was forced again to announce that the company performed below analysts' expectations ($.24 versus $.31 per share) and would do so again in the following (and her last) quarter ($.35–.39 versus an anticipated $.41–.47 per share). She "angrily called the performance 'clearly unacceptable,'" and summarily fired three high-ranking HP executives.[13] HP's share price fell to $16.90.

Under her successor, Mark Hurd, HP's revenues and profits have exceeded expectations in every quarter, spectacularly so, by margins of 30 percent, 38 percent, and 51 percent.[14] The share price has risen as high as $53.48, more than triple what the price had been under Fiorina. HP announced $8 billion share buybacks in 2005 and again in 2006, a sign of robust financial performance.[15] In the third calendar quarter of 2006, under CEO Mark Hurd, HP overtook IBM to become the world's largest technology company, with expected revenue of $92.1 billion,[16] which in the following year grew to $111 billion. HP followed that acquisition with another, of Electronic Data Systems (EDS).

A Comparison

The Fiorina scenario sounds familiar. The previous corporate governance poster girl, Jill Barad, rose from an entry level position to CEO in 12 years, only to have the Mattel board of directors oust her from office after a short tenure. Like Barad, Fiorina was flamboyant—a buzz followed her. Employees called Barad "Princess of Power" and "Bossy Barbie." HP engineers, too, had names for Fiorina: "Armani Carly," and after she ordered massive job cuts, "Chainsaw Carly."

Barad, too, consistently promised too much in terms of revenue and earnings. Barad also attempted, and failed, at a high-quality acquisition (Hasbro versus PwC Consulting). On the rebound, to prove her mettle, Barad caused her company to make the "big dumb acquisition," The Learning Company. Fiorina took her company into a merger with Compaq Computer, which almost everyone criticized. The numbers are bigger at Hewlett-Packard but the parallels between Ms. Barad's and Ms. Fiorina's careers are striking.

Biography

Carleton (Carly) Fiorina is the daughter of Madelon Juergens and Joseph Sneed. Joe Sneed was a professor of law at various law schools before serving as dean of the Duke University School of Law. In 1973, President Nixon, a Duke law graduate, appointed Sneed to the United States Court of Appeals for the Ninth Circuit, based in San Francisco, where he went on to an illustrious career as a federal appellate judge.

Carly went to grammar school in Ithaca, New York, while her father taught at Cornell, and high school in Durham, North Carolina, while her father taught at Duke. She matriculated at Stanford, where in 1976 she received her degree in medieval history. While at Stanford, she spent a summer at Hewlett-Packard. She started law school at UCLA but dropped out. Much to the dismay of her father, she told him that she was "adverse to precedents."[17] A few years later (1980) she completed an MBA at the University of Maryland and, sometime after she had been in the working world, a second advanced degree from the Sloan School of Management at MIT.

She began her career as an account executive for the AT&T Long Lines Division. She thrived in sales, rising to a position with an oxymoronic title of senior vice-president, global marketing—Atlantic and Canadian regions. She also married Frank Fiorina, an AT&T executive who had two young daughters. Carly, as well as Frank, had short prior marriages.

When the split up of AT&T was imminent, Ms. Fiorina spearheaded the spin off of Bell Labs, Western Electric and parts of other divisions into Lucent Technologies: "Fiorina got plucked from a sea of senior men to direct the strategy, orchestrate the IPO, and lead the search for a name and a corporate image."[18]

Lucent went public in April 1996. Although since surpassed by Google and other offerings, Lucent's $3 billion share offering "turned out to be the biggest, most successful IPO in U.S. history."[19]

Lucent in the Sky with Diamonds

With Lucent independent, Ms. Fiorina collected a passel of corporate titles: vice-president, corporate operations, and group president, global service providers. One of her great successes was in the consumer products division, which in 1998 achieved $19 billion in sales under her leadership. Her Lucent mentor, Rich McGinn, termed her "wickedly smart," praising her "unorthodox ways of thinking and her innate knack for selling."

Her meteoric rise at Lucent was not without pratfalls, but they managed not to come to light until after she had begun at HP. One was a joint undertaking with Phillips, NV, the large European conglomerate. Fiorina pushed hard for the venture, which quickly deteriorated and then unraveled completely in one year, causing a $1.5 billion loss. Fiorina never acknowledged failure. "She just packed her bags and walked away," without so much as a farewell to those who had worked beneath her in the joint venture.[20]

In retrospect at least, Lucent executives lay at Fiorina's feet channel stuffing[21] and other improper revenue recognition, as well as an extension of over $8 billion in vendor financing to dubious credit risks. Lucent had to write off the entire amount, which marks the visible start of its unending tales of woe, which Chapter 5 chronicles. One Fiorina biographer goes so far as to say that if HP board members had known about what Fiorina had really done at Lucent, they would never have hired her as HP's CEO.[22]

In July 1999, Ms. Fiorina left Lucent, before its prolonged downward slide, and took up the CEO title at Hewlett-Packard, succeeding Lew Platt.

From Murray Hill to Palo Alto

The HP board had narrowed its list of 100 CEO candidates to four, including Carly Fiorina, based upon her "super sales woman" image. The board required each of the four finalists, who included two women who were high-ranking HP insiders, to sit for psychological assessments, a three-hour interview, and a 900-question test. Such extensive psychological evaluations of CEO finalists were unusual, especially in the fly-by-the seat-of-your-pants high-tech area.

Ms. Fiorina's shortcoming was her background in telecommunications rather than computers. In a later interview, she recalled the sales pitch she used to convince the HP board:

> Look, lack of computer expertise is not Hewlett-Packard's problem. There are loads of people here who can provide that. I've demonstrated an ability to pick up quickly on the essence of what's important. I know what I don't know. And I know that our strengths are complementary. You have deep engineering prowess. I bring strategic vision, which HP needs.[23]

Hewlett-Packard made the announcement of Ms. Fiorina's selection on July 17, 1999. She became the first woman CEO in the *Fortune 25*. She received a $100 million "welcome package." After a torrent of media coverage, Ms. Fiorina disappeared, to begin mapping out her plan for change at HP.

Hewlett-Packard

Fiorina came to a company with deep roots, a distinct culture, and a storied history, about which she seemed to be only dimly aware.

Seemingly, all astounding successes in the Silicon Valley began in garages, as HP's did. Steven Jobs and Steven Wozniak, both former HP employees, built the first Apple computer in Wozniak's garage. A Silicon Valley joke is that, before the announcement of a technological breakthrough, the promoter has to acquire a garage and move the engineer's bench there so that the last component may be inserted and the breakthrough announced in the driveway.

The original garage story dates to before World War II, when in 1938 William Hewlett and David Packard, Stanford University classmates, flipped a coin to see whose name would go first in their partnership. They borrowed $538 from their engineering professor, Frederick Terman, and set to work in Hewlett's garage. Built in the garage at 329 Addison Avenue, the inaugural product was an oscillator which generated audio signals for defense and communications applications. Hewlett and Packard used a kitchen oven to bake enamel on the oscillator's metal cowlings. They designated the oscillator the HP200B to make it seem the product of a mature company, selling eight to the Walt Disney Company for $71.50 each. Disney used the oscillators in developing the soundtrack for *Fantasia*.

Bill Hewlett and Dave Packard were inventive. "In the beginning, we did anything to bring in a nickel," Mr. Hewlett recalled. "We had a bowling lane foul line indicator. We had a thing that would make a urinal flush automatically . . . We had a shock machine to make people lose weight."[24]

By 1947 Hewlett-Packard had revenues of $1.5 million. Packard had the business acumen, becoming the company's public face. Hewlett was the technology geek. He was happiest rubbing shoulders with the company's engineers, which he called "management by walking around." "Management by walking around" became an element of the "HP Way"—a set of informal management principles that many businesses have emulated since the early Silicon Valley and high-tech days.[25] At least two famous business books, *The HP Way* and *Built to Last*, describe management at HP.[26]

HP developed test equipment and other measuring devices, first gaining public attention with its calculator. "Walking around," Mr. Hewlett challenged engineers to develop a calculator that would fit a shirt pocket. In 1972, the product, known as the HP 35 because it had 35 keys, reached the market. Almost overnight it replaced the slide rule, which generations of engineers had worn in cases suspended from their belts:

> Employees were expected to take pride in anything and everything they did. The managers themselves, starting with Hewlett and Packard, understood the work on a technical level [and] could evaluate the quality of their employees simply by walking around . . . The essence of the HP way was integrity and commitment. HP, from the beginning, aspired to be more than just another business. The goal was profit, as it must be in all businesses, but it was also the development of a sense of mission.[27]

Going Public

Bill and Dave, as they were known, took the company public in 1957, selling shares of stock to the public, on a widespread basis, by means of investment bankers acting in an underwriting syndicate. By virtue of their HP sharehold-ings, Bill and Dave became wealthy. By 2000, William Hewlett ranked 26th on *Forbes's* list of the wealthiest Americans, with an estimated $9 billion fortune. The garage where William Hewlett and David Packard began became a state landmark. Hewlett-Packard became known as "The Company That Invented Silicon Valley."

Hewlett and Packard fostered the communal spirit that characterized the early days of the Silicon Valley, then simply the Santa Clara Valley. They encouraged other entrepreneurs through investments and joint ventures. They provided incipient entrepreneurs with management skills they needed to form companies.

Bill and Dave remained simple men, engineers at heart. They decreed that several basic principles would characterize their company, among them: 1) treat all employees with respect; 2) plan for the long term; 3) hold bureau-cracy to a minimum; and 4) never pursue sales for sales growth alone. To encourage innovation, they divided business units which grew too large, creating a new "product group" whenever an existing unit grew too big. Everyone who received a company car, including Bill and Dave, got a Ford Taurus.

Company engineers at the HP Corvallis, Oregon facility developed the inkjet dot matrix printer, supposedly in a workshop no bigger than a large closet, to be followed by engineers at the Boise, Idaho facility, who developed the laser printer. The company became the number two producer of personal computers and the leading producer of printers. Revenues doubled between 1993 and 1997. The company sold its 100th million inkjet printer, and all the ink cartridges and other supplies that went with it. Annual sales reached $50 billion, the number of employees 89,000. The company had 87 autono-mous businesses and 130 product groups.[28]

The engineering focus, the autonomy within the company, and the lack of marketing buzz ("Built to Last") ultimately became a source of stagnation. An observer said of Hewlett-Packard that HP would market sushi as "cold, dead fish." In the late 1990s, insiders said that HP was "sick and endangered," "suffocating." HP was mired in the personal computer age when everyone else had moved on, embracing the internet boom, according to *Forbes* reporter Quentin Hardy:

> HP suffers from turf battles, complacency and slow growth, analyzes decisions endlessly and sends no clear message to a fast-moving market. The maker of big servers doesn't run on "Internet time" and hasn't tagged itself to the Web boom, even as rivals like Sun Microsystems zip by. HP is preoccupied with products when it must focus, instead, on customers.[29]

HP was derisively characterized as part of "the clueless establishment." The disunity of myriad product and business groups led to different HP logos and

100 brand names. HP could not put a figure on advertising costs because costs were spread over far-flung business unit budgets within HP. Since 1995, HP revenue growth had declined—26 percent, then 22 percent, 12 percent, and finally 10 percent in Lewis Platt's last year, while before "HP had grown faster, for longer, than any company in American history . . . an average of 20.2 percent between 1958 and 1995."[30] HP's share price remained in the high seventies while Cisco, Intel, Oracle and Sun share prices shot through the roof.

CEO Carly Fiorina Arrives

After her early management retreat, in summer 1999, Carly Fiorina emerged center stage. She kicked off a $200 million image building advertising campaign, featuring herself. She filmed the first spot in front of the garage where Bill and Dave had developed their first products, touting "the innovative spirit of HP." She appeared on television—Morning Show with Carly, Tom Brokaw with Carly, Japanese television with Carly, CNBC with Carly.

On the *Today Show*, Ms. Fiorina proclaimed to correspondent Jamie Gangell that she did not believe that her gender had ever held her back. Stating that "I have spent a lifetime believing that the most important thing is to focus on what's inside the package," Ms. Fiorina vehemently denied the existence of a glass ceiling, stressing that "a competitive industry cannot afford sexism."[31] Ms. Fiorina refused to accept the title "role model for women."[32]

In December 1999, Carly Fiorina appeared on the cover of *Fortune*, with the headline "The Cult of Carly." Inside, the article bore a second title—"All Carly, All the Time"—dubbing her activities "The Carly Show." "Travels with Carly" described her use of corporate funds to purchase a $45 million Gulfstream IV so that she "could project her image worldwide."

The Gulfstream jet, of course, represented a quantum jump up from the Ford Taurus Bill and Dave drove. HP had always used corporate aircraft in a plebian way: as a taxi service to take engineers and managers to and from its remote outposts in Corvallis, Boise, or San Diego. In fact, immediately before Fiorina had arrived, CEO Platt caused HP to sell off two plush jets as unneeded. Fiorina reversed all this: HP would now use its aircraft in a patrician way. She caused HP to buy the Gulfstream and curtail the taxi service. On one trip alone, using the Gulfstream, Fiorina made eight stops in the United States, five in Asia, and five in Europe—*in one week*. She gave 47 speeches outside the company in one year and 70 in another. She gave high-profile, gang-buster presentations each year at the annual Comdex high-tech trade show in Las Vegas. She appeared on 40-plus magazine covers in her first year alone.

Reviewing her early activity as CEO, one business editorial wondered: "Whose brand was she building anyway?" Her predecessor as CEO, Lew Platt, opined to no one in particular: "[H]er celebrity style is strange to me. I'm of a different era."

Cruising in her Gulfstream at 40,000 feet, Carly was perceived by HP employees as rendering lip service only to Bill Hewlett's "management by walking around." Nonetheless, Fiorina went on record to "[stress] the importance of networking with all levels, saying, 'The worst thing a CEO can do is get disconnected from reality, from the rank and file.' "[33]

In contrast, and more accurately, Fiorina believed that visibility for herself and for a CEO were good for the company, a value she put stock in throughout her career. "It's very important that people know what you're doing. That's how they know what you're capable of."[34] Some agreed with Carly Fiorina's views about self-promotion. "In technology, the CEO really needs to create a buzz around the company," a Paine Webber analyst said "[and] Carly is a buzz machine."[35]

Inside Hewlett-Packard

Ms. Fiorina orchestrated a make over of HP. She tore up the company-wide profit-sharing plan in favor of strict performance-based bonus systems. She decreed that under the plan HP would perform evaluations twice yearly so that HP salespersons would be less likely to coast after they had achieved sales goals for the year.

As has been seen, in a three-day retreat with senior managers she came up with four groups to replace HP's 87 business units. Two front-end groups would focus on consumer activities (marketing, sales, service) and two back-end organizations would devote themselves to designing and manufacturing, respectively, computer products and printer products. In place of the traditional HP, "a collection of stand alone products and producers," the Fiorina HP would become "a customer-focused and integrated provider of information appliances, highly reliable IT [information technology] infrastructure, and e-services."[36]

Insiders perceived there to be both good and bad in the redesigned HP. Some executives worried that managers would feel that they could "not wield 'real authority' if they couldn't control both product development and marketing. 'It took some of the glory, if you wish, out of the job,' " said a recently retired HP executive.[37]

Under the old regime, however, HP products had competed against each other. HP's laser and inkjet printers, accounting for 40 percent of revenues, used incompatible software and network connections, making it difficult and expensive for customers to, say, upgrade from an inkjet to a laser. With its design teams consolidated under the Fiorina regime, HP was able to introduce a fully compatible line of printers.

HP's $20 billion printer business included 60 percent of the inkjet and laser business worldwide. HP sold the printers at margins of 15 to 20 percent. It then sold annually $9 billion in printer supplies. The margin on ink, one of those supplies, was 50 percent.

Yet, of the 15 trillion pages printed each year in the United States alone, only 3.5 percent were printed in desktop publishing. Most corporations still printed, say, a sales brochure using a traditional offset press, shipping the brochures to offices around the company, where the offices keep brochures in a box at the back of a closet or in a file drawer.

Under Fiorina's reorganization, HP developed the strategy of enabling corporations to transmit digital copies of a brochure to offices, to be produced when needed, on HP printers. The print-on-demand method worked for books, magazines, annual reports, and newspapers as well. The Fiorina reorganization facilitated the expansion of the printer market, thus making the "product portfolio" stronger.[38]

HP's product portfolio, computers, servers, and printers, put HP at the intersection of three important vectors: e-services and e-commerce, the internet, and appliances. Besides printing brochures from headquarters, an HP appliance could print stamps from the Postal Service, package stickers from Fed-Ex, and concert tickets from Ticketmaster.

Too Fast a Track?

Fiorina's bold moves might have been too much, too soon: she trod on many toes. In her televised public appearances she "promised to make HP a great company once again." But HP, of course, had never ceased being great. It had not fallen into an abyss.

A manager at the laser printer division noted that "[t]he feeling was, here was Carly, who wasn't a long time in the H-P culture, who doesn't understand our business and the H-P Way, and doesn't understand our strengths, particularly in businesses that were viewed as successful for so long."[39]

In an early appearance before HP workers, Carly shouted "Send me 'The Ten Stupidest Things We Do,' " and walked off the stage.[40] Based upon results and employee satisfaction in a job well done, pre-Carly, Hewlett-Packard seemed to many to be far removed from a place in which "stupid things" were done:

> Fiorina set in motion plans to change nearly every aspect of the company. It would be organized differently, market its products differently, do R & D differently, set strategy differently, deal with customers differently, and reward its employees differently . . . [W]hat Fiorina wanted to do was like trying to change the engine of a 747 in flight . . . perhaps most remarkably, she would do it all on her own.[41]

"The HP way," Ms. Fiorina explained to a reporter, "has become an excuse for all sorts of bad habits, particularly slowness and risk aversion . . . Preserve the best," she said, "reinvent the rest."[42]

No Consistency: Promises and Misses

Early in her tenure, in fall, 1999, CEO Carly Fiorina raised Hewlett-Packard's projections of revenue and earnings growth from 10–13 percent to a "firm" 15 percent.

In November 1999 (Hewlett-Packard is on an October 31 fiscal year), HP missed Fiorina's projections: 1999 revenues were up 10 percent but earnings were flat, up 1 percent from 1998.[43]

On May 16, 2000, HP announced that, as of end of second quarter, revenues were up 15 percent, and earning per share up 15 percent, in line with Fiorina's projections. "We are confident about our momentum going forward," she stated.

In August of 2000, HP's third quarter results were spectacular. Revenues were up 15 percent, earnings per share were up 37 percent. Fiorina: "Based upon our confidence, we're splitting our shares [2 for 1]."

Shortly thereafter, the HP board awarded Ms. Fiorina the title of board chair. HP share price reached $103.94,[44] peaking shortly thereafter at (pre-split) $107.

On November 13, 2000, HP reported revenues up 17 percent and earnings up 9 percent for fiscal 2000. Fiorina raised the ante once again. She set a goal of 17 percent growth in revenues profits for 2001.

Two months later, on January 11, 2001, HP had to announce another "miss" (HP first quarter revenues were flat, earnings up only 6 percent), followed by another miss on April 18, 2001 (for second quarter, 2001, revenues to be down 2–4 percent, earnings to fall 56–67 percent). An HP spokesperson (not Ms. Fiorina) stated: "The U.S. downturn in the consumer market is now spreading to other regions [of the world]." The chronology thereafter:

- May 16, 2001, earnings in second quarter down 62 percent.
- June 6, 2001, at a press conference, despite recent poor performance, Ms. Fiorina projects 10–12 percent growth in revenues and earnings.
- A leading bond rating agency (Moody's) downgrades HP's debt securities.
- HP share price hovers in low thirties.
- September 4, 2001, Ms. Fiorina announces $24 billion acquisition of Compaq Computer. HP share price falls 19 percent and an additional 3.5 percent the following day.
- HP share price reaches a pre-September 11 low and bottoms out at $15.50 on September 17, 2001.

All at once Hewlett-Packard tumbled from the ranks of the "nifty fifty" or "one decision" stocks (the only decision an investor ever has to make is buy).

Carly Fiorina may not have been around long enough to have learnt her lesson about projections of future economic performance—under promise and over deliver. Alternatively, her background was in industries (telecommunications, high tech) and fields (sales) to which those lessons were thought not to apply and optimism was the order of the day.

But, surely, in her cadre of advisers, Ms. Fiorina must have had someone who could have given that advice and schooled her on the lessons of financial history. That no one appears to have done so may be a sign that her lampoon of the "HP Way" and comments about "stupid things we do," coupled with "All Carly, All of the Time" may have come back to haunt her.

The Big Dumb Acquisition? The Compaq Merger

On September 4, 2001, Ms. Fiorina, representing Hewlett-Packard, and Michael Capellas, representing Compaq Computer, announced their plan to merge the companies, to be consummated in early 2002. The events leading up to merger were a textbook example of "how not to do it," a reverse road map:

1. The merger seemed to make no strategic sense either to casual onlookers or industry analysts. The HP Compaq merger represented a pendulum-like swing from high-end aspirations (PricewaterhouseCoopers Consulting) down to the low end, the "junky" part, of the business.
2. Ms. Fiorina indulged in her penchant for rosy forecasts, predicting 20 percent earnings growth in the year following the combination of the two companies.[45]
3. She failed to consult members of the Hewlett and Packard families, plus related foundations, which owned over 18 percent of HP's stock. In fact, she oversaw the elimination from the HP board of all four representatives of the families: David Packard, Susan Packard Orr, and Hewlett son-in-law, Jean-Paul Gimon before and Walter Hewlett after the merger announcement.[46]
4. She agreed to "deal protection" known as a termination, or "goodbye," fee of $675 million, payable to the prospective merger partner (Compaq here) if deal did not close. The $675 million amount, while barely within tolerances in relative amount (2.75 percent of $24.5 billion) in the beginning, became oversize (3.55 percent) as the HP share price and the worth of the merger declined to $19 billion. The fee made it very difficult for HP to abandon the merger or for individual directors to oppose it.

Immediate Reactions

Based upon the announcement, Moody's lowered HP's debt rating two levels because HP was buying a lower quality company. The press compared Carly Fiorina to the "thousands of CEOs [who] have fancied themselves as Morgans-in-the making, shelling out trillions of dollars in a quest to gorge themselves to greatness":

The latest glutton is Carly Fiorina, the CEO of Hewlett-Packard. Last week she announced that H.P. would spend twenty-five billion dollars to acquire Compaq Computer . . . Both H.P. and Compaq have struggled during the economic slowdown . . . But Fiorina insisted that uniting the two firms would solve their problems, creating a company with the size and scope to dominate existing markets . . . This was about as smart as betting all your money on a long shot after a bad day at the track.[47]

Of Compaq Computer, it was said that Ms. Fiorina was "apparently overexposed in impressionable childhood years to the story in which the imprisoned handsome prince is released from a toad's body by a kiss from a beautiful princess."[48] Compaq is a slow growing, unprofitable company in a troubled industry. "Alas, it's a toad that's going to stay a toad," according to one financial columnist.

Projections of 20 percent earnings growth for the merged entity seemed irresponsible. In the fourth quarter ending October 31, 2001, HP's revenues fell 89 percent from the previous year, although the company remained marginally profitable.[49]

Compaq had not earned money in three years, laying off people, firing CEOs and restructuring constantly, losing $2.3 billion since 1998. Compaq forecast that, due to competition from Dell Computer, 2001 sales would decline $10 billion, to $33 billion.[50]

Further Reactions

Perhaps Ms. Fiorina's greatest gaffe was in not consulting the Hewlett and Packard children, along with trustees of the charitable trusts that founders William Hewlett and David Packard created. The David and Lucille Packard Foundation was then the fourth largest in the United States. Eighty percent of its assets were invested in HP shares. The Hewlett Foundation was similar.

More extraordinary, after not being consulted, one by one the intensely private members of the founders' families came forward publicly to oppose the Hewlett-Packard Compaq merger. First was Walter Hewlett, a director of HP who had in September voted in favor of the merger. Speaking on his own behalf, and on behalf of the William and Flora Hewlett Foundation, he told reporters that "This is a bad transaction . . . It would be better if it ends sooner."[51] After hiring consultants to advise them, the Packard children and the Packard Foundation joined the Hewletts.[52] David Packard, a professor of Greek at UCLA, came forward as the family spokesperson. Noting that under Fiorina HP had already laid off 6,000 employees, Mr. Packard keyed in on the human dimension:

[M]r. Packard strongly suggested that the merger was a cruel departure from the values and corporate culture nurtured by the founders, William Hewlett and David Packard.

"The announced logic of this merger plan ... depends on massive employee layoffs," at least 15,000, probably more. While he acknowledged that the founders never guaranteed job security, Mr. Packard added, "I also know that Bill and Dave never developed a premeditated business strategy that treated H.P. employees as expendable."[53]

Last of all, about the time of the merger announcement, when Ms. Fiorina had bound HP to payment of a $675 million terminations fee if HP abandoned the merger, she asked HP employees to take a voluntary 10 percent pay cut. True to the HP Way, a majority of them agreed to do so.[54]

Amid this barrage of criticism, aimed not only at the Compaq merger but at Ms. Fiorina herself, Walter Hewlett announced that he planned to solicit other HP shareholders to vote in opposition to the merger with Compaq—an extraordinary happening (a sitting director publicly opposing his own board of directors) in corporate America.[55] Carly Fiorina and HP won that proxy fight marginally with 52 percent of the votes cast.

Walter Hewlett also filed suit in the Delaware Chancery Court, alleging that, in order to get the Compaq merger approved by a majority of the HP shares, Fiorina had engaged in illegal vote buying (from Deutsche Bank) and had made misleading statements in urging HP shareholders to vote for the merger. He lost in his bid to obtain an injunction. Fiorina saw to it that HP did not re-nominate Walter Hewlett for a seat on the HP board. The last representative of the founding families disappeared. HP and Compaq consummated their merger on May 6, 2002.

More Promises, More Misses and Removal

Carly Fiorina did give a justification for the Compaq merger: the scale (size) that would come with it. "We were far too dependent on Microsoft [for software] and Intel [for semi-conductors], yet we negotiated with them from a position of weakness because our volumes weren't sufficient to give us the same clout as Compaq or Dell."[56] So the merger was not in pursuit of additional sales for sales' sake, which Hewlett and Packard had foresworn. A combined HP Compaq could bargain, achieving considerable cost savings and rack up large earnings gains.

HP under Fiorina never captured the synergies the merger portended. HP again missed projections Fiorina had made, in the third quarters of 2003 and again in 2004. Board members and analysts praised Fiorina as an architect of corporate strategy but wondered about her ability to oversee execution of that strategy.

Fiorina refused, however, to countenance employment of a chief operating officer (COO), who could pay attention to details while Fiorina traveled, gave speeches, and developed strategy. At a February 8, 2005 board meeting at Chicago O'Hare Airport, ostensibly a planning session for the upcoming HP shareholders' meeting, the board summarily ousted Carleton Fiorina from the CEO and board chair offices at HP.

In her autobiography, Fiorina made much of the machinations of individual directors, calling the HP board "dysfunctional" and board members' actions "amateurish and immature."[57] Be that as it may, the reasons the board removed Carleton Fiorina seemed clear, even though she denied them:

- She continued to make rosy projections of earnings and profit growth, missing them less often but missing them nonetheless, most recently for the third and fourth quarters of calendar 2004.
- She remained obdurate about not hiring a COO when a celebrity CEO such as Fiorina cries out for a complementary second-in-command.
- On her watch, even though integration of HP and Compaq had been highly successful, saving $3.5 billion, the new entity had not been able to achieve growth in operating earnings, which her successor has done, in spectacular fashion, since Fiorina left the company. In her autobiography, Fiorina unequivocally states that "[b]usiness is about producing results."[58] At HP she never produced them.
- Her public persona, her travel, her speeches, and her overweening egoism, at first a novelty, had become a distraction. Her successor was the exact opposite, flying under the radar as "a low profile problem solver" who has led HP to unprecedented revenue and profit growth.[59]

The Good and the Bad—The Good

Surprise of surprises, the sale of personal computers caused HP revenues to resume their upward trajectory, and with them profits and the HP share price. "Strong sales of laptop computers" pushed profits up 51 percent in early 2006.[60] HP beat analysts' estimate every quarter since Mr. Hurd took office. "One of the surprises was how profitable [was] the company's computer division in which Dell is the company's chief rival."[61] "PC sales played a large role" and "strong worldwide sales of personal computers" permitted HP to perform above analysts' forecasts in the second quarter of 2007.[62] In early 2008, HP raised its profit forecasts again, noting "the torrid pace of sales growth in the personal computer market," up 24 percent worldwide and 37 percent in laptops.[63] Parents who could afford to do so seemingly bought a laptop for every child over ten. Retailers sold out of HP computers in the 2007–08 holiday shopping seasons.

The merger for which analysts and the press maligned Carly Fiorina worked as she said it would work. HP became a much larger and more profitable corporation. The drawback is that it occurred not in 2003 or 2004, as Fiorina predicted, but in 2006, 2007, and 2008, after the HP board had removed Fiorina.

It is also not quite accurate to say, as Fiorina does, that she designed and put in place the platform upon which HP has achieved such good results. Her telescoping of 87 HP departments into four was an adverse reaction to CEO Rich McGinn's actions at Lucent, when he separated one business into 11 different "corporations."[64] Successor Hurd has undone some of Fiorina's reorganization, decentralizing HP once more, and that has played a part in the recent successes.

Tentative Teachings

Don't Too Much a "Tall Poppy" Be

Australia is an egalitarian country. One manifestation of that spirit is the tendency to cut down anyone who has become a "tall poppy." Americans do much the same, taking down a notch or two those who "have become too big for their britches." It behooves a woman who seeks to rise to the higher heights of an organization to avoid accumulating a reputation as a tall poppy, or "too big for her britches."

In the end, tall poppy status contributed to Fiorina's downfall. She traveled too much, in her biography describing travel to Korea, Belgium, France, Switzerland, the Netherlands, Brazil, and China for Lucent alone.[65] For HP the "Fiorina Palooza" jetted to 18 HP and customer sites on three continents in one week.

Her purported rationale seems correct: "I've found that if I really want to know what's going on, you have to travel. The farther from headquarters you get . . . the more you find out about what is actually going on."[66] She only indirectly shows awareness that she overdid it, by feigning indignation at criticism: "The CEOs of Lucent, Cisco, IBM, Dell, Sun Microsystems, Microsoft, Compaq, Oracle, GE, 3M [and] DuPont all flew in corporate jets . . . Nevertheless, my travel on a company plane was reported as evidence of my disrespect for the HP Way, my 'regal' nature, my 'distance' from employees."[67] She insisted on a provision in her employment contract that HP would provide her with jet transportation of all travel, personal as well as business, which corporate governance guru Nell Minnow termed "the Rolls Royce of aircraft provisions."[68]

Ms. Fiorina is disingenuous. She talks of the media invitations she turned down[69] but never about all those she accepted, the countless feature stories about her, the magazine covers which featured her, the 60 or more off-campus speeches she gave each year, her monthly telecasts to all HP employees, and more. At time her ego knew no bounds. She set herself up for a come-uppance.

Be Assertive

Again there is a ying and a yang about everything. The yang is to be a poppy, just one that is not too tall. Corporations need symbols and alter egos, especially as a company is a fictional being which needs humans to act for it.

Sometimes the symbol is the logo (Coca Cola) or a product (Xerox or Scotch Tape). Often the alter ego is a celebrity spokesperson (Ronald Reagan for General Electric). Sometimes it is the CEO.

Advice books urge women in business careers to take on speaking engagements while on the way up. Appear on magazine covers or in feature stories if you can. Catalyst's Sheila Wellington advocates women hiring a publicist or a speaking coach.[70] Corporations want to feel that a rising executive can represent the company in a competent, if not accomplished, fashion anywhere, at any time, in the most complex of transactions or problematic of circumstances. The public persona that comes through, and that it does come through, in speeches or the media, give higher ups confidence that a rising executive has the right qualities.

Just don't overdo it. Carleton Fiorina overdid it, like no other CEO in the current era. By reverse implication, her example serves as model of "what not to do" on the way up.

Avoid being Lopsided

Learn about revenues, profits, forecasts, and share prices, as well as sales. The chronicle of Jill Barad's tenure at Mattel highlights her fixation with marketing the Barbie line of dolls. At Lucent and at HP, Fiorina's experience and interests, while primarily in sales, were broader. She was interested in making herself the image of Hewlett Packard. She was interested in being the architect of business organization and strategy. But both women failed to give the necessary attention to revenues, profits, forecasts, and share prices, and this deficiency led to their downfalls.

Fiorina's autobiography mentions HP's share price once, toward the very end. Her thinking generally on the subject of share prices misses the mark:

> A CEO's job is to manage the company . . . The stock price has to take care of itself . . . A company's stock price is important, but in my opinion, a company's stock price has become too important.[71]

She gives HP's share price short shrift when reflecting on five years as CEO: "The only clouds on the horizon were the press and the stock price."[72] If so, it was a rather large, ominous cloud—HP's share price hovered near an all-time low for the several years of her tenure. Perhaps the HP board exercised too much forbearance, but in January 2005 they expressed to Fiorina "their legitimate concern about the stock price [and] the perception of the performance of the company."[73]

At the opposite extreme, nothing is worse than an executive who pulls up a company's stock price five or six times a day. A rising executive, as well as one who has arrived, must learn about such matters, and put them in the proper perspective. Directors are willing to appear patient but revenue and sales growth, meeting forecasts, and share prices are never far from board members' consciousness. Any woman who aspires to be a CEO has to develop a feel for that.

Fiorina is similarly casual about missing forecasts. She points out that in 23 quarters with her as CEO, "HP only missed 3 quarters of significance."[74] What is of significance is a subjective judgment. Further it is up to the board, not the CEO, to make that judgment. HP missed more than three quarterly forecasts in Fiorina's time at HP. Her lack of understanding about forecasts and share prices, combined with her blaze approach to them, contributed to her fall from grace.

A CEO's Performance isn't a Popularity Contest

Parenting isn't a popularity contest either. Parents have to dole out tough love on frequent occasion. So, too, for managers rising through the ranks. Carleton Fiorina regarded the HP-Compaq merger vote as a litmus test for her popularity. She caused pollsters to take company-wide surveys, placing great faith in "ongoing surveys [which showed] that the majority of employees supported the deal." She relied too much on "beauty contests."

A CEO cannot Ignore Extreme Employee Displeasure, or Lack of Popularity, Among Significant Employee Sectors

Engineers, managers, and employees in the HP printer facilities in Oregon and Idaho, which comprised the bedrock of HP's financial performance, detested Fiorina and hated the proposed Compaq merger. Rather than attempting to placate them, or allay their fears, Fiorina blew them off, opining that they did not know what they were talking about:

> Walter [Hewlett] and David [Packard] would commission "employee" surveys at four company locations in the Pacific Northwest where tradition ran deep. . . . [T]he methodology was flawed and the results were not statistically reliable [according to Fiorina] yet the results of these surveys were presented to the press with great fanfare and as evidence that a "majority" of employees opposed the deal.[75]

Shareholders approved the merger. Fiorina won the battle, but lost the war. Her failures to listen or consult fostered undying enmity among key HP employee sectors, contributing greatly to her downfall. Besides, it is poor management style, for a CEO or for a manager who aspires to become one, to ignore extreme displeasure or unhappiness in some segment or quarter of the operations under their supervision.

Keep Your Ego in Check and Learn to Partner

Psychologist Michael Maccoby makes the case that "productive narcissists" make the best corporate CEOs.[76] Carleton Fiorina was such a CEO, the celebrity wannabe who must always be center stage, loves to travel, make speeches, and be pictured on magazine covers. She was bold and inventive as an architect of corporate strategy and organization. "[A] narcissist personality . . . needs to partner with an obsessive," Maccoby concludes.[77] "[T]hink of Steve Ballmer [second at Microsoft to Bill Gates], Roy Lane [second to Larry Ellison at Oracle], and Colleen Barrett [second to Herb Kelleher at Southwest Airlines]—in building the company, watching the bottom line, and managing people."[78]

Fiorina was weak, very weak, on execution. During her tenure, HP did not show signs of the benefits of her merger or her management. The company missed key consensus analyst forecasts. Directors told her that she needed a complementary second-in-command. Analyst Rob Enderle wrote that "Carly's strength was one of vision, but her weakness [is] one of execution."[79] Fiorina herself recognized the need to partner: "Leaders are candid and courageous . . . they bolster their weaknesses by relying on others with complementary skills."[80] But that advice was for others, not for her. "Asked if she would consider hiring a chief operating officer, Fiorina said icily in an interview: 'I'm running the company the way I think it should be run.' "[81]

Fiorina's refusal to consider a second-in-command, despite repeated requests to hire one, put her squarely in opposition to many of the HP directors. It also contributed to the failure of HP to perform as it should have earlier on and its run away financial success under command of "low key problem solver" Mark Hurd.[82]

A Wrap

Carly Fiorina is an icon, one for whom it is unfortunate that her arms are not longer so that she can pat herself on the back more. Her autobiography is remarkable. It expresses no doubt about a single decision she made or action she took in over five years, save perhaps that she acted too quickly in laying off thousands of HP employees.[83] Yet at best, her performance was mixed. According to many, it was poor.

Worse than that, she trashes every person whom she perceives failed to support her or who stood in her way. Michael Capellas, the CEO of Compaq, was "abusive and incoherent" and "counterproductive."[84] Directors' behavior was "amateurish and immature." David Packard's anti-merger *Wall Street Journal* advertisements were "misogynist manifestos that sound like they were written by the Unabomber."[85] "None of them were fighting fair," she says of everyone who opposed the merger. She casts aspersions on the HP rank-and-file; if they were not with her, they were against her. "All the HP employees who'd ever resisted change suddenly had a champion in Walter Hewlett."[86]

Fiorina saves the highest heaps of trash for Walter Hewlett. Walter "hadn't been really qualified [to be a director] in the first place and he didn't contribute much at meetings."[87] Maybe "he hadn't paid enough attention" at meetings.[88] His opposition to the merger was "an insult to board deliberations"; he was a liar.[89] She made light of him as "an academician and a musician . . . neither profession made [him] qualified to countermand the decision of an entire board."[90]

Her out-of-control ego and lack of meaningful analysis makes after-the-fact evaluation difficult and hides from ready view the positive things she did accomplish. It also gives some guidance as to a subject that is not a topic for this book—what to do after you have become a CEO. Be more candid, gracious, and charitable to those who oppose you. Regard them as rivals or competitors, yes, but not as enemies, as Carleton Fiorina has done.

Early in 2009, Carly Fiorina underwent surgery for breast cancer, from which she is currently recovering. She, like Meg Whitman (Chapter 7), is mentioned as a potential Republican candidate for US senator of California in 2010.

3   A CEO Success—Andrea Jung at Avon Products

"Ding dong, Avon calling!" was a familiar refrain in 1950s television. Avon's representatives went door to door. Avon ladies would reappear to deliver cosmetics to housewives in living rooms. Now, no one is at home. Avon's direct selling has, in the United States at least, become a horse and buggy method of marketing.[1] When Andrea Jung became the CEO at Avon Products, she took leadership of an organization with an antiquated, indeed, horse and buggy, business plan.

"Avon Calling" still works in many of the other 130-plus countries in which Avon "has coverage," doing business through sales representatives. Jung has realized and capitalized on that. Avon's sales are increasing in less developed parts of the world, such as South America and East Asia, even if there has not been consistent growth in the United States. Seventy percent of Avon's business is overseas.

This domestic and foreign scenario confounded two CEOs at Avon Products, the 115-year-old direct sales company. CEO James Preston stepped down in 1997, giving way to Charles Perrin, CEO of Duracell, brought in to be a miracle worker. Perrin lasted 18 months. After disappointing earnings in the fourth quarter of 1999 sent Avon's share price to a new $23 low, Avon announced "early retirement" for Mr. Perrin at age 53, appointing to the CEO position a female marketing whiz, Andrea Jung, age 42.

A Layered Approach to Business Methods

Jung went right to work restructuring Avon sales channels. By 2000, Avon had an expanded array of sales outlets under which consumers could purchase Avon products in five different ways:

1. As always, from their Avon representative, of whom there are 700,000 worldwide.
2. From kiosks in shopping malls across the United States, many of which will be franchised to Avon sales representatives.
3. Through store fronts franchised to Avon sales representatives.
4. In large retailers' stores, where consumers will be able to purchase Avon's

beComing line of cosmetics, originally to be marketed in a strategic alliance with Sears Roebuck.[2]

5. By email and over the internet, but again, from Avon representatives, tens of thousands of whom have become "web enabled."[3]

This is the work of a determined CEO who quickly developed solutions to confront the conundrum Avon has always faced, namely, how to sell its products in a myriad new ways, reaching young consumers and working women, without undercutting Avon's army of faithful reps. Now the Avon rep "instead of saying 'ding dong' [will say] 'you have mail.' "[4]

In addition, the array of products is broader. It includes "Beauty Plus," which consists of jewelry, watches, accessories, and apparel. "Beyond Beauty" is third product line consisting of gift and decorative, home entertainment, and health and nutrition products. Customers may purchase Barbie dolls and Barbie doll accessories from Avon reps.

Early in her tenure, Andrea Jung added 46 percent to Avon's research and development budget, with the command to bring blockbuster products to market faster. Ms. Jung told her R&D head: "You've got two years [instead of three in which to bring new products to market]. I need a breakthrough and that's the goal."[5]

Andrea Jung got what she wanted. Avon's anti-ageing cream, "Retroactive," was a hit, grossing $100 million in its first year. Avon has also begun selling "a slew of other new products—vitamins, jump ropes, yoga mats, and aromatic therapy oils—under a line called Wellness."[6]

In mid-2000, Avon announced that under Ms. Jung sales were up 9 percent with profits increasing 2.5 percent. In early 2002, when the stock market was deep into a down market, Avon Products' share price hovered at or just below $50, a high for the preceding year, and a high for the preceding decade.

In 2005–06, Avon's growth slowed, to only 7.6 percent in 2006. Jung cut employee ranks by 10 percent and management ranks by 30 percent. She again cut the number of products in the Avon catalogue. Sales began rising briskly (12 percent in mid-2007) and the stock responded.[7]

Remarkable but not Flamboyant

Avon's new CEO has always been a determined person. In the fourth grade, she was set on getting a box of 120 colored pencils. Her parents promised her the pencils if she received straight "A" grades—no "A–" grades," much less "B" grades. So young Andrea Jung holed up in her room, studying, missing birthdays and tennis parties. At the end of the year she delivered straight "A" grades. She got the full set of pencils. "I'll never forget that," CEO Jung says.

She is the product of determined parents. Her father is Hong Kong Chinese, her mother from Shanghai. Both parents emigrated to Canada, meeting at the University of Toronto. Her father went on to obtain his master's degree at MIT, later becoming a leading Toronto architect. Her mother became one of Canada's first women chemical engineers, all the while maintaining her proficiency as a classical pianist.

Andrea, the first of their two children, was born in Toronto in 1959 and still maintains her Canadian citizenship, despite having grown up in the United States. In 1962, Andrea's father accepted a professorship at MIT. The Jung family relocated to Wellesley, Massachusetts, where Andrea matured into a super achiever.

As a youth, she had a regime of piano lessons together with Saturday morning Mandarin Chinese lessons. She played the piano regularly until the demands of motherhood and being CEO combined to deprive her of the playing time. Many people who meet CEO Jung comment on her exceptionally strong handshake, which she attributes to her 37 years of strenuous piano practice.[8]

CEO Jung "[b]y her own admission . . . was never a natural student," although the facts would say otherwise. Andrea went from Wellesley, Massachusetts, to Princeton, where four years later she was graduated *Magna Cum Laude* with a Bachelor of Arts in English Literature. She was bound for law school but decided first to gain experience in business. So she attended a career fair at which she interviewed with and was offered a job by Bloomingdale's.

Patient but not Passive

Andrea Jung turned out to have found her calling in retail. Moving through the Bloomingdale's management training program, Ms. Jung hooked up with a mentor, who happened to be Bloomingdale's first female vice-president, a tactful business woman, and a working mother. Barbara Bass helped Andrea overcome, at least in part, her "childhood Asian submissiveness." Andrea has explained to younger women in business: "Some people just wait for someone to take them under their wing. I've always advised that they shouldn't wait. They should find someone's wing to grab onto."[9]

Partly on Barbara Bass's wings, Ms. Jung rose rapidly. By the mid-1980s, she was in charge of intimate apparel (lingerie), with the rank of vice-president. Her mentor, though, suddenly departed Bloomingdale's to become CEO of I. Magnin, the San Francisco department store chain. When invited, Andrea Jung joined Bass, moving from New York to San Francisco in 1987. She rose quickly to the position of senior vice-president at I. Magnin. She married, shortly thereafter giving birth to a daughter. But, by 1991, Andrea was divorced.

Also, in 1991, Neiman Marcus recruited Andrea to become executive vice-president of the ritzy Dallas department store chain. She was just 32 and reluctant to leave San Francisco and her mentor. On the other hand, "It was a terrific opportunity . . . It was a larger company and a bigger job."

She was, among other things, in charge of all women's apparel. She jetted regularly to Paris for the fashion houses' runway shows. But she disliked it. Nieman Marcus did not need the creativity Jung had previously developed, marketing products to all income levels. She was marketing products to deep-pocketed consumers in the United State's highest income brackets. "Only three percent of Americans can afford to shop regularly at Neiman Marcus without mortgaging their homes two or three times over," one wag had joked. Andrea was "stagnating." She had also fallen in love again, this time to Michael Gould who was on his way to New York to become president at Bloomingdale's.

Andrea Jung married Michael Gould, 15 years her senior, left Neiman Marcus, and moved to New York in 1993. Casting about for a challenge, in May 1993 she accepted a position consulting in marketing at Avon Products. Gould was her connection. He had been running the Giorgio Beverly Hills perfume business for Avon before accepting the job at Bloomie's. Seven months later the Jung consultantship blossomed into a full-time position as head of marketing.

Management Positions at Avon Products

David H. McConnell had formed the California Perfume Co. in 1886, with a view to selling perfume door-to-door to ladies of the Victorian era. The first Avon lady, a Ms. Albee of Winchester, New Hampshire, sold a package of assorted perfumes to a New England housewife, making Ms. Albee the first of several million Avon ladies. The company, however, did not become Avon until 1939, when it selected that name for its broad generic appeal.[10]

In 1993, when asked to evaluate Avon's readiness to enter direct selling, Andrea found most products "unprepared." Avon had struggled to enter the internet age, primarily because managers did not anticipate how fearful traditional, brisk-and-mortar sales reps would be about B-to-C ("Business to Consumer") commerce over the internet. When the company put the address for its website on the Avon catalogue, sales representatives covered it over with their address labels, fearful that e-commerce would undermine direct sales. The experience, that personnel in brick-and-mortar settings believed B-to-C efforts would upstage them, seems clear today but was largely unanticipated then.[11] Jung saw what was happening. She caused Avon to remove the web address from catalogues. In addition, she had to scrap packaging, substituting redesigned packages, hire a new advertising agency, and reduce the Avon catalogue 40 percent.

Despite the troubles, Andrea Jung liked Avon: "I felt that all the things I wanted for my career were right here at Avon." Women form one quarter of the company's board of directors and nearly half its senior officers.

> [T]here is no glass ceiling to squelch [my] advancement. I'm very select-
> ive in the companies I work for . . . I started at Bloomingdale's because it

was committed to developing women. When I went to I. Magnin in San Francisco, it was to accompany a female CEO and because there's a strong Asian population in that city. I never encountered a glass ceiling because of my race.

Then Avon CEO James Preston promoted Jung to vice-president global marketing. In 1997, when Preston stepped down, there were four inside candidates for CEO. The board of directors bypassed all four, going outside to hire Charles Perrin, who had no experience in retailing to women. Two of the four pretenders to the CEO chair left the company. Ms. Jung stayed, accepting the board's offer of the COO (chief operating officer) position. In that capacity, she traveled widely, obtaining an invaluable feel for the variety of environments Avon faced in its truly global business.

A Remake of the Company

After ten years of leadership by Andrea Jung, Avon has a future. Many women cannot afford Estee Lauder or Lancôme cosmetics. Avon develops and prices its products for that under-served niche, the middle class. Under Jung, Avon has developed new and varying ways in which to reach them.

"Let's Talk" has replaced "Avon Calling" as the motto. Fifty percent of Avon's reps have internet access. The resistance of the 1990s, when reps stickered over the website address, has dissipated. There are now 15,000-plus "e-reps" selling online.

There are not 15,000 websites. Avon has a template which each e-rep adapts. Avon calculates a $1.00 plus cost for processing a paper order. The comparable cost for an electronic order is $0.30 per customer, maybe even as low as $0.20. "Anything we can get off paper has a significant cost advantage," COO Susan Kropf states.[12]

In 2000, after Andrea Jung had described her remake of Avon, a Paine Webber (now UBS Securities) analyst told clients "Her business plan has a high probability of disappointment." In 2001, Avon's sales were up 5 percent while profits increased 11 percent and the share price kept knocking against the all-time high. Longer term, there will be fewer bumps in the road for Avon, because Jung has caused Avon to diversify, both in sales channels and geographically. Each of the 139 countries in which Avon does business is likely to scroll through phases in their development in which one or another of Avon's, and Jung's, marketing methods will do well.

In the United States, internet sales may quickly rise to become 25 percent of the market, although Jung predicts that the figure may not go much higher because, especially in cosmetics, women like to try products and talk to other women who vouch for or criticize the product.

In countries such as Malaysia, Singapore, and other East Asian nations with rising per capita income, and after the East Asian economic crises of 1998–2003, the time may now be opportune to substitute traditional retail for direct selling, through franchises to Avon reps or strategic alliances with existing retailers. In other countries, such as Indonesia, India, Brazil, or Russia, direct selling through Avon reps may not be horse and buggy at all.[13] The health of the direct selling method "remains very important to us," central to Avon's business method.[14]

Work–Life and Personal Growth

Growing up in a Chinese–Canadian family, Andrea Jung's environment imbued her with post-Confucian values, for example, the teachings that "the shiny nail is the first to feel the sting of the hammer" and that each person has a fixed place in a cosmic order. She has herself described the difficulty in surmounting her "childhood Asian submissiveness." Avon co-workers said that at first they found her "aloof" and "detached."[15] Now an Avon V-P says "I see a leader who's willing to tell the story of her heritage, her grandmother [who died of breast cancer] to her daughter. She's more comfortable in herself."

Sheila Wellington of the NYU Stern School of Business finds that generally "[W]omen are reluctant to stand out. . . . Nevertheless, stand out is what you need to do."[16] Overcoming the hangover of Asian and post-Confucian values, as well as any reticence indigenous to her gender, Andrea Jung has stood out.

She is determined that Avon will be a leader in supporting breast cancer research. Avon reps have raised over $55 million per year, toward a goal of $250 million.[17] In her family, when her mother's mother was dying from breast cancer at the young age of 63, no one would talk to her about the disease. Now the granddaughter regularly takes center stage in "The Race for the Cure."

Ms. Jung has formed CEO advisory councils of top ten performers around the globe and meets regularly with them. She addressed 13,000 Avon reps at their convention in Las Vegas, sandwiched between entertainment by Engelbert Humperdinck and aerobic sessions led by chubby exercise guru Richard Simmons. "Avon is first and foremost about you," she proclaims, "I stand here and promise you that that will never change." Ms. Jung wraps up with the amazing declaration: "I love you all!" bringing 13,000 whistling, stomping women to their feet.

Ms. Jung explains: "I grew up in a traditional Asian household. It was more reserved." Ten years ago, she explains, she would not have brought her daughter to work. If she had to take her daughter to a pediatrician's appointment, she would tell co-workers that she had a business appointment.

Today she tries to set a different example. She walks her daughter and adopted son to the bus in the morning. She is at home by 7:30 for dinner with her children. Her daughter regularly visits her mother's Avon offices and, for an occasional treat, Avon's Fifth Avenue Spa. Says a fellow woman director, "She's the kind of woman that most women aspire to be . . . [b]ut you're always asking, 'Oh my God. How does she do it all?'"

Visible and Biting Criticism

Not all has been smooth. Following the great 30-month bear market of April 2000 to November 2002, during which Avon's stock held its value, the Avon share price fell, from $45 in February 2005, to $25 in September of that year, when most other share prices were rising. Moreover, the Avon price stayed there for 14–15 months. In 2006, Jim Cramer, the animated television stock analyst, and author of the best selling *Jim Cramer's Stay Mad*[18] put Andrea Jung at the top on his "CEO Wall of Shame." Before tens of millions of viewers, Cramer regularly questioned Jung's abilities, calling for her resignation.[19]

Atop revenues increasing at 12 percent, in 2007 Jung and Avon announced a "pretty aggressive and bold" $2 billion stock buyback plan, without any bank borrowing. "Management could be signaling confidence in its ability to generate substantial free cash flow in the future," thought Professor Anant Sundaram of the Tuck School of Business at Dartmouth.[20]

Avon's stock price rebounded to $43. Cramer recanted, admitting that he was wrong about Jung and Avon and that stock would be an investment well-suited for holding through a recession.[21]

Tentative Teachings

Side Stepping within the Corporate Sector

As much as any woman CEO in office, Andrea Jung and her career pattern exemplify the pattern many of the experts recommend. "Be patient, but not passive" is the mantra they urge upon aspiring women.[22] By that, those experts assure their readers that the best career pattern is to work steadily up through the ranks of one, two, or perhaps three corporate hierarchies (three for Andrea Jung), until they enter into the pool from which companies choose senior managers and directors.[23]

Empirical research, however, shows that at least as far as directorships are concerned, the advice which experts dispense is wrong. Sixty-two percent of women directors in the *Fortune 500* "side step" onto corporate boards from successful careers in academics, not-for-profits, government, consulting, their own businesses, or law practice.[24] Your best chance of being a woman director at a large U.S. corporation is to be a tenured professor in business, law or health sciences at an elite university. For example, one study found that 13 women professors at Harvard held 21 corporate directorships.[25]

Your worst chance is to "be patient, but not passive": only nine women have risen vertically through the ranks of one company to become a corporate director. So the advice is wrong, pretty much flat wrong, at least as regards directorships.

For senior management positions, including elevation to the CEO level, the prevailing advice may be more on point. Andrea Jung's career pattern indicates that "be patient, but not passive" may be better advice, when the grail is a CEO position, especially when combined with a degree of side stepping among organizations, as Jung has done.

Develop a "Can Do" Reputation

Another piece of advice applicable to all who aspire to high positions and which Andrea Jung exemplifies is to "develop a reputation as one who can solve problems."[26] Throughout her career, Jung has done that but perhaps most illustrative is what she did in her early days as CEO. She confronted a predicament, namely, the seeming obsolescence of Avon's direct selling methods, coupled with retention of sales reps, the resolution of which had befuddled three previous CEOs. She did not forsake Avon's traditional direct selling but emphasized it more in markets in which that selling method had greater potential. In turn she developed a menu of marketing alternatives which have great potential in different markets at different times.

You can have Children

Further, you can raise those children hands on while still being a CEO. Jill Barad has two boys. Andrea Jung has a daughter and an adopted son. Carleton Fiorina is mother to two adopted girls. These women began a re-examination of the prevailing wisdom that, as a woman progressing upward in business, you cannot have children, or will be forced to give short shrift to parenting.

A Conclusion

"She bit off a lot. The challenges are great," says Legg Mason investment manager for Robert Hagstrom. But "at this point, it would be very hard to give her anything less than A's." Robert Sellers of Aberdeen Asset Management agrees: "It's a textbook study of how to turn around a company."[27]

Andrea Jung is more in the limelight than some other successful women CEOs this book chronicles but she relies on the same skill set that those CEOs do: hard work, analytical ability, staying in touch with the consumer, and the courage of their convictions after they have made a decision, however radical it might be. She does not rely on a "buzz machine" or "All Andrea, All the Time," or on "big (dumb) acquisitions," as other high-profile CEOs have done. At this point in her career as CEO, she has proven her entitlement to another boxed set of 120 colored pencils.[28]

4 Plowhorse—Marion Sandler at Golden West Financial

Certain business leaders believe that by becoming a celebrity CEO they enhance the corporation's public persona. Splashy acquisitions, such as Mattel's acquisition of The Learning Company, or Hewlett-Packard's of Compaq Computer, add to the mark a CEO has made for herself. At Hewlett-Packard, "The Cult of Carly" and "All Carly, All the Time" cemented Carleton Fiorina into her place among celebrities. Six months after her entry into the CEO suite, Carly Fiorina appeared on the *Forbes* cover as a "super hero savior" of Hewlett-Packard, a company that had not met with any failure, had a proud corporate culture/brand, and needed no savior.[1]

A Conclusion First

Good to Great: Why Some Companies Make the Leap . . . and Others Don't[2] has been continuously on the business best-seller list from 2001, when it appeared, to at least 2009, an extraordinary run.[3] Applying various screens to 1,500 public companies, author Jim Collins selected 11 companies as organizations that had moved from "good to great." Collins reviewed the management styles of those companies' CEOs:

> The real issue at hand is not male or female, but the type of leadership. [W]e systematically analyzed leaders who took good companies and made them great. All the good to great leaders were the opposite of Ms. Fiorina . . . They deflected attention away from themselves, shunned the limelight and quietly focused on the tasks at hand. One described himself as "more plowhorse than showhorse" . . .
>
> [T]he most effective leaders never make themselves the center of attention . . . Indeed, the very best ones overwhelmed us not with their ego, but with their humility.[4]

Mr. Collins concluded that Ms. Fiorina's later "failure lies in her inability to become such a leader and not in the utterly irrelevant fact that she is a woman."[5]

Collins is right but also wrong. Gender appears to have played a significant part in setting women executives up for failure. Women in business have few role models. Out of a sense of insecurity, they overcompensate. They feel they have too much to prove, too soon. Jill Barad came on with feigned bravado and "puff publicity." Carly Fiorina's "buzz machine" had much to do with her being only one of two female CEOs at the time. Gender may not be "irrelevant," as Collins asserts.

The More Modest Shall Inherit the Earth

A role model opposite Jill Barad or Carly Fiorina for women in business could be Marion Sandler, a plowhorse in Collins' lexicon. By virtue of day-to-day management skill, combined with efficiency, frugality, and a steady stream of small, well-thought-out acquisitions, she built Golden West Financial into the second largest thrift institution in the United States (after Washington Mutual), company 421 in the *Fortune 500*. From 1963, when she and her husband bought a controlling interest in Golden West, to 2007, she oversaw an increase from $38 million to $127 billion in assets, a growth rate of 460 percent per annum, sustained over 40 years. Golden West's market capitalization reached $18 billion when, in May 2007, Wachovia Bank acquired Golden West for cash and stock valued at $26 billion.[6]

Marion Sandler is a depression era child. Her parents were Russian immigrants who settled in Maine, where they built up a middle-class existence through a hardware business. They had five children: four boys and one girl. Having endured a depression and a world war, the single girl, Marion Osher, matriculated at Wellesley College in 1948, graduating four years later. She made her way to New York City where she earned an MBA at New York University (NYU).

Even armed with an MBA, in the 1950s Marion Osher had few avenues open. She took a position as an assistant buyer at Bloomingdale's, a common career path for women. After two years, Marion tried an uncommon career path. She applied for a securities analyst position with the Wall Street firm of Domminick & Domminick, a retail firm which no longer exists. The Domminick partners felt constrained to hold a meeting to entertain her application because the firm had never hired a woman before, other than to "man" the receptionist's desk.

As a securities analyst, Marion followed the savings and loan industry. The business was easy to understand. Both the states and, through the Federal Home Loan Bank Board (FHLBB), the federal government regulated the business, most importantly the interest rate on savings deposits. S&Ls thus paid out, say, 4.5 percent on deposits and lent to home purchasers at, say, 6.5 percent. Managing thrift institutions was simply a matter of managing the "spread," the difference between what the government said could be paid out on deposits and what came in as the form of interest home owners paid. Because they could not compete on interest rates, thrifts competed offering toasters, binoculars, or luggage. A spread of 1 percent was necessary to pay staff salaries, overheads, and other expenses. Two percent meant excellent profitability. Most S&Ls hovered between those extremes.

Marion Osher divined how easy it might be to manage an S&L to good profitability. But she did not act upon her insights. She continued covering the industry for Domminick, determined to become the first woman partner. In 1961, she married Herbert Sandler, an attorney.

After five years' employment, she approached her supervising partner at Domminick about the partnership track. He made it abundantly clear that she could not become a partner at Domminick. In fact, Ms. Sandler now recalls, the other "partners laughed." "In those days, there was no beating around the bush. It was very clear a woman couldn't become a partner."[7]

Go West, Young Woman

Frustrated in her career ambitions, after one more year at Domminick and two at Oppenheimer & Co., Marion Sandler decided to emulate her parents' "do it yourself" approach. She persuaded her husband of the ease of management in the S&L industry. They canvassed the field to find an S&L in which they could invest.

California was then in its second post-war boom. Developers were opening tract housing projects by the scores. Young home buyers needed fistfuls of financing. Based upon their analysis of the S&L industry, Marion and Herbert acted upon Horace Greeley's exhortation, "Go West."

Once in California, husband and wife continued to pore over the financial statements of publicly traded California savings and loans. They found a prospect in Oakland, California, a two-office S&L with $38 million in assets (loans outstanding).

For an S&L, accounting is somewhat counter intuitive. Much of the cash and cash equivalents (treasury bonds, etc.) are at the beck and call of depositors, payable upon demand. Hence, deposits are not assets (cash) but liabilities (amounts owed to depositors). By contrast, promissory notes, backed by mortgages on residences, entitle the S&L to a stream of interest income and payments on principal. Loans, and the paper instruments which represent them, are the assets.

For $4.1 million, the Sandlers purchased a controlling interest in a California S&L that held $38 million in mortgages and some tables and chairs, give or take an adding machine. To finance their stock purchase, they borrowed from family members. They christened the sleepy company "Golden West Financial," which they thought nicely symbolized their aspirations for success in the California market and the savings and loan industry.

As co-owners, Marion and Herbert Sandler determined that they would share the executive suite. Marion would supervise the liability side (deposits, depositors, and savings). Herbert would be in charge of the assets side (lending). Marion Sandler thus became a rarity for her time, a female CEO.[8]

Ms. Sandler knew the business from her securities analyst days. It was a simple business, with two products, passbook savings accounts and fixed rate mortgages. She turned a watchful eye toward wasteful expenditures and watched the "spread." "We keep our business simple, very simple," Marion remarked.[9]

The Savings and Loan Business

When Golden West began acquiring other savings and loans, Marion personally conducted the feasibility studies and, later, the due diligence. Due diligence is a business word for the process by which a buyer assures herself that, in rough terms, she is getting what she thought she acquired, not necessarily as much in terms of price as in terms of serviceability. A buyer who hopes that she is purchasing a reliable used car, or one who assures herself that the home under consideration will shelter her family, presenting few surprises, as well as the purchaser of an entire corporation, engages in due diligence by taking the car to a mechanic, or checking the foundation, the rain gutters, and so on.[10] Due diligence in a corporate acquisition may be time consuming but is very necessary.

As a former securities analyst, Marion Sandler was capable of undertaking the necessary due diligence, which she did. In that way, Golden West did not pay the high fees investment bankers or lawyers charge.

In the highly regulated environment of that era, thrifts could not open new branches on a whim. They had to make extensive filings with regulatory authorities. They would have to demonstrate that public necessity and convenience militated in favor of a financial institution at the corner of Hollywood and Vine, or Geary and Fillmore. Applicants had to prepare area maps with locations of all competing institutions in a 10-mile radius, as well as traffic analyses. Most S&Ls hired firms of attorneys. At Golden West, Marion Sandler prepared the maps and drafted the filings. As an attorney, Herbert handled negotiations, drafted leases and contracts, and appeared at hearings. Together, Herbert and Marion kept overheads low, maximizing the portion of the "spread" that went to profits and minimizing the portion that went to expenses.

As the business grew, Marion had to turn her attention to adding management. She sought out intelligent, trustworthy employees. Discussing the management team and the way in which she put it together, Ms. Sandler explains that "[w]e have high standards, we're analytical." Members of the team she put together worked at Golden West for 30 years.

In 1968, Marion Sandler returned to Wall Street. Golden West Financial did its initial public offering (IPO). The frugally managed savings and loan was then publicly held, ready to begin its climb to the *Fortune 500* ranks.

The Quest for Liquidity

The year 1974 saw a slump in the home mortgage market. Those S&Ls which survived the downturn did so by packaging mortgages for sale in the secondary market to mortgage wholesalers, who later sold debt securities backed by pools of home mortgages. Previously, thrifts retained the mortgages created by their customers. Those thrifts would quickly run out of funds for further lending, stuck with an illiquid mortgage portfolio. By freeing up capital tied up in those mortgages through selling them, a thrift threw off the albatross around its neck that its in-house mortgage portfolio represented, thus vastly increasing liquidity.

Because it had become so easy to wholesale on the back end, up-front originators (retailers) extended credit to persons with poor repayment prospects (purchasers of gargantuan suburban homes). The prospect of defaults on those loans later lead to the "subprime mortgage mess," which in 2008–09 has rippled through the most distant corners of our economy.

The entry of federal chartered corporations (Fannie Mae, Freddie Mac, Ginnie Mae) on the scene as wholesalers of 50 percent of the mortgages in the United States has also standardized the backbone for mortgage loans (same application, appraisal forms, note, form of mortgage). Standardized backbones and increased liquidity have made home mortgages costs cheaper than they used to be, saving trillions of dollars to homeowners.

From the standpoint of an S&L CEO such as Marion Sandler, the development has been a two-edged sword. Because there are many more eligible prospects for mortgages, a manager must exercise more discipline in choosing among them. The spread, always thin, has narrowed throughout the industry. The premium for adept management has increased.

Back to the 1970s

In the late 1970s, rampant inflation and high interest rates came to prevail. Many S&Ls fell into the trap of short-term borrowing of funds at high interest rates to fund long-term, fixed-rate mortgages. When short-term interest rates continued to climb, S&Ls faced the prospect of "negative spreads," paying out more than they took in as interest.

Marion Sandler and Golden West avoided the phenomenon by careful matching of interest rates and maturities. What she borrowed short term, she invested short term, in government securities or certificates of deposit from other financial institutions. If funds came from depositors who bought floating rate certificates of deposit, Ms. Sandler ensured that the funds went into instruments that were equally interest rate sensitive. "All S&Ls deal with the same ingredients," Ms. Sandler said at the time, "[b]ut our recipe is different."[11]

Golden West caught flack. By escaping the trap of borrowing short term and investing long term, Golden West pulled back from the home mortgage market in which by their charters S&Ls are supposed to function. One competing executive charged that the Sandlers "went against an 'unspoken rule' that FHLBB advances should bolster the housing market rather than be used [in] an arbitrage play." But another observer, a former FHLBB official no less, disagreed: "If I had been running an S&L in that environment, I would have been pleased to have done what Golden West did."

Deregulation

Fixed ceilings on the interest rates thrifts could pay limited the competition among them. Limits on competition within the savings and loan industry had not, however, prevented competition from other quarters, namely, money market funds brokerage firms and mutual fund complexes. Money market funds paid market interest rates, provided check books, and otherwise greater accessibility to funds. A massive outflow of funds from S&Ls, and commercial banks as well, known by the jaw-breaking term "disintermediation," occurred.

The solution was to lobby Congress. Congress had recently deregulated the airlines; deregulation was the Reagan Administration's talisman. The Garn St. Germain legislation, named after Senator Jake Garn of Utah and Representative Ferdinand St. Germain of Rhode Island, deregulated the S&L industry.

Now thrifts, free of regulation, could pay any interest rate they wished. They began to chase money market dollars, offering competitive interest rates rather than toasters, on a proliferating array of products, including variable rate certificates of deposit and interest bearing checking accounts.

Be careful what you wish for. Those S&Ls paying out much greater (deregulated) amounts of interest were stuck with staid mortgage portfolios that yielded far less than the S&Ls were paying out in interest. Negative spreads, which had been seen from time-to-time in the late 1970s, took on an air of permanence.

S&L managers had to invent schemes to increase the interest they received. Many caused their member-owned institutions to convert from member-owned (mutual) form to shareholder-owned corporations. They then went public, selling shares, using the funds investors had paid for shares to fund the shortfalls negative spreads had created. Other managers went to junk bond king Mike Milkin. They used depositors' dollars to buy 13 and 14 percent junk bonds from Milkin's Drexel Burnham Lambert, hoping to pull up the average yield of the portfolio, which now consisted of a mix of low-paying "safe" mortgages and high-paying risky junk bonds.[12]

Desperate for higher yielding investments, S&L managers made out-of-area loans to riskier borrowers who were willing to pay up-front loan fees and higher interest. It seemed as though every S&L financed (and, after foreclosure, owned) a golf course in Texas.

Little worked. The savings and loan crisis blossomed. Congress formed the Resolution Trust Company to rescue hundreds of failed thrift institutions. The Federal Home Loan Bank Board morphed into the Office of Thrift Supervision, pursuing scores of S&L managers and directors for breaches of their fiduciary duties. The government-backed insurance corporation for thrifts, the Federal Savings and Loan Insurance Corporation (FSLIC), had to pursue rogues, who got control of failing S&Ls, looting them, and hiding assets offshore, in the Cayman Island, the Bahamas, Turks and Caicos, the Netherlands Antilles, and more. Many institutions went out of business. The number of thrifts (S&Ls) in the United States declined from 4,500 to 1,000.

Golden West in Times of Trouble

Under Marion Sandler, Golden West Financial sailed through the crisis. Ms. Sandler realized early on that, just like a supermarket, operating an S&L is not a high margin business. Executives are managing an ever-narrowing "spread" out of which must come all expenses and profits, if any.

Golden West retained a high percentage of the mortgages they received. They confined themselves to "mortgages on modestly priced single family homes. No junk bonds, no loans for shopping centers, golf courses, or million-dollar mansions."[13] Golden West kept fixed rate loans to a minimum; it utilized its own brand of adjustable rate mortgage (ARM), which adjusts monthly rather than yearly or longer. It became famous for "Pick A Payment" mortgages under which borrowers could choose interest only, or smaller and minimum payments, for a time, to see them through a period of financial difficulty.[14]

Golden West based interest rate adjustments on its own internally generated Cost of Savings Index based upon its cost of deposits, thus carefully matching loans with cost of funds. Monthly adjustments meant no huge overhangs. Many other S&Ls faced waves of prospective defaults as rates adjusted dramatically upward after several years, suddenly presenting over extended homeowners with large increases in monthly payments.[15] Golden West felt few of the seismic dislocations emanating from the adjustable rate mortgage crises.

Golden West at any Time

S&L managers must concentrate on the cost as well as the revenue side. Golden West had no Gulfstream such as Hewlett-Packard had. The Sandlers flew economy class, as did their employees. Golden West had no executive dining room; most days CEO Marion Sandler ate a sandwich at her desk. Golden West's branch offices were three times smaller than the industry average, although the company utilized celebrity architects such as Frank Geary or Eric Haeslop to design some of its 475 branch facilities. Based upon his research, Dean Witter's S&L analyst concluded that "there's not a financial institution that comes close to [Golden West's] operating efficiency."[16]

Marion Sandler's frugal management style meant that Golden West Financial never had to chase high yields through purchase of junk bonds or high-risk out-of-area loans. Golden West chugged through the days of disintermediation and the S&L crisis just fine. Until Wachovia acquired it, of the 20 largest S&Ls in the 1980s, Golden West Financial stood as the only survivor from the list.[17]

Under the banners of its World Savings and Loan Association and World Savings Banks, in 2006 Golden West Financial had $20 billion in mortgage originations, $4 billion in revenues, $500 million in profits, and 475 offices in 38 states, gathering deposits in nine states and lending in 38. At 75, Marion Sandler opines that "[r]eal power is being able to sustain it."[18] Says another time-tested female executive: "It doesn't come down to hype or how many magazine covers you were on . . . It comes down to do you have a product that is of value to customers in the marketplace?"[19] Those values, and accompanying reliance on frugality and efficiency, mark one of the differences between a Jill Barad or a Carleton Fiorina and the leading female CEO of a half generation earlier, Marion Sandler.

At the end of her very successful career, Marion Sandler grows wistful. She does not see women making the progress the experts prognosticate or which the statistics ballyhooed by organizations such as Catalyst, Inc., would indicate.

> [W]hen I go to industry meetings, I don't see other women and I don't see them on the programs. . . . It is still tough for women to make it. You have to be in the right place at the right time. And you have to be terribly talented—a lot better than the male competition.

Advising young women, Marion Sandler can only tell them to follow her lead: "[B]uy the company or build your own."[20]

Tentative Teachings

Education Is Important

Marion Sandler was graduated from Wellesley, as was Paula Rosport Reynolds (Chapter 6); Andrea Jung, as well as Meg Whitman (Chapter 8) were graduated from Princeton. All 21 women in this book were graduated from college, many of them from universities and colleges with elite status.

MBA (Graduate School in Business) and Financial Literacy are Important

Ms. Sandler was graduated from what has become the Stern School of Business at NYU. Another counterintuitive finding of this book is that a majority of women CEOs (16, in fact) have graduate degrees, the MBA degree in all but one case (a JD in law). Most, but not all, have demonstrated that they possess the financial acumen which is necessary for anyone who holds the top spot. The MBA degree started them in that direction; often further experiences helped take them to where they needed to be. For instance, Marion Sandler worked several years as a New York securities analyst, covering the savings and loan industry.

Keep a Low Profile and an Even Keel

In contradistinction to Jill Barad or Carleton Fiorina, with an Andrea Jung perhaps in the middle, Marion Sandler represents the antipode on the flamboyance spectrum. She ate her lunch at her desk; she flew commercial (coach); she insisted upon low overheads; and she lasted a very long time (over 30 years as CEO). She oversaw ever-rising levels of revenue and profits, and ended with a killer sale of the company for $26 billion. She reaped great financial rewards, greater than any other female CEO in this book, by being a plowhorse rather than a showhorse.

Resist Feeling Insecure

Be aware of the dangers which may lurk in overcompensating for gender. Marion Sandler appears to have done so, contributing to her great success.

Disposition of the Sandler Wealth

Post-acquisition, the Sandlers have donated $1.3 billion from the Wachovia sale to the Sandler Family Supporting Foundation. They have signaled their intention to give away everything they received for their 10 percent share of Golden West. So far they have funded stem cell research, the UC Berkeley Human Rights Center, and ProPacifica—a nonprofit organization specializing in the type of investigative journalism that has all but disappeared in an age of declining newspaper publishing and a fixation with the internet, tweeting, Brittany Spears, Paris Hilton, and celebrities.[21]

For its part, Wachovia, mired in the subprime mortgage mess, expresses "buyer's remorse" over its "big dumb acquisition"—the $26 billion Wachovia paid for Golden West just weeks before the mortgage and credit crunches began in earnest.[22] Near insolvency, with losses estimated at $36 billion on the mortgages acquired from Golden West alone, Wachovia accepted $40 billion in government bailout (TARP) funds. It was not enough: early in 2009 Wachovia had to seek the protection of a merger with the healthier Wells Fargo & Co. and the nation's fourth largest bank (Wachovia, which had swallowed up Golden West) disappeared.

On television's *Sixty Minutes* news program, whistleblowers excoriated the Sandlers' stewardship of Golden West: under the "Pick a Payment" option, homeowners could select monthly payment amounts that would not even cover the interest, ballooning principal loan balances to amounts that never might be repaid. Screening of credit risks in World Savings branch offices was said to have been non-existent. Seemingly, however, neither the Sandlers nor Golden West hid these and other deficiencies from view. Wachovia could have uncovered them in a thorough due diligence exercise which, evidently, Wachovia failed to perform. The Sandlers seem financially secure even if somewhat tarnished by allegations against their company.

5 Anne Mulcahy at Xerox and Patricia Russo at Alcatel-Lucent—Fix It CEOs

More than any other female CEOs, Anne Mulcahy and Patricia Russo are alike. A year apart in age, from large families (five children in Mulcahy's case, seven in Russo's), each grew up near New York City (Long Island and Trenton, NJ). Both are excellent athletes. Citicorp's Sandy Weill proposed Russo, with a 12.5 handicap, as a first woman member at Augusta National Golf Club.[1] Mulcahy and Russo attended Catholic universities (Marymount, Tarrytown, NY and Georgetown, Washington, DC). Both began their careers in sales. Anne Mulcahy became a "lifer" at Xerox, beginning there 33 years ago. Patricia Russo worked for IBM for eight years before switching to AT&T and Lucent, with 17 months away as president of Kodak (second to CEO Daniel Carp), before Lucent lured her back with the CEO position. Both Mulcahy and Russo reached the top of organizations which were in great difficulty, with revenues falling and awash with losses. Mulcahy has turned her company (Xerox) around while Russo's (Alcatel-Lucent) still struggles, finally causing her to resign as CEO, in Summer 2008.

CEO models, or examples thereof, come in waves. In the 1990s, the celebrity CEO was in vogue. Jack Welch at General Electric and Bill Gates at Microsoft typified the breed. Jill Barad and Carleton Fiorina were the headline women of the times, celebrity CEOs as well.

A phalanx of "Mr. And Ms. Fix-Its" followed. Fix-Its papered over the excesses of the 1990s, and consolidated gains that corporations had made. Mulcahy and Russo reside firmly within the Fix-It group. *Business Week* headlined its feature on Mulcahy "She's Here to Fix the Xerox."[2]

Further Similarities

Both, too, belong in a subgroup of Fix-It CEOs: their charges were to rescue falling angels, Xerox and Lucent. Despite a series of heart-stopping events, including ten consecutive quarters of sliding sales, Mulcahy persevered. When the board appointed her CEO, Mulcahy remembers, "I was getting condolences [rather] than congratulations."[3] Management theorists and securities analysts agree that Xerox has turned the corner: it has become profitable once more, it has resumed dividends, and its share price has risen.[4] In 2005, Catalyst named Mulcahy "Woman of the Year."[5]

At Lucent, Russo had to preside over 13 consecutive quarters of not only decreasing sales but also losses. The company cut 115,000 jobs. The share price declined from a high of $64.69 in 1999 to less than a dollar in 2001, at which point the New York Stock Exchange threatened to invoke its regulations for delisting when shares' price falls below $1.00. Quarterly sales were cut roughly in half, from approximately $4 to $2 billion.

After a brief resurgence late in 2004, the downward slide at Lucent commenced once more. Russo negotiated a $13.5 billion merger with Alcatel, the French telecommunications giant, with Russo to be CEO of the new entity and Alcatel CEO Serge Tchuruk to be board chair. Losses continued at the new entity. Alcatel-Lucent cut 16,500 additional jobs, when projections had been for 9,000. The additional job cuts must be read against the background that Russo and her predecessor, Harry Schacht, had reduced Lucent's headcount by a staggering 114,500, from 150,000 to 33,500 (30,000 by the Avaya spinoff into a separate public company and the remaining 84,500 by outright job cuts). The merger seemed to have been nothing but re-arranging deck chairs on the *Titanic*.

Mulcahy enjoys better times now, but she endured a three-year parade of horribles. Russo has endured an unending skein of bad news. Both CEOs have endured by knowing when to duck. They never promised more than they were certain they could deliver, although Russo's certainty proved to be ill-advised once or twice.

They have been modest, although now in rosier times Mulcahy has become a trophy director, with board seats at Aetna Insurance, AMR, Citicorp., Electronic Data Systems (EDS) (later acquired by Hewlett-Packard), Target, and Xerox, as well as not-for-profit Catalyst, Inc.[6] Unlike Jill Barad, Mulcahy and Russo never have been flamboyant. Unlike either Barad or Carleton Fiorina, neither has sought the limelight. They both typify the Fix-It CEO.

ANNE MARIE MULCAHY

An Extremis Situation

In her first months as CEO at Xerox, Anne Mulcahy suffered through the latter portion of a steep downward slide in Xerox's share price, from $64 in May 1999 to $6.00 in June 2002. In fact, the Xerox share price had fallen from $63.69 to $4.93 in *one year* (2000) alone.[7] Mulcahy ordered workforce reductions resulting in 22,000 of 96,000 employees losing jobs.[8] She had to shut down promising product developments in what amounted to corporate infanticide.[9] Xerox had to restate four years' profits (1997–2000), the result of a Securities and Exchange Commission (SEC) accounting probe.[10] In April 2002, Mulcahy's Xerox paid a $10 million SEC fine, the largest then on record.[11] Just when she thought the bad news was behind her, Mulcahy had to hear from PricewaterhouseCoopers that the accounting write-offs would be double those predicted earlier, $6 billion versus $3 billion.[12]

For her first several years, Mulcahy worked all day, every day, from 6 am until 7 pm, continuing to make telephone calls after she arrived home in the evening.[13] She confessed to pulling her car over on the Merritt Parkway on her way home to rest her speeding heart. Through it all, a gaffe or two aside, Mulcahy kept her balance. She remained resolute in her intention "to fix the Xerox." The Xerox view is that Mulcahy will go to heaven as "Saint Anne."

The Predicament at Xerox

The company dominated the copier and document handling business well into the 1990s. Although Xerox's products were expensive, everyone used them. Then, while Xerox dealt with CEO succession problems, accounting woes, and an SEC investigation, Xerox lost its dominant position. Beginning in the late 1970s, low-cost providers such as Cannon and Ricoh gained market share. Giants such as Hewlett-Packard and a newly merged Konica-Minolta entered the field. Still later Kodak and the Dutch company Oce competed with Xerox. Oce announced that it "was on plan to grab at least a 20 percent share of the high speed copier market."[14]

Loss of market share in equipment sales and leasing packs a triple whammy. By losing equipment market share, Xerox lost significantly more in the follow-on market of inks, toners, and paper, which constantly renews itself after a copier manufacturer has gotten its foot in the door through installation of machines. Over time, from the 1970s, when Cannon and Ricoh first entered the market, until Mulcahy became CEO in 2001, Xerox's share of the copier market fell from 90 percent to 13 percent.

Early Black Marks

Ms. Mulcahy's first gaffe was a rookie mistake. Analysts had been clamoring for a remake of Xerox, into another IBM, which Louis Gerstner had remade into a provider of end-to-end business solutions, including profitable consulting. Ms. Mulcahy thought she was telling analysts what they wanted to hear when, in October 2000, she called Xerox's business plan "unsustainable." The stock plunged 26 percent in one day. "I figured being honest would make us credible," she said. "I made a roaring mistake."[15] She did not realize how fickle analysts may be, especially when searching for a pretext to justify dumping a stock.

As CEO, Mulcahy made another very public miscue in her dealings with the SEC. Disregarding lawyers' advice, Mulcahy negotiated the Xerox SEC settlement herself. "Maybe it [improper recognition of lease revenues for large copiers] didn't happen on my watch, but I am the most senior spokesperson, the one who can make a commitment about what we will do from now on," she reasoned.

Her direct participation was correct. One reason the SEC came down hard on Xerox was SEC staff perceptions that Xerox was uncooperative. For two years, Xerox representatives tried to lead the SEC to believe that the accounting problems were limited to Xerox's Mexican subsidiary, which was not true.[16]

Rather Mulcahy goofed when she requested a face-to-face meeting with SEC Chairman Harvey Pitt. The press excoriated Pitt for holding the meetings. Pitt also met with KPMG's CEO Eugene O'Kelly, when KPMG had been Pitt's client in private practice. Cynics thought that Pitt was polishing his client list for the day he returned to private practice.

Mulcahy compounded her goof by discussing the Xerox case with Pitt during their face time. One rule lawyers and judges follow is never to discuss a pending or recently decided case, on social or "meet and greet" occasions. Mulcahy met with Pitt on December 7, 2001, while the Xerox matter was pending, discussing it with him. The meeting became public news in May 2002.[17]

Mulcahy and Xerox did not come off well in the incident, but it was Chairman Pitt whom the press roasted.[18] Both the *Wall Street Journal* and Common Cause cited Pitt's conflicts of interest and poor judgment in the Mulcahy and O'Kelly meetings, calling for him to resign, which he later did.[19]

Mulcahy Biography

Anne Dolan was born on Long Island on October 21, 1952. She had four brothers who helped make her into a self-professed "gym rat." Her father worked as a publishing executive. From college, after two years at Chase Manhattan Bank, she entered the workforce at Xerox in 1976 as a sales rep.[20] In 1992, she became vice-president for human resources.

Bucking the prevailing view, which holds that human resources positions are dead ends, especially for women, Ms. Mulcahy moved up from human resources to chief staff officer under CEO Paul Allaire. She then became vice-president for customer operations with responsibility for South and Central America, Europe, Asia, Africa, and China. Xerox named her a senior vice-president in 1998.

Biographical details cannot convey Mulcahy's intense feeling about all matters Xerox. She has worked for the company practically all her working life, and she, along with Susan Ivey at Reynolds America (Chapter 6), are the only prominent female CEOs this book features who have done so. Her husband, Joe Mulcahy, is a retired Xerox sales manager. Her brother, Tom Dolan, is president of Xerox's new Global Solutions Services. "The good news or the bad news is she has the soul of Xerox."[21]

CEO Succession

During the latter part of Mulcahy's assent, a high-stakes drama was playing itself out at Xerox's headquarters in Stamford, Connecticut. In 1969, Xerox had moved its senior executives from Rochester, New York, where the company's roots and principal facilities were, to the fashionable Stamford address.

In Rochester, Xerox had unparalleled success in the 1960s and 1970s. Its 914 copier, which President Joseph Wilson took 14 years to develop, introducing it in 1959, was the best-selling industrial product of all-time, as of the time 914 production ceased in 1973.[22] Entire college endowments and substantial personal fortunes rested upon an investment in Xerox, which in 1906 had begun in Rochester as Haloid Co., a photographic supply company.

In the early 1970s, Xerox patents began to expire. Japanese competitors such as Cannon and Ricoh were then first able to move onto Xerox's turf. Xerox Parc, a research facility located in Palo Alto, California, near Stanford University, was an epicenter of invention. Xerox engineers developed the user-friendly icon commands that converted the personal computer into a user friendly tool. Steven Jobs and Apple Computer used Xerox icons to develop the Macintosh operating system.[23] Xerox did not. "For a good twenty years now," an ex-Xerox executive observed, "Xerox executives have been restructuring, revamping and repositioning virtually nonstop."[24]

Paul Allaire, another Xerox "lifer," had joined the company in 1964. He disengaged Xerox from a costly 1980s diversification into insurance. As CEO, he cut costs and introduced new products, including Xerox's first digital copier. Xerox re-branded itself from the copier company to the "Document Company," which would help organize the entire paper flow that desktop publishing and other technological advancements had bought into the picture.

As the choice of a successor to Allaire loomed, Xerox's board selected an heir apparent to train in a number two position, as president and chief operating officer. They chose G. Richard Thoman, who had spent his career working with IBM's Louis Gerstner: at McKinsey & Co., American Express, RJR Nabisco and, finally, at IBM. Thoman was to be a change agent, to devise a new vision on the hill for Xerox.

Thoman failed badly. Xerox missed the SOHO (small office, home office) fad. Thoman decided to take on Hewlett-Packard's printers but a decade too late. He pushed multifunction digital machines (scanner, fax, printer, copier) but, again, it too was too little too late.

Xerox had a serious case of the bloat. Wags called the oversized bureaucracy "Burox." Thoman did not cut. Instead, he ordered six months' study, which recommended a modest 10 percent cut (8,000 jobs). He also reorganized the sales force along functional lines (industries versus geographical territories), which had the Xerox sales force up in arms.

"I can't emphasize enough how mandarin and isolated the (Xerox) headquarters culture became over time," noted a Xerox retiree. At Xerox, executives at all times maintained "a patina of fake collegiality," masking from view a political and manipulative headquarter's culture.

Thoman was a "policy wonk." He was incapable of small talk but relished free wheeling, intellectually charged discussions. At Xerox, he should have done exactly the opposite—kept up the small talk in public and relegated the free wheeling discussion to behind closed doors. As a result of the mismatch with the Xerox culture, Thoman came across as arrogant and out of control.

What really undercut Thoman was not his strategic error, or his indecision on Burox and bloat, or his reorganization of the sales force, or the clash of his personal style with the Xerox culture, but the continuing specter of predecessor Paul Allaire. Allaire had become chairman of the board when Thoman ascended to CEO. Not content to limit himself to board meetings, Allaire negotiated a protocol by which, as board chair, he attended senior management meetings. His shadow presence undercut Thoman.

Thoman was gone 13 months after he had become CEO; Allaire was back in as CEO.

The Mulcahy Succession

For three years, political intrigue distracted Xerox from what it should have been doing. Then Anne Mulcahy became CEO in August 2001; she succeeded Paul Allaire as board chair in January 2002.[25] Anne Mulcahy was different from Thoman, Allaire, and other Xerox executives in at least three ways, all of which signaled an end to political intrigue.

One, Mulcahy was an unabashed cheerleader. No mandarin-like inscrutable behavior from her. Nor would she tolerate that behavior from other of her executives.

Second, she was unpretentious. When compared by the press to Hewlett-Packard's Carly Fiorina ("All Carly, All of the Time"), Mulcahy replied "I'm not as famous as Carly and I want to keep it that way."[26] Mulcahy was half hard-nosed executive, half sensitive mother, who attended her sons' high school track meets and gave every Xerox employee their birthday as a day off—as a reward for sticking through Xerox's tough times.[27] During the period of re-computing Xerox's 1997–2000 earnings, Mulcahy telephoned her financial people several times a day. She told them to take Memorial Day weekend off. "I heard the strain in their voices, and I knew I had to ease up."

Third, she has been decisive. "She is fair and direct . . . She makes hard decisions quickly and never looks back," says Gary Bonadonna, director of the Needletrades, Industrial and Textile Employees, which represents Xerox's rank-and-file.[28] Mulcahy herself says, "there needs to be far more innovation and receptivity to new ideas. I have very little time for endless debate and consensus."[29]

Turning Xerox Around

Some of the steps Mulcahy took in her effort to turn the once mighty ship around are as follows:

- She has outsourced Xerox's manufacturing to Singapore.
- She sold a half interest in a joint venture to Fuji Film for $1.3 billion, raising cash and exiting the venture.
- She has caused the administrative side of equipment leasing to be farmed out to GE Capital through a joint venture, Xerox Capital Services.
- She cut the payroll by 22,000.[30]
- She moved the corporate headquarters from high-priced Stamford to more modestly priced Norwalk, Connecticut.
- She caused Xerox to sell to GE Capital, the Xerox financial arm which provides vendor financing to Xerox customers, and, in the process, raised $557 million.[31]
- As president and COO, Mulcahy closed the purchase of Portland, Oregon Textronix color printing division for $925 million. It has proven to be a success, a steady source of revenues and profits for Xerox.

"She has proven personable and decisive," says Denis Nayden of GE Capital. More importantly, cost cutting permits Xerox to sell products for half the price they used to command. For example, the Phaser 6100 office color printer now sells for $699, which "helps Xerox compete with Cannon, Ricoh, and Hewlett-Packard for the more profitable sales of ink, paper and services."[32] In 2003, battling to "counter an image that it sold only highly sophisticated products at premium prices," Xerox launched a new office printer–copier that sells for less than $900, less than half the price customers had been paying for a comparable Xerox machine.[33] "[The] changes enable Xerox to compete head-to-head with rivals like Cannon and Ricoh for the first time in years in the $52 billion office copier market."[34] Xerox will never return to a 90 percent market share but it is competitive once again.

Mulcahy on Mulcahy

She knows that she got where she is by being, in her words, "an unpretentious workhorse."[35] Maggie Wildrotter, CEO of Citizens Communications, prefers holding up Mulcahy to a flashy Carleton Fiorina "for up-and-coming female CEOs," as "an example of grace under pressure . . . who has stunned Wall Street and her peers by saving a company many had written off."[36] Mulcahy deflects such praise, saying she "was lucky to inherit a company in which 'enlightened leaders' long ago built an infrastructure . . . that has created a diverse team of leaders at the top." "I feel fortunate because this is a company that understood the value of inclusiveness before it was in vogue . . . [b]ut you have to keep focused on it. [It] doesn't happen by accident."[37] Interestingly, and contrary to the advice books, Mulcahy thinks that advancement of women in business isn't "about mentoring programs or diversity programs at companies—it starts with a CEO who is willing to have a diverse leadership team run his or her business." At Xerox, she co-founded a Woman's Network, as did Brenda Barnes (Chapter 7) when she became CEO at Sara Lee Corp.[38] Among other things, through meetings, a Woman's Network permits women managers to associate with and get to know one another.

More important to Anne Mulcahy than mentors is the setting in which her parents raised her. "[D]inner was a time to be provocative, to discuss politics, religion, current events, anything that was contentious. You had to participate, you had to be armed with information from reading newspapers." From those experiences, "I learned that you can disagree, even fight, without confusing theoretical arguments with personal attacks."[39]

She also grew up "in a gender neutral household." "For me, it always felt absolutely natural to be the only woman in a room full of men." "I grew up in a home that did not differentiate between being a man or being a woman. I had four brothers, but I was never assigned 'female' responsibilities. I wasn't the one who cleaned up the dishes every night. . . . Today, I realize how unusual that is, but as a kid, it seemed perfectly normal."[40]

PATRICIA RUSSO

Another Glamor Company Gone Bad

Patricia Russo, now an ex-*Fortune 500* female CEO, was also at the helm of a fallen angel. Lucent Technologies' share price had fallen from $80 to $7.10 when Ms. Russo took office,[41] and went as low as $0.58, in October 2002. Through retirement buyouts, asset sales, spinoffs of divisions, and layoffs, Lucent slashed its workforce from 120,000 to 56,000 at the time Ms. Russo returned,[42] and continued down to 33,500 under her tenure. Lucent, once a darling of the high-tech telecommunications sector, lost $16.2 billion in 2001,[43] and $11.8 billion in 2002.

What happened? In line with the wisdom prevailing of the 1990s, Lucent got "big fast."[44] It made acquisitions which proved to be duds. It spent great sums on fiber optic manufacture only to have Canada's Nortel Networks eclipse it with a differing technology. The internet and e-commerce never achieved a fifth of their potential, leaving miles of fiber optic cable unused in the ground, bandwidth that the United States will not need for decades, and smothering a market for which Lucent had prepared.

Lucent also financed the purchase of telecommunications equipment by scores of wannabe telecommunications and internet service providers, which all went belly up, paying little, if anything, on their debts to Lucent. Vendor (Lucent) financing for purchases by Winstar, Global Crossing, Jato, One.Tel, and others reached $8.4 billion in 2002. All of those companies entered bankruptcy, never paying Lucent a cent:

> By early 1999, the company's outstanding bills began to climb as Lucent began easing up on its credit terms. Rather than insisting that customers pay their bills in 30 days, [Carleton] Fiorina [then a Lucent vice-president]'s salespeople would let customers slide for 90 days or longer if they placed an order. Salespeople were pressured to get customers to buy immediately rather than put it off—a tactic that essentially borrowed from future quarters to make the current one.[45]

Lucent had an obsolete product mix. It still had an excess of supplies for the copper wire circuit switched networks. Ericsson, Nokia, and Nortel stole the march on Lucent in supplying the wireless market.

Legal Troubles

Like Xerox, Lucent has been the subject of an SEC investigation into accounting irregularities. Lucent had come out of the cold in December 2000, confessing to the SEC that it had improperly booked $679 million in revenue. The previous August, the Lucent board sacked CEO Richard McGinn on whose watch the improper revenue recognition had occurred.[46]

In a suit for wrongful dismissal, former president for North American sales, Nina Aversano, claimed that Lucent had forced both her and Patricia Russo to resign from their positions at Lucent because they had objected to inflated revenue reports.[47] Russo denied the story and quietly departed, to Eastman Kodak in Rochester, where she was to be president and chief operating officer.

Seventeen months later she was back at Lucent, as CEO. Kodak analysts lamented her departure, calling her "a positive force in a negative environment" and "the most articulate leader they've had in years" at Kodak.[48]

After sacking CEO McGinn, the Lucent board turned to the previous CEO, Henry Schacht. Schacht put in place a business plan to cut Lucent's size in half and to sell no more to wannabes. Under his plan, Lucent would sell only to major telecommunications companies such as Verizon, SBC, and Bell South. Schacht implemented much of his business plan before he approached Ms. Russo about returning to Lucent. Lucent gave Russo a $29.9 million "golden hello" to lure her from Kodak.[49]

In the Saddle

Russo's business plan was simply to implement Schacht's plan. She argued that an "outsider's strategic ditherings are the last thing shell shocked Lucent employees need right now . . . the company requires a CEO who will stick to the basics."[50]

As they did with Anne Mulcahy, the press often compared Russo to the other star who had emerged from Lucent, Carly Fiorina. After the comparison, many came to call Russo "the anti-Carly."[51]

Co-workers and the press described Russo as "intense but reserved, the very antithesis of the back-slapping CEOs to whom companies often turn when they are looking for a quick fix. She is the ultimate corporate type—a familiar face at Lucent's headquarters." She was a "straight shooter," who gave subordinates bad news or good news without varnish. Reporters often found Russo snacking on M&Ms in her office.[52] When she returned to Lucent from Kodak, she carried only a thin briefcase—no oriental rugs, Audubon prints, or Chippendale furniture. When the press asked her about that, she replied "I travel light." Associates described her as "grounded" and "low key."[53]

Patricia Russo's skill set meshed nicely with Henry Schacht's business plan. One large telecom's CEO said of Lucent: "They need someone who knows the industry, the personnel, and the field organizations," concluding that Russo fitted the bill of particulars outlined.[54] In her first few weeks as CEO, Ms. Russo made 19 personal calls on major Lucent customers.[55] Patricia Russo seemed the quietest, most controlled of the six women CEOs in the *Fortune 500* when she took office. More than Anne Mulcahy, or perhaps even Marion Sandler at Golden West Financial, Russo seemed "within herself." She knew her limitations.

The Limits of Management Skill

For all her evident abilities, Russo had been unable to resurrect Lucent. There were gaffes. She forecast that Lucent would be profitable by 2003. It was but not until its fourth fiscal quarter, ending September 30, 2003.[56] Meanwhile, Jim Kelleher, analyst for Argus Research, spoke for many when he noted a "resumption of their credibility problem," leading to a conclusion that "I just won't buy the stock."[57]

Then, after six quarters of modest profits, in 2004 Lucent slipped into the red again. In addition to European competitors, such as Ericsson, Siemens, and Nokia, new entrants from China, such as Huawei and ZTE, emerged as principal players in an already crowded wireless market. Lucent's biggest subscribers, Verizon and AT&T, found themselves losing fixed line subscribers not to wireless but to cable companies. Product purchasers, such as Bell South, merged with other entities (AT&T); they withdrew from purchasing in any quantity while they digested the merger.[58]

Thus was Lucent brought to the brink of its own merger. Alcatel and Lucent had discussed a $22.8 billion merger, when Lucent was a much bigger company, in 2001.[59] Alcatel, a global company with only 12 percent of its sales in France, and a bigger one than Lucent, with 58,000 employees, seemed a good fit for Lucent, which had re-invented itself, with half its revenue from wireless equipment.[60]

A Season for White Elephants in Telecommunications

The parties billed the Alcatel-Lucent transaction as a "merger of equals," which it clearly was not. The headquarters would be in France where Russo would move. All the new corporation's senior managers, save Russo, would be French. The new board would consist of Russo, Tchuruk of Alcatel, six directors from Lucent, six directors from Alcatel, and two new directors who would be European.[61] "Alcatel is worth $8 billion more than Lucent. That's typically a t-a-k-e-o-v-e-r."[62]

Critics were not kind: this merger of equals "is a synonym for d-i-s-a-s-t-e-r in English, d-e-s-a-s-t-r-e in French." The merger closed in September 2006. It has been red ink and additional job cuts (16,500) since. The revenue shortfalls have been said to be "astonishing."[63] The merger has "all the ingredients of being a disaster," said analyst Per Lindberg of Dresdener Kleinwort.[64]

Alcatel-Lucent lost $3.8 billion in 2007 but revenues had increased 18 percent. There were signs that, once the partners had digested the costs associated with the merger, the new company could return to profitability.[65] Russo, though, will not be there. A French shareholder, Michel Tiphineau, had warned Alcatel executives that Ms. Russo had struck an ominous note by saying "au revoir," or goodbye, rather than "a bientot," or "see you soon."[66] More substantive is a reporter's prognostication:

> [M]s. Russo is being thrown into a tight-knit management team in France with very few of her own people. The chief financial officer, the chief operations officer, and the head of human resources are all Alcatel veterans. You can just imagine how loyal they will be to Ms. Russo when she tries to go after Alcatel employees while trying to achieve the job cuts the companies have promised . . . So here's a prediction: Ms. Russo will not be the chief executive of the combined company in 36 months. An Alcatel executive will be.[67]

Ms. Russo describes how she has survived as long as she did: "You can't let the snowball roll over you."[68] Yet, given the toll all the job cuts and losses have to have taken on her, the prediction that she would not be in office by 2009 seemed a viable proposition, even for one as even keeled and understated as Ms. Russo has been.

On her part, she has "consistently said she has no plans to leave,"[69] until July 2008, when she confirmed predictions, announcing that she would step down as CEO when the Alcatel board appointed a successor, which it did in September, with a $9.4 million severance package and $740,000 annual retirement for Russo.[70] The high-level resignation was seen as "an admission that the merger has failed to deliver on its promise to create a global player in telecommunications equipment." In 2007–08, Alcatel again had six consecutive quarters of losses.

The company's "dual identity" proved to be a burden: "It was a permanent balancing act: if an American gets this job, a French must get that other job . . . [A] new boss coming in from the outside will be able to start from scratch."[71] French employees criticized Russo's lack of a technical background and "lack of effort to brush up on high-school French." Russo remained chipper to the last: "She said she wasn't the manager to lead the company" after the merger and ensuing reorganization: "The Marines that land on the beach and secure it aren't necessarily the same ones you want there to keep the peace and build hospitals and schools."[72]

Tentative Teachings

Line Experience, while Important, may be Overrated

In some cases, the lack of line experience is a pretext search committees use to exclude women. Before rising to become CEO, Anne Mulcahy spent the greatest amount of her time as vice-president for human resources, a so-called pink collar job which companies often reserve for women executives. Pat Russo had a sales background. Nonetheless, at the penultimate stage of any high-level candidate review, search committees are looking for any excuse to shorten the list. Lack of line or any other similar experience throughout the course of a career may be the pretext they were looking for.

Changing Careers often Aids Career Advancement

Changing employers and sectors (e.g., profit to not-for-profit, or profit to government) may have a beneficial strategic effect, as Pat Russo's departure to Kodak shows. By contrast, too much "side stepping" may give off the appearance of a lack of stability or "careerism," a characterization Meg Whitman (Chapter 7) narrowly avoided. Anne Mulcahy proves the exception to the rule. She has spent virtually her entire career at the same corporation, Xerox.

Mulcahy at Xerox and Russo at Lucent are Paradigmatic "Glass Cliff" Case Studies

This recently articulated theory, to be discussed in Chapter 12, holds that, while boards today are more likely to choose a woman as CEO, boards are much more likely to take a chance on naming a woman as CEO when the company is in the midst of tough times, or in an extremis situation. Xerox with Anne Mulcahy and Lucent with Pat Russo bear witness to the theory, as does Avon with Andrea Jung, and as do several of the corporations with women CEOs in chapters that follow (e.g., Reynolds America with Susan Ivey (Chapter 6), Sara Lee Corp. with Brenda Barnes (Chapter 7), Rite Aid with Mary Sammons (Chapter 8), Carol Bartz at Yahoo! (Chapter 9)).

Know when to Duck, know when to Admit Error, know when to Apologize

Jill Barad and Carleton Fiorina were never able to do these things. They had short tenures as CEOs. By contrast, Mulcahy and Russo lasted much longer. Neither made quantified projections or, for the most part, generic ones either. Through periods of red ink, massive layoffs, downsizing, and poor stock market performance, they kept low profiles.

Balance becomes more Important as You Rise toward the Top

Anne Mulcahy never misses an athletic event in which her sons participate. Pat Russo keeps her hand in several sports, as does Mulcahy. Russo plays golf to a competitive handicap. While a woman or other executive may relegate balance to third or fourth on her list of priorities in mid-career, which may be a judicious choice, as women reach for the very top balance seems to become a top priority again. These two women CEOs (Mulcahy and Russo) have a degree of balance in their lives as CEOs; it seems an ingredient of their success.

Dedication is not just about Long Hours and Hard Work

Anne Mulcahy has been called "the soul of Xerox." Pat Russo has spent much of her career at AT&T and its successor, Lucent. Undoubtedly they work long hours. But the type of dedication they exhibit and which got them to the CEO suite is different. They believe in the companies they lead: their people, their products and services, and their future. They make that evident as CEOs and they have made it evident on their way upward.

Be Decisive

CEO Richard Thoman at Xerox couldn't make decisions. When finally he made them, he pulled his punch and made tepid moves that satisfied no one. Both Mulcahy and Russo had to make drastic downsizing plans and implement them. They have done so with as much sensitivity as they could muster yet they made them as swiftly and efficiently as possible. "I have little time for endless debate and consensus," says Mulcahy.

Exhibit Grace under Pressure

If you ask another person "how are you," many will respond "I've had a lousy day," or even worse, with an earful, or litany, of troubles. By contrast, the unpretentious, less egocentric and graceful will always turn the question around, responding "Fine. And how are you?" Later they may or may not unburden themselves of stress of carrying so many intractable problems and predicaments with them. Both Anne Mulcahy and Pat Russo are unpretentious workhorses who at all times have exhibited grace under pressure.

You can't let the Snowball roll over You

Because she has that elixir of grace under pressure, Pat Russo has made this one of her mantras. When senior executives give an aspiring executive a test to turn around a product, a plant, division, or subsidiary, as well as when a woman becomes the CEO of a company in a turnaround situation, she has to take on the challenges of the job one by one and set about as the problem solver, the one who can fix it if anyone can. They can't let themselves be overwhelmed. For an executive in that situation at some point in her career, and many will find themselves given such a challenge, a good first place to look would be the predicaments Anne Mulcahy and Pat Russo faced and the manner in which each responded.

6 Go Where They Aren't

Susan M. Ivey—Reynolds America, Inc., Paula Reynolds—Safeco Insurance Co., and Patricia Woertz—Archer Daniels Midland, Inc.

These women made their marks in male environments—not just which men dominate but which male managers populate exclusively. Susan Ivey spent her 27-year career in tobacco, rising to become CEO of the industry's second largest producer, Reynolds America. Paula Reynolds rose through the ranks of the utility industry, before becoming CEO at Safeco (insurance and the *Fortune 500*). Patricia Woertz spent 29 years in oil and gas (Gulf Oil, Chevron, then Chevron-Texaco), before the Archer Daniels Midland board of directors appointed her CEO of the agribusiness giant, "supermarket to the world."

"Going where they (women) aren't" is not for every woman. Yet these women show that, with sufficient ability and self-confidence, ambitious women are able to counter-program, rising further and more rapidly than they would have in fashion, travel, publishing, retail, food or other industries with more significant female representation in management.

SUSAN M. IVEY

The Tobacco Culture

Susan Ivey is the only smoker among the 21 women this book chronicles. She began her career in tobacco because she was a smoker. She could not find Barclay menthol cigarettes in Louisville, so she telephoned Barclay's producer, Brown & Williamson Tobacco (B&W). Marketing officials told her that B&W's hometown, Louisville, had no distributor for the brand. Ivey wanted to sell, according to her, something she "had a passion for: cosmetics, alcohol or cigarettes." Admiring her forthright approach, the B&W managers hired Susan Ivey.[1]

Ivey didn't come from tobacco country. Raised in New York, after graduating from the University of Florida in 1980, she followed her boyfriend, who obtained a position at General Electric's Louisville manufacturing facility. While she worked by day, first at Lanier Business Products Co., and then in her entry level position at B&W, at night Ivey studied for an MBA at

Bellarmine College, the local Jesuit university. After she received her degree, she moved quickly into a succession of management roles at B&W, which sanded off any rough edges: district sales manager, brand director, and vice-president marketing.

Her next steps were international ones, with B&W posting her to the parent corporation in England, British American Tobacco, plc (BAT). She served there 1990–94, followed by two years as a marketing director in Hong Kong. Back in London, Ivey held several posts, including director of marketing for China, head of international brands, and senior vice-president marketing. In 2001, back in the United States once more, she became president and CEO of B&W, the BAT subsidiary.[2]

R.J. Reynolds Tobacco and B&W, which BAT had spun off, merged in January 2004, to form Reynolds America. Susan Ivey became CEO of the merged entity, which began trading on the New York Stock Exchange as Reynolds America, Inc. (RAI).

Industry Ups and Downs

Internationally, cigarette consumption continued to increase. Ivey's career benefited from that through the 1990s.[3] She enabled BAT to capitalize on international trends by rejuvenating old trademarks. In China, for example, she oversaw the re-launch of the State Express 555 brand. She breathed new life into the Lucky Strike and Kool labels.[4] At RAI, she oversaw the switch to "an every day low price" strategy for formerly premium brands such as GPC and Viceroy to undercut competitors' premium brands. She thus also cut out costly rebate and incentive programs for those labels.

Domestically, cigarette consumption took a different path. In 1998, state attorneys general of 46 states reached a $368.5 billion settlement of a civil suit against the major tobacco companies, which included B&W.[5] Forced to pay their share of the settlement, bound by the settlement's marketing restrictions, and confronted by a decline in cigarette consumption generally, the majors faced a considerable backdraft. Into the vacuum so created, smaller companies, not parties to the settlement, marketed cheaper discount brands, with great success. Between 1998 and 2003, B&W's domestic market share fell from 15 percent to 10.6 percent.[6]

Although Susan Ivey's watch at the time was, fortuitously, the international markets, when she became RAI CEO, she had to face a domestic situation that had deteriorated. For example, in 2003, Reynolds Tobacco's domestic sales were off 13 percent from the year before. The company faced not only an onslaught of discounted brands but also a bevy of lawsuits by smokers and their survivors. In the third quarter of 2003, Reynolds posted a $3.5 billion loss.[7]

CEO Ivey turned those numbers into RAI's favor. She caused RAI to acquire Conwood Company, the nation's second largest manufacturer of smokeless tobacco products, with a 25 percent market share and a growing demographic, for $3.5 billion. Her marketing prowess has returned five of RAI's cigarette brands to the top ten domestic brands. In 2007, RAI earnings increased 12.6 percent, to $4.57 per share, and dividends increased 13.3 percent, to $3.40 per year. She caused the board to adopt a policy of paying out 75 percent of current income to shareholders in the form of dividends. Until the market crunch of 2008, the share price increased 127 percent since 2004, compared to 32 percent for the Standard & Poors 500 overall.[8] In 2007, *Fortune* listed CEO Ivey as the 24th most powerful business woman in the United States.[9]

Work–Life and Susan Ivey

A woman CEO of a German public company has suggested that maybe in this day and age woman are having children late in life, at a time in their lives when what always is an episodic event in any life seems even more precious and special. If women had their children earlier, they might take child bearing and rearing more in their stride, returning for an uninterrupted stint at their careers.[10]

Susan Ivey is the opposite. Children came into her life when she was 38 years old, advanced in her career. In 1997, she married Trevor Ivey, whom she met in Malaysia while she was working in London for BAT and he was based in Taiwan for the same company. He had two sons, then ages 13 and 16, by his first marriage, at the time he and Susan married. In fact, children did not come front and center in her life until two years later. Susan and Trevor did not keep household together until 1999, after Trevor had retired from BAT.

Trickle Down at Reynolds America

Susan Ivey may be more powerful than 24th among business women in the United States, at least to women executives at Reynolds America. Nineteen women serve as Reynolds America corporate officers under CEO Ivey. Four of the seven highest officials at the company are women: Susan Ivey, chair and CEO; Julia "Judy" Lambeth, executive vice-president and general counsel; Ann Johnston, vice-president for human resources; and Susan Wilson, vice-president and general auditor. Three of 12 board members are female, as is true of only 14 percent of America's public companies.

Ivey herself seems schizophrenic about the development. On the one hand, she maintains that promotion decisions are not gender based, the result of a strict meritocracy to RAI.[11] On the other, Ivey is fanatical about measurable results in the hiring and promotion of women and has urged progressiveness in the makeup of upper management.[12]

Commentators urge myriad reasons for a trickle down effect when it does take place at a particular company. First, better mentoring by women, who are now in the upper management ranks, enables women below to progress better. Second, adverse reactions to women as co-workers fall markedly as their proportion increases in the work center or management group. Third, better information about women and roles they can play corrects previous information biases and asymmetries, leading to hiring and promotion of additional women.[13]

Certain companies have had women CEOs for a number of years but virtually no visibility for other women. Hewlett-Packard under Carleton Fiorina and Rite Aid under Mary Sammons are examples. Few other women broke into the upper management ranks under those two CEOs: no trickle down occurred. At Reynolds America, under CEO Susan Ivey, a trickle down (a robust trickle down at that) has taken place. The difference is not due to any specific factor (increased mentoring, elimination of information asymmetries). The difference is due to tone at the top. Susan Ivey has set the right tone at Reynolds America.

PAULA ROSPORT REYNOLDS

Go Where They Aren't

In 2002, Spencer Stuart, the executive recruiting firm, studied the utility industry.[14] More than half of women managers the study surveyed found the energy industry to be the least appealing of ten industries. They called the energy industry "an old boy network," "boring," "not female friendly." The Spencer Stuart report concluded that "[t]he industry's leadership culture is rooted in male-dominated disciplines, such as engineering, making it difficult for women."[15]

Twenty-four years earlier, in 1978, Paula Rosport saw the utility industry's characteristics as advantages. The reason she choose her first management job out of Wellesley College, after a short stint consulting, in energy and utilities was "because there were no women and I'd be unique."[16] "Research consistently finds that male-dominated industries are especially prone to gender stereotyping and that women . . . report facing specific barriers to advancement."[17] Paula Rosport Reynolds found great success there, spending 27 years in the utility industry before becoming the CEO at Safeco Insurance, 363rd on the 2007 *Fortune 500*.

A Side-Stepping Career

She achieved that success by changing jobs and changing companies, always within the utilities industry, with some frequency, another common ingredient of successful careers for women.[18] She began with the large San Francisco utility Pacific Gas & Electric Co., spending 16 years there and rising to senior vice-president, then moved to Pacific Gas Transmission, which built and operated pipelines. Many of her jobs were line jobs, including heading up construction of the Alberta-to-California pipeline, at the time the longest natural gas pipeline ever built.

Reynolds moved to Houston in 1995, where she became president of PanEnergy Power Services. In 1997, PanEnergy, the parent corporation of Reynolds's subsidiary, merged with Duke Power. Ms. Reynolds became president and CEO of Duke Energy Power Services, a larger entity resulting from the merger of two similar subsidiaries.

In 1998, she moved again, this time to Atlanta, Georgia, where she became president and chief operating officer (COO) of Atlanta Gas Light Company, soon to rename itself with the fancier appellation AGL Resources, Inc. She became CEO of AGL in 2000. AGL moved aggressively through acquisitions (Virginia Natural Gas, NUI Corp.) to become the second largest natural gas distribution company in the United States, ranked 717th on the *Fortune 1000* by 2006, when CEO Reynolds left AGL for Safeco in Seattle.[19]

Women and other minorities may move to get out from underneath a glass or plexiglass ceiling that retards their upward progress in their current company. There seems to have been a bit of that in Paula Reynolds's career: "I picked up and moved every time there was a new opportunity—because your odds of getting to the top at any corporation are low no matter who you are. The best way to improve your chance of success is by moving."[20] Such moves nearly always impose a human cost on those around the side-stepping manager: Reynolds's son refers to himself as "a corporate vagabond."

Her frequent moves also seem to be in keeping with one of her theories of management, that is, "the half life of a leader." Beyond an initial period of observation, which may last five or six months, a leader's effectiveness is the highest at the beginning of her tenure and, like the irradiated material, has a half life thereafter, diminishing in effectiveness as time progresses.[21] The first implication is to set an agenda and accomplish goals early. The second implication is to change positions or seek promotions to coincide with projected decreases in efficiency.

A Near Trophy Director

One of Paula Reynolds' less praiseworthy characteristics seems to have been an inability to say "no" to seats on other corporations' boards. Her popularity may also be reflective of how few women have risen to prominence in business. While not a straight up trophy director, Paula Reynolds has been a "serial" trophy director. She has sat on boards at Coca Cola (2001–07); Air Products & Chemicals, Inc. (2001–04); Circuit City Stores Inc. (2001–03); Delta Airlines (2003 to present); Anadarko Petroleum Corp. (2004 to present); and the Seattle Art Museum (2007), as well as Safeco Insurance. Paula Reynolds may be a very capable director but her presence on so many boards, albeit serially, arouses suspicion that she permits herself to be used as a token.

Mentoring and Trickle Down

Being a serial director was the yang of it. The ying is that one of Reynolds's most praiseworthy characteristics is that she has been a help and inspiration to other women managers wherever she had been. She has benefited them in more formal ways as well, shepherding them upward through promotions and positions with greater amounts of authority, not easy in the male-dominated utility industry:

- At Duke Energy, Paula Rosport facilitated promotion of Gianna Mansueto Howard to a position in which she became responsible for construction of a new electrical power plant, a very successful venture for Duke.[22] "[N]ot only did [Gianna] have the skill to understand the risks and make it happen, she managed to infuse everyone involved with a deep energy and enthusiasm," sang the superior about the subordinate.
- At AGL, Inc., Rosport mentored Catherine Land Waters, who went on to become a senior vice-president, crediting Rosport with her success.[23] Again, Rosport reciprocated with unstinting praise: "[She had] kind of a sponge quality . . . [a]nything you put in front of [Catherine] she's going to absorb, from arts to engineering."
- Susan Sitherwood, who went on to become vice-president Southern Operations at AGL, talks of having been mentored: "Leadership from someone like Reynolds creates an opportunity for success . . . Everybody needs good role models, a line of sight for their aspirations, Paula provided that."[24]

No statistics seem available for Paula Reynolds leadership at AGL, as they are available for, say, Susan Ivey's at Reynolds America. The anecdotes such as those above do demonstrate that under Paula Reynolds as CEO not only mentoring but also a trickle down takes place as well.

Trickle down also accords with Reynolds's management philosophy: "The strength of an organization, as she sees it, is its ability to make its dissenters its leaders. That's why the best leaders embrace out-of-the-box thinkers and diversity of thought."[25] She likes to leave as much room as is possible for junior managers to create and contribute their ideas: "An important lesson of leadership is to learn to subordinate yourself in various ways."[26]

According to Suzanne Sitherwood, Paula Reynolds has a "non-stop passion for diversity." Talking of her achievements at AGL, Reynolds boasted: "Since 1999, we've more than doubled the participation of minorities in our executive team and we have increased by 40 percent the number of women in our executive team . . . This is probably the only place in America that is not a cosmetics company where you have a CEO and a COO who are women."[27]

Reynolds at Safeco

Paula Rosport became Reynolds in October 2005, after her marriage to Steve Reynolds, the CEO since 2002 of Puget Energy, the Northwest electric and gas utility. Paula Reynolds had a bicoastal marriage until she became Safeco CEO in January 2006, when she moved to Seattle and the CEO couple took up housekeeping.

At Safeco, Reynolds seemed too busy for any mentoring of women or trickle down to take place. She succeeded a highly successful Safeco CEO, Mike McGavick, who rescued a nearly moribund company, leaving to pursue a political career.[28] After taking over, Reynolds caused Safeco to sell off its high-rise headquarters building in Seattle's university district, moving corporate operations into leased space. She moved the place of trading for Safeco shares from over-the-counter, on the NASDAQ, to the New York Stock Exchange.

Financial performance was flat. After a peak of $68 in 2007, the Safeco share price slipped back to the low forties and stayed there. *Fortune* listed Reynolds as one of its six underperforming female CEOs in 2007, removing her from "Fortune's 50 Most Powerful Women." She initiated job cuts and a stock buyback program. Evidently, however, Reynolds was unable to get all the sand out of the gearbox. In April 2008, she engineered the sale of the company to Liberty Mutual Insurance of Boston for a so-so $68.25 per share, or $6.2 billion, effective September 2008.[29] Seattle lost a proud local company, retaining only the name on the major league baseball park (Safeco Field). Reynolds moved to New York to take a position with AIG supervising the gargantuan government bailout of that company.

PATRICIA WOERTZ

Even Earlier Beginnings

Paula Reynolds started her quest after college, as have most other women CEOs. Pat Woertz began hers *in grammar school*. While other parents were preparing to take children to Disney World, Pat Woertz's parents took her on industrial tours: a window manufacturing plant, a Heinz ketchup factory, a U.S. Steel mill, Gulf Oil and Mellon Bank headquarters facilities. Her mother, Vi, was a school librarian for whom summers were for education. Pat did not groan as many other children would. She enjoyed it: "I've always enjoyed seeing how things are made."[30] Those early immersions in seeing how things are done, or how they are made, also prepared her for a corporate culture in which engineers and males dominate.

Woertz formulated a desire to become a corporate CEO from an early age. She stayed close to home (Pittsburgh) for college, majoring in accounting at Penn State (she later got an executive MBA at Columbia). She then spent three years in public accounting, with the Pittsburgh office of Ernst & Young. She jumped to Gulf Oil Co., then a Pittsburgh institution, beginning a 29-year career in the petroleum industry. Again, going where they aren't, immersion into the worlds of accounting and auditing better prepared Pat Woertz for a corporate culture many women would find adverse.

She had her three children early, ignoring the advice of a "knuckle dragging boss" at Gulf Oil, who actually said, "Get yourself fixed and expense it."[31]

Twenty-nine Years in Oil and Gas

In 1983, T. Boone Pickens made a hostile takeover bid for Gulf Oil, after having obtained "greenmail" payments for the shares he had obtained in earlier hostile bids for Cities Service and Phillips Petroleum.[32] Pickens chased Gulf into a defensive $14 billion merger with Chevron of San Francisco and Houston.

Woertz already was in Houston, Gulf having transferred her there a few years earlier. The plan of merger required the new larger Chevron to rid itself of duplicative facilities: a pipeline, a refinery, and 4,000 service stations. Managers put Woertz in command of the "clean team," charged with making the divestitures. "It was a turning point in my career," she remembers. "I learned about M&A and how to value assets and how to work with investment bankers."

She and her family moved to Chevron headquarters in San Francisco, where she went through a string of positions: finance manager, Chevron information technology (1989); strategic planning manager for Chevron (1991); and president, Chevron Canada (1993), which necessitated another move, this time to Vancouver, British Columbia. Within Chevron, senior managers regarded the Canadian posting as a proving ground for rising stars.

In 1996, Woertz and family returned to San Francisco, where she went through a further succession of jobs, ending up as CEO of Chevron Products Company, responsible for 8,600 employees, 8,000 service stations, and six refineries. She had risen further than any woman ever had at Chevron, although her experience had been limited exclusively to "downstream operations." In oil patch culture, real power, replete with the roustabout mentality, reside "upstream," in exploration and production, where beachhead production in Kazakstan and drilling in the North Sea better capture the spirit of the industry.

Chevron merged with Texaco in 2000. Woertz became executive vice-president, effectively chief operating officer, in charge of downstream operations in 180 countries, 26,000 employees, 25,000 service stations, 20 refineries, 2.2 million barrels of production daily, and $80 billion in annual revenue. Thereafter, though, the new company stumbled, with downstream earnings falling from $1.1 billion to $43 million in the first half of 2002. Woertz cut jobs and trimmed operating expenses by $500 million, restoring profitability. She later told students in a 2005 speech at the

University of Pennsylvania's Wharton Business School that reorganization, with the inevitable job cuts that accompany it, "underscores the shadow side of creativity. Nothing is created without something being destroyed."

A less charitable view from a former Chevron insider is that Woertz's overweening ambition and lack of engineering expertise caused her to fault people rather than equipment and processes which had malfunctioned. In fact, a criticism which many level at her is that her ambition has been outsized for all of her career. Many former co-workers brand her "hyper ambitious."

Archer Daniels Midland

Local journalists ascribe to ADM "a bit of a Mafioso image."[33] George Archer and John Daniels formed the company over 105 years ago. But they did so in the small downstate Illinois town of Decatur, where it remains headquartered, and the company has suffered from its insularity ever since.

Dwayne Andreas took over as CEO in 1970. In 27 years, he increased revenues 31-fold, from $450 million to $14 billion by 1997 (today its annual revenues exceed $40 billion). He also caused the company to hire, among others, his brother, his sons, and two nephews.

Critics bashed ADM in a number of ways besides nepotism. Under Andreas, ADM became the archetypical political corporation. Andreas leased the suite which adjoined the one that the U.S. Ambassador to the United Nations uses at the Waldorf Astoria in New York. Andreas convinced Andrew Young, George H.W. Bush, and Bob Dole, as well as other politicians and former ambassadors to serve on ADM's board, which *Business Week* ranked the worst performing board in the United States. Wags swore that ADM stood for "All Dwayne's Men."

In 1997, a federal court found Dwayne Andreas's son, Michael, an ADM vice-president, along with several other ADM executives, guilty of price fixing. The judge fined ADM $100 million and sentenced Michael Andreas to three years in prison. The title of one book about ADM, current at the time, seemed to capture it all: *Rats in the Grain*.[34]

Nonetheless, the Andreas clan maintained their grip. Dwayne's nephew, G. Allen Andreas, succeeded Dwayne as CEO in 1997. Added to nepotism, criminality, and influence peddling arguably was sexism. In 2005, Allen Andreas publicly stated that "[m]y bias, because of the specific nature of this company, is to stay with someone inside," namely, a male successor.

Woertz at ADM

The ten-person ADM board overrode Allen Andreas's preferences, naming Patricia Woertz CEO in April 2006.[35] ADM became the largest U.S. corporation, which *Fortune* ranked 56th, with a female CEO, taking over from Hewlett-Packard, which *Fortune* ranked 19th but which had deposed its woman CEO, Carleton Fiorina, in 2005.

Progressives applauded Woertz's appointment: "By God, if you knew the culture there. Bringing in an outsider, a woman no less, into a company that's a bastion of lifers and good ole' boys—I can't tell you what a huge change that is."[36] Others were more circumspect. A director remarked that he was impressed with how well Woertz understood ADM's businesses. Her predecessor, Allen Andreas, announced, perhaps ominously, that he would remain chair: "I'll be directing the direction and scope of our activities."[37]

Taking over ADM at this time, when agribusiness is at a historic high, is "a bit like taking over a technology high flier" in the mid-1990s.[38] A principal ADM product, high fructose corn syrup, was up 23 percent in one year. ADM's price-earnings multiple expanded from 12 to 19, with the share price reaching the high forties. On the other hand, corn and soy beans prices, which ADM must pay, rose at all-time highs. Fueled by rapidly rising food prices across the board, the entire world faces a food crisis of drastic dimensions.

Under Woertz, ADM has had to confront that. Bedeviled by high raw material costs in 2008, ADM 2008 profit fell 61 percent and the share price from near 40 to $25.87.[39]

Then there is ethanol. ADM is building the world's largest ethanol plants in Cedar Rapids, Iowa, and Columbus, Nebraska, capable of producing 55 million gallons yearly. ADM's new CEO seems ambivalent. "I've always supported free trade and commerce," she says on one hand. "There are subsidies in every industry" and "You live by the rules of the game," she notes on the other, at least if questioners remind her that the federal government pays $0.51 subsidy for every gallon to ethanol producers such as ADM. Scores of senators and representatives trip over one another to fund ethanol production and to win the farm vote. When farmers clear land and use fuel and fertilizer to plant and harvest corn, and producers such as ADM use it to produce ethanol, the environmental harm and even out-of-pocket cost is much greater for production of ethanol than for production and use of traditional fossil fuel.

Woertz seems to know this but cannot admit it openly. "It is clear that there is an energy positive in producing ethanol," she states for public consumption. She quietly explores the feasibility of ethanol manufactured with sugar, which is up to eight times as efficient as production with corn. She has pushed ADM in its development of corn-based biodegradable plastic, a green product that could replace oil-based plastics, which are not biodegradable and which litter land fills and beaches.

The greatest oddity early in her ADM career is that she has caused ADM's Washington, DC, representatives to register as lobbyists. Even though ADM spokespersons were ubiquitous, they were always behind the scenes. If ADM wanted a change in legislation, or a subsidy modified, a dozen farmers' organizations, who were registered as lobbyists, would come forward. Woertz commanded that ADM finally be forthright at what occurs, formally registering its people on Capitol Hill. "No more lobbying by proxy," Woertz has decreed.

Woertz as a Woman CEO

She seems invisible. Even more so, she exhibits the "Queen Bee" mentality, relishing being, and remaining, the only woman in a male culture.[40] "Her focus," she says, "is on leading the company, not her status."[41] "I've always been gender-blind in my career," she tells reporters.[42] Although it is still early in her CEO tenure, Woertz has brought with her no evidence of a trickle down, either at ADM, Chevron-Texaco, Chevron, or Gulf Oil.

Pat Woertz is an example for younger women to follow. She has had a successful career in an industry which men operate, almost exclusively. She has become CEO of the 56th largest corporation in the United States, in yet another industry which men populate. Still, she is not the success Susan Ivey and Paula Reynolds have been. Those women have accomplished all Pat Woertz has, and more. They have not only been a role model for younger women to follow but also throughout their careers they have gone to extra lengths to blaze a trail for women who might follow. While not being overly aggressive, for that may well be counterproductive, they have done what they could, and then some.

Tentative Teachings

Go Where They Aren't

The choice is not for everyone but every woman in business should give thought to it, either initially or after her first or second promotion. Certain industries remain male dominated but the instances of outright or even subtle discrimination, while not eliminated, are vastly reduced. This is the twenty-first century. Susan Ivey in tobacco, Paula Reynolds in utilities and then insurance, and Pat Woertz in petroleum and agribusiness are the generation following the pioneers. Their successes herald the elimination of hurdles and obstacles that existed only 15–20 years ago, which will continue to fall.

Go Where They Aren't—Part II

Recent studies indicate that young women are no less adept at math than are boys. The fatalistic attitude that "girls are no good in math," which many parents and teachers perpetuate, is overdue for a phase-out. So, too, with mainstream financial subjects at the university and graduate school levels: corporate finance, accounting, auditing, stocks and commodities, money and banking, and so on. Pat Woertz majored in accounting, beginning her career with a large national accounting firm. Her background gave her an undoubted head start, establishing credibility for her in a male-dominated industry. The trick is to master and apply technical expertise while at the same time retaining perspective, that is, ability to appreciate that there is a bigger picture and to be able to see what it is and what it might become.

More Side Stepping

Paula Reynolds went through a succession of positions at Pacific Gas & Electric, Pan Energy Corp., and AGL Resources before jumping to the insurance business as CEO. Pat Woertz began at Ernst & Ernst (now Ernst & Young), went to Gulf Oil, then to Chevron (via merger), then to Chevron Texaco (again via merger), finally jumping to an agribusiness giant and a CEO position. By contrast, Susan Ivey spent nearly her entire career with Brown & Williamson, which became half of Reynolds America, the company she now heads.

The Half Life of a Leader and Her Ideas

This observation, by Paula Reynolds, is that after an initial indoctrination period, leaders are most creative, productive, and able to be effective at the start of their tenure in a management position and that those abilities decrease thereafter. When either of two events occur—one, the rising woman executive butts into what she senses may be a glass ceiling, or, two, she senses that the half life phenomenon is taking hold—she should give thought to changing jobs, changing employers, changing industries, or even side stepping to a different sector. Many people are very much like plants: they need to be re-potted periodically or, more accurately, they need to re-pot themselves.

Don't be a Trophy Director

One drawback to Anne Mulcahy is that, after her dazzling success at Xerox, she has let herself become a trophy director, serving on boards at Xerox, Aetna Insurance, AMR, Citicorp, EDS, and Target. Paula Reynolds has let herself do something of the same, serving on boards at Safeco, Coca Cola, Air Products, Circuit City, Delta Airlines, and Andarko Petroleum. In this day, no one can serve effectively on more than two or perhaps three other boards of directors. These women's service on a multitude of boards, as well as Brenda Barnes's service on seven corporate boards at one time (Chapter 7), has several effects. One, it raises the specter of tokenism, as the odds are great that trophies cannot be effective directors when occupying so many positions. Two, trophy directors crowd out other deserving women who may be just as good but merely not as visible as the trophies are. Three, as fellow CEOs, they are not necessarily considered the best type of directors any more and, further, are allowing themselves to be complicit in a scheme whereby sitting CEOs game the system, leading to ever higher levels of CEO compensation, by stacking boards with fellow CEOs. Four, when independent directors, on the board and through committee membership, are supposed to be working directors, very few individuals can perform the necessary tasks if they sit on four, five or six boards. The latter is doubly or triply true when the trophy director has a day job as the CEO of another corporation.

Make Dissenters into Leaders

Encourage out-of-the-box thinking. Leave room for juniors and subordinates to create and to contribute. These are some of the management precepts these women CEOs have taped to their bathroom mirrors.

Eschew the Political Model

Or, at least, make it transparent. Pat Woertz no longer insures that the ADM board staffs itself with politicians and retired ambassadors. She cannot escape ADM's dependency on ethanol and government subsidies but she has taken steps to make it above board. Reliance on political participation and influence is a telltale sign to many investors and to the market. A celebrity board, like a politically stacked board, is the gasp of a none too effective CEO attempting to stall their ultimate demise. Celebrity boards under Conrad Black at Hollister International, James Robinson at American Express, or James Agee at Morrison-Knudson are examples. In the same way, Dwayne Andreas's staffing with politicians postponed discovery of the illegalities and influence peddling that was going on at ADM. Then, too, many modern CEOs realize how fleeting can be success that was gained through political intervention or influence.

7 Two Additional CEO Portraits

Brenda Barnes—Sara Lee Corp., and Meg Whitman—eBay, Inc.

It is traditional to save the best for last. This book reverses it, saving the worst for toward the last (worst in very good group, mind you). Joined by Mary Sammons, profiled in the next chapter, Brenda Barnes (Sara Lee Corp.) and Meg Whitman (eBay, Inc.) are placed near the bottom of the 21 female CEOs this book portrays, for various reasons.

Meg Whitman is everybody's "golden girl." She presided over ten years of phenomenal growth at eBay, the online auction company. She is a graduate of Princeton and Harvard Business School. She literally is golden (blonde). She is informal yet precise, disarming in her manner. She is a candidate for governor of California in 2010.[1] But she should have been a poster child for her role in a practice known as spinning. Instead, she escaped adverse publicity for her participation in a practice that symbolized corporate greed.

Underwriters desirous of eBay's future custom reserved shares for CEO Whitman's accounts in over 100 "hot issue" IPOs (initial public offerings), most of which were sure-fire money makers. Because the shares were scarce, in demand during the tech stock craze and likely to rise quickly in price once in the market (because demand outstripped supply), the shares were clamored for by public investors, resulting in "hot issues." *Sub silento* underwriters reserved, and later allocated, substantial numbers of these shares to corporate bigwigs, especially CEOs such as Whitman.

Investment banking firms allocated to Whitman more hot issue shares than any other CEO. Whitman made millions with no effort. Later lawsuits forced her to disgorge profits but the disgorgement was a pittance of $3 million for a CEO who made $15.6 million per year and whose net worth exceeds $1.4 billion. Other than the lawsuit, Meg Whitman escaped notice for her part in a chapter of greed. Not only did she escape adverse publicity but she also retained her crown as queen of women CEOs, perhaps justifiably, perhaps not.

Brenda Barnes ranks low on the list because she let herself become a trophy director. Before she became a CEO, she served on the boards of seven major publicly held corporations, seemingly unaware that she was being used as a token and not cognizant of the manner in which she crowded out other deserving women who aspired to be directors.[2] Her membership on seven boards tied her with four other women for second place on the trophy director list in 2005. Barnes herself may have believed that she could do a thorough job as a director at seven major companies but most corporate governance experts would regard her belief as unrealistic.

BRENDA BARNES

Humble Beginnings

She was born in a Chicago suburb as Brenda Czajka, the third of seven sisters. Her father worked as a pipe fitter at the International Harvester plant in Melrose Park, Illinois. He spent many of his waking hours remodeling and expanding the bungalow in which his family lived, instilling in his daughters, including Brenda, a strong work ethic.

She matriculated at Augustana College, a small Lutheran school in Rock Island, Illinois, 150 miles southwest of Chicago, on the Mississippi. She was a driven student who majored in economics and business. Her college friend Joan Kemma remembers: "Brenda would always wrap things up. She would speak in bullet points, almost like a memo."[3] "She didn't join a sorority, didn't do cheerleading." She was dedicated to being a student.[4]

Upon graduation, she returned to Chicago, taking a transition job—night shift with the U.S. Postal Service. Being a postal service employee taught her about how not to manage: "I felt like they [her bosses] had a whip in their hand. It's the old school of management. Not a lot of fun."[5]

She left to pursue two pathways. One, she went to work in marketing for Chicago-based Wilson Sporting Goods, Inc. Two, she enrolled in the MBA program at Loyola University. In the late 1970s, PepsiCo was reaching beyond the soft drink business to become a conglomerate. It acquired a number of fast food companies (Pizza Hut, Taco Bell), which under Indra Nooyi it later divested.[6] During that time, PepsiCo also acquired Wilson Sporting Goods.

In 1980 PepsiCo shipped a newly graduated MBA, Brenda Barnes, to Texas, where PepsiCo's Frito Lay snack food division was located. She spent eight years there, marketing Frito's Rold Gold Pretzels and Funyun onion rings. Finally, PepsiCo gave her a line job. She went from marketing to heading up PepsiCo's newly created western region. "This was a big time operating job, and a very unconventional job for a woman," recalled Craig Weatherup, PepsiCo's CEO, who had become a mentor to Barnes.[7]

Managing half of PepsiCo's U.S. operations was a seemingly all-consuming job. She traveled 30, 40 and 50 percent of the time. Nonetheless, she and her husband, Randy Barnes, also a PepsiCo executive, raised two boys and a girl. The eldest son and the daughter are now in college. The youngest, Brian, remains at home.

Barnes progressed upward. She became president, North America for PepsiCo. In that job, and in her previous position at PepsiCo, she proved herself an effective leader, able to motivate and inspire a workforce of over 10,000, mostly blue-collar male employees. Then, in 1996, with no warning, she quit.

The "Betrayal"

Male chauvinists everywhere loved the irony. Here was a capable, high-profile woman on the fast track who suddenly opted out, ostensibly to spend time with her family. Newspaper business sections ran titles such as "Superwoman Is Coming Home," "Superwoman Is Dead," and "Goodbye Superwoman."[8] A *London Times* editorial recounted her meteoric rise and the abrupt termination, concluding that "Women belong at home and some are beginning to realize it."[9] Feminist scholars and career women were critical. Barnes had failed to advance sexual equality in the highest levels of the workplace when she had an opportunity to do so.

When women "opt" out of professional practices or management tracks in business organizations, many say that in part they have done so because their families, particularly their children, need their undivided attention.[10] "[A] cottage industry of academics, self-help experts, authors, corporate recruiters, networking groups, and consultants . . . [also] say the biggest problem [for women] is balancing the demands of a high-level job with family obligations that often far surpass those of typical male executives."[11]

Barnes has an interesting slant on this. She says that she opted out, and that other women do so as well, because they need their families, the one group of persons likely to give them unconditional love and not the other way around: "I was selfish; I did it for me. They [her children] would have survived, they would have been fine. They're great students, they have good hearts, I think they're grounded, they work hard."[12]

The Great Side Step

Another way to view Brenda Barnes's career progression is not as a betrayal at all. Instead, hers was a career move that better positioned her to become CEO of a major public company—a feat which she did accomplish, and one in her hometown of Chicago, to boot. Not only was it a side step but it may also have been a calculated and shrewd side step.

Brenda Barnes did not go home to stay with her children. She took positions on seven boards of large corporations, which she actively sought, becoming a trophy director *par excellence*. She also became a part-time professor at Northwestern University Kellogg School of Business, which publications such as the *Wall Street Journal* rate as one of the top five MBA schools in the United States.[13] From mid-fall 1999 until late spring 2000, she served as an interim president at Starwood Hotels, a large publicly held company. She didn't "retire" at all.

Brenda Barnes dissembles. To business writers, she admits only to membership on three boards, but the proxy data companies file with the SEC indicate that she served on seven boards at once. Whatever the number, Brenda Barnes positioned herself beautifully for a second side step.

There is nothing wrong with *what* she did. There may be leveled several criticisms at *how* she did it. She did it without suffering any loss in prestige or income, contrary to appearances she seems to have intended. In that regard, and others, she was perhaps less than forthright, letting others believe that she was retiring from active business life and letting others believe that she served on three rather than six or seven boards.[14]

Not everyone lays down a blanket condemnation of trophy directors. Writing in the *Journal of Corporation Law*, Professor Lissa Broome believes that:

> the trophy director category . . . might be better segmented into the following subcategories: "celebrity director" (someone who is lending her name . . .); "retired director" (someone who has retired from a significant position and is remaining active . . .); and the "professional director" (someone who . . . [has] a great deal of flexibility and free time . . .). It is important to distinguish between these categories. [T]he retired and professional directors may add valuable insights to board deliberations.[15]

Brenda Barnes fits both the retired and the professional director descriptions. No matter what the posture of the trophy director, however, Professor Broome does not deal with the sheer impossibility of any person doing adequate, let alone exemplary, service when they are serving on seven boards, receiving largish paychecks from seven corporations. For that reason, several of the services, such as Corporate Library, Risk Metrics Group (formerly Institutional Investors Services (ISS)), Glass Lewis Advisers, or Proxy, Inc., which advise institutional investors on how to vote share blocks, recommend votes against (withhold authority) director candidates who serve on excessive numbers of corporate boards.[16]

Appointment as CEO

One day after Carleton Fiorina "resigned" as CEO of Hewlett-Packard, on February 15, 2005, Sara Lee Corp. named Brenda Barnes its CEO.[17] Ms. Barnes very quickly caused the company, once known as Consolidated Foods Corp., to move its headquarters from high-profile downtown Chicago to low-profile (and lower cost) Downers Grove, a Chicago suburb. Barnes has tried to take the company back to its core competencies in food products, divesting subsidiaries in bras, pantyhose, and underwear (Wonderbra, Playtex, and Hanes). Earlier (2001) the company divested itself of Coach, a retailer of premium leather goods.[18] She announced further plans to rid Sara Lee of its European meats and U.S. retail coffee units. Mostly through divestitures, she reduced the Sara Lee head count from 150,000 to 50,000 employees. She pledged to turn Sara Lee "into a tightly focused consumer products company churning out 12 percent margins."[19]

Sara Lee now focuses on three divisions in which Barnes believes the operating margins, and thus the profits, will be greater: food products (Jimmy Dean sausage, Ball Park Franks and, of course, baked goods); beverages (Douwe Egberts coffees); and household and personal care products (Sanex shower gel and Kiwi shoe polish).[20] Barnes told the *Chicago Tribune's* Greg Burns that, as of late 2007, she and Sara Lee were sticking to plan. "I'm even keeled, I'm not panicked, because I feel we have a plan. Our history is not fantastic. In the end, the numbers have to demonstrate the change."[21]

So far the numbers are not there. Barnes and Sara Lee seem to be imprisoned in a down elevator, stuck between floors. Sara Lee's share price peaked around the time the board of director appointed Barnes, in February 2005, at $25 per share, up from $19 per share 15 months earlier. Since that time it has been a downward slide, to a low of $8.68 in 2008–09. Earnings per share were positive but not spectacular, at $0.84 for 2007, until a $975 million loss in the second quarter of 2008. Operating margins lag far behind 12 percent, at 6 percent in good times and lower still as high raw material costs (food) cut into margins.[22] CEO Barnes seems to have learned little from the demises of Jill Barad at Mattel and Carly Fiorina at Hewlett-Packard, who made rosy projections which their companies never achieved. At Sara Lee, though, so far "no one is calling for a management shakeup, because analysts and investors seem to agree that no matter who's in charge Sara Lee will be a tough ship to turn."[23]

A Broader Trickle Down under Brenda Barnes?

On her watch, Barnes has not pointedly added to the diversity in Sara Lee's management ranks. She did launch a "woman's network," which attracts several hundred to its meetings. She has also made achievement of diversity a metric in computation of bonuses: "There's a lot of tendency to check the boxes on stuff like this. That's not enough. Did the numbers change?"[24]

Unwittingly perhaps, however, Brenda Barnes's elevation at Sara Lee has played a role in a broader trickle down in the Midwest, across the region and across companies. In 2006, the *Chicago Tribune* reported that 35 of Chicago's 50 largest public companies did not have a woman among their top wage earners. Fifteen of Chicago's top companies had no senior women executives at all. Across the Midwest, no large public company in Michigan had a woman director and in Ohio the number of women directors had decreased. "We're going backwards," said Lyn Fitzgerald of the Chicago Network and United Way.[25] Some attributed the backsliding to "diversity fatigue": executives at many companies have let their attention to diversity issues, including the appointment of women, wane after so many years of attention.

As Brenda Barnes's and Pat Woertz's appointments at Sara Lee and ADM took hold, and Irene Rosenfeld at the newly spun off Kraft Foods (Chapter 9), the statistics improved. The number of Chicago corporations with no female directors decreased to one (Nalco Co.) as Brunswick, the bowling equipment and machine tool company, named a woman to its board. In 2006–07, Chicago corporations Tenneco, Wrigley, Nalco, Smurfit-Stone Container, and Ni-Source all added women to their senior management groups. Only seven of Chicago's 50 largest companies (Illinois Tool Works, CNA Financial, Office Max, Anixter International, Old Republic, Pactiv and Unitrin) had no female executive officers.[26]

Chicago is a bellwether for a broad spectrum of the Midwest in education, art, music, journalism, publishing and business—the Mecca for millions, from Denver to Pittsburgh, and from Kentucky to Northern Minnesota and Michigan. It is "not some corporate Lake Wobegon."[27] Brenda Barnes in Downers Grove, Pat Woertz downstate in Decatur, and Irene Rosenfeld in Northfield, as capable women CEOs of large publicly held companies serve as examples, sending a message to a geographical area far larger than Chicago or Illinois.

MEG WHITMAN

Side Stepper or Job Jockey?

Meg Whitman has pushed it to the limit. She has had employment with more business organizations than any woman CEO this book portrays. She began with an MBA from Harvard Business School in 1979. Her entry-level job was with a brand management team at Proctor & Gamble. Her husband, neurosurgeon Griff Harsh, obtained a residency in San Francisco. Whitman left Proctor & Gamble for a consultant's position with Bain Consulting's California office, where she came to know Mitt Romney, later to be governor of Massachusetts (to whose presidential campaign she contributed), and John Donahue, whom she recruited for eBay and who became her successor as CEO.[28]

She added to her "old economy" resume in 1989 when she moved to the Walt Disney Co. as vice-president of strategic planning and later senior vice-president of marketing for consumer products division. Her husband moved back to the East Coast, accepting a position at Massachusetts General Hospital in Boston. Whitman took a position at Stride Rite Corp., in Lexington, Massachusetts, where she resurrected the Keds division (tennis shoes) and then, while president of the Stride Division, oversaw the introduction of the Munchkin line of baby shoes.[29]

By this time, Whitman and her husband had two sons. She left them behind in Boston to join a not-for-profit, Florists Telephone Delivery (FTD), as CEO. While there she oversaw FTD's conversion to a for-profit corporation which later was acquired by United Online (2008). In 1997, after two years in the Midwest, Whitman went back to Boston, where she added yet another to her "Whitman's Sampler" of corporate positions: general manager of the preschool division at publicly held Hasbro Toys. She played roles in marketing Hasbro's Playskool, Mr. Potato Head, Barney, and Teletubbies, among others.[30]

eBay Hires a Grown Up

Pierre Omidyar worked as a manager for a Silicon Valley software producer, living with his girlfriend.[31] Collecting and trading Pez (a small, round, hard candy like a Tic Tak) dispensers inspired Omidyar to conceive of an online trading forum. Online barter exchanges (e.g., ITEX) existed (two used washing machines for four free nights at a hotel) but not auction services (two washing machines for the highest bidder willing to pay cash). Those subscribers who listed items for sale would be in charge of the entire transaction, including shipping the item and collecting the payment. Buyers and sellers would rate each other on the timeliness and other aspects of the transaction. It was a cross between a virtual flea market and an online person-to-person auction site.

Omidyar used a first generation, local internet service provider to host the website. He quit his day job, opened a tiny office in San Jose, and approached Sand Hill Road in Palo Alto where many of the venture capitalist firms, including Kleiner Perkins, the paradigm, have offices. He sold 22 percent of his company to Benchmark Partners for $5 million. He opened the site on Labor Day, 1995.

New economy startups joke about the need for adult supervision but many firms have added an older, more experienced business person as CEO, especially as a prelude to their initial public offering (IPO).[32] Netscape added Jim Barksdale and Apple Computer brought in John Sculley from PepsiCo. eBay hired a headhunter, Ramsey Beirne, Ossining, New York, to find an adult.

Ramsey Beirne had Meg Whitman's name on the short list of potential CEO candidates. She requested that they drop her name, appalled by the appearance of a company (eBay) which seemed to run an online version of the classified ads. Robert Kagle, the partner at Benchmark in charge of eBay matters, insisted that the recruiter try Whitman again. They did and she took a flier on a "virtual firm." She joined eBay as CEO in February 1998, and took it public in an IPO the following September.

Management Challenges

One challenge was to superimpose order on a structure without a structure, a few steps removed from anarchy. None of the eBay managers made appointments, either on their own or others' calendars. The firm mirrored the values it instilled in subscribers—everyone was empowered to make decisions and everyone trusted everyone else to do the right thing. It was free form all the way. Whitman kept the good and discarded the bad. She encouraged open communication, winning the trust of the engineers and code drafters who were not accustomed to being heard. She installed what she terms the "no penalty culture." Any person can try out an idea or make a statement without fear of retribution or sanction.

She kept the informality. No "Carly Armani," Whitman kept to khaki and denim, albeit stylish and befitting a Silicon Valley CEO. She worked from a cubicle amongst eBay's other open plan cubicles. She did not retreat to a CEO inter sanctum.

At the same time she kept the informality, she introduced requirements for status reports, project plans, cost-benefit analyses, and other management decisional tools. Management theorists and eBay veterans praise her skill at imposing old economy methods, or at least the helpful ones, in a new economy milieu, without destroying the spirit of the company. They label it as one of her greatest contributions to a growing eBay.

She also found that a manana spirit resulted in an under-investment in technological architecture. Soon after her arrival, the eBay website went down for 8 hours, prompting user outcries. In turn, part of that failure resulted from the inability of the marketing persons to communicate effectively with information technology specialists and engineers. Whitman introduced a train analogy:

> [We] began to speak about a unit of production as a train seat. For example, it used to be that the train left once a week with six seats. . . . These analogies allowed someone like a marketing manager to discuss projects in terms of their technology needs. The manager might say, "This will take roughly sixteen seats." And we can come back and say, "There is no way we can get that, so let's rework so it takes only eight seats."[33]

Whitman continued carefully to blend old-school, old-economy discipline with the fast-paced, seat-of-the-pants methodology of an internet start-up. She used simple methods: train analogies and weekly staff meetings but they worked. eBay grew from 35 to 15,000 employees.

Early on she had to confront social responsibility issues: should eBay allow the sale of firearms and of pirated computer games on its website? Her friend, Howard Schultz, alter ego of Starbucks, convinced Whitman that it was not on keeping with "the character of the company." eBay banned their sale on the site.[34]

A Serial Acquirer?

Jeffrey Sonnenfeld of the Yale School of Management calls the failed CEOs of a few years ago "serial acquirers, tacking companies on to their core businesses in order to bolster their financial holdings."[35] He singled out Bernie Ebbers at WorldCom (60 acquisitions in 16 years), or the Rigas father and sons at Adelphia Communications (acquisition of countless cable television systems).

But Sonnenfeld ignores successful "serial acquirers," such as Bill Gates at Microsoft, or John Chambers at Cisco. They caused their companies to make scores of acquisitions each year, in one case over 90 in less than five years. Even an institution as conservative as Wachovia Bank went through a period of "furious growth," with 80 acquisitions of other financial institutions over seven to eight years.[36] Acquisitions may be the only way for a company to grow in a maturing industry (a city or town can only support one cable company, or one internet backbone). A prevailing business philosophy has been to "Get Big Fast."[37] CEO Indra Nooyi, a Yale School of Management graduate, told fellow panelists that PepsiCo "considers as many as 30 acquisitions globally *at any one time.*"[38]

A central achievement of Meg Whitman's ten-year reign at eBay has been to be a "serial acquirer," helping eBay "get big fast." The acquisitions on her watch include:

- Butterfield & Butterfield, a land-based San Francisco auction house.
- Kruse International, a dealer in collector automobiles.
- Half.com, a company that sells used goods at fixed prices (no auction).
- Billpoint, a firm which handles monetary transactions for eBay subscribers.
- Skype, an internet calling firm which eBay acquired for $2.6 billion, only to write off $1.7 billion in 2004.[39]
- Craig's List, a website listing classified ads and preferred providers in 450 cities worldwide (part owner).
- PayPal, a firm which performs functions similar to Billpoint, giving site users confidence and safety in their exchanges of money and merchandise.
- Stubhub, an online facilitator for the sale of tickets to concerts and sporting events.

Meg Whitman proves Sonnenfeld wrong. Serial acquisitions, such as those Whitman helped engineer at eBay, are a laudatory way to grow a company, especially in the era of globalization and even with a stumble (Skype for eBay) or two along the way.

Spinning

Again, spinning is the preferential allocation of shares in hot issue IPOs to CEOs and other senior managers who will likely profit from receipt of those shares, and who are likely in the future be in a position to direct underwriting and acquisition business to the investment banking firm arranging the alloca-tion. Writers have identified a number of investor and market harms that spinning causes. One is that what the issuing corporation and the underwriter represent to be a public offering is only partly that, as they have assigned a portion of the offering to favored "bigwigs."

Two, spinning helps the rich get richer while members of the public complain that it becomes more expensive for them to become shareholders, because they must acquire shares at the later, higher market price, also paying a broker's commission, rather than at the lower offering price, with no commission. With underwriters having carved out numbers of shares, spinning them to influential clients, members of the public among whom a strong appetite for the shares remains must purchase them in the aftermarket, at higher prices.

Three, the right to bestow underwriting business on a particular underwriter or underwriters belongs to the corporation, not the CEO. In corporate law parlance, the right to receive preferential treatment is a corporate opportunity. Executives such as Whitman who receive the shares in their account have "diverted" or "usurped" a corporate opportunity.[40]

Whitman, the lead candidate to be the spinning poster child, claims not to have known, but it seems disingenuous. How could a knowledgeable business woman receive share allocations and reap windfall profits in nearly 100 companies, over several years, without recognizing what was going on? Shareholders sued Whitman for usurpation of corporate opportunities. Whitman and eBay quickly settled the suit for $3 million plus attorney's fees.[41] Whitman remained on lists of the most admired women in business and "the most respected CEOs," not just in the United States but around the world.[42] She received no flak; her Teflon shell protected her.

The Golden Girl

The media barely touched her because she has been so successful at eBay (although it has fallen on harder time since she left). The company had $7.7 billion in 2007 revenues. eBay has 248 million users worldwide.[43] The shares have reached dizzying heights. Since the IPO in 1998, an initial investor would have seen a 5,600 percent return at the stock's high.[44] The shares have settled back into the teens recently, and as low as $9.91 in the market slump.[45] (Whitman received 14.4 million shares for $0.03 apiece when eBay hired her.) Her personal wealth exceeds $1.4 billion. Corporate circles have associated her name with CEO searches at 3-M Corp., MacDonald's, and other major companies. She was on the short list to succeed Michael Eisner as CEO at Disney but withdrew when she surmised that the Disney board already leaned toward Robert Iger, who got the job.[46] She is a Republican candidate for governor of California. She has given Princeton $30 million, which the university is using to construct undergraduate housing that will be named after her (Whitman College). It's all almost too good to be true.

Near Trophy Status

Another Whitman fault is that she comes close to being a trophy director, serving on boards at Proctor & Gamble, eBay, DreamWorks Animation, SKG, and GAP. She is a trustee of Princeton. Only her resignation from the board at Goldman Sachs, occasioned by the spinning scandal (Goldman allocated many IPO shares to Whitman accounts) saved her from super trophy director status.

No evidence of a trickle down exists at eBay. Whitman does not appear to have extended herself to have eBay hire women or mentored women herself. She did not see to the addition of women directors to the board, as have Andrea Jung, Marion Sandler, Ann Mulcahy, and other women CEOs at their corporations. The record is devoid of any Whitman statements on the issue. Other evidence indicates that she is a man's woman. Staff at eBay call Whitman's conference room "Blondie's Room."

As a woman CEO, Whitman is a mixed bag, despite the unstinting praise she garners in some quarters. Her role in the spinning chapter, her trophy director status, and her gender neutrality put her down the list of women CEOs even if otherwise the assessment is a favorable one.[47]

Tentative Teachings

Do not be Greedy

Accept only properly approved (board approved) salary and perquisites. Do not accept IPO allocations in other companies, backdated stock options, spring-loaded ones (option grants timed to precede, or front run, the release of favorable corporate news, thus increasing the executive's potential for profit), or excessive housing, travel, or other perks. Meg Whitman's acceptance of IPO allocations to her account puts a cloud over her head that should remain for the rest of her career, despite her achievements. Steven Jobs and all he has done at Apple are diminished by his receipt of stock options backdated to a time when the market, and therefore his exercise price, were lower, and his profit upon exercise greater. Executives such as the Tysons at Tyson's Foods have received from the board's compensation committee stock options which were "spring loaded," granted shortly before favorable news became public, pushing the stock price and the executives' profits upon exercise upwards. These instances of what appears to be unbridled greed leave a stain that is indelible.

Children Increase in Worth as You Rise toward the Top

Surprisingly, you may need your children more than your children need you, especially as you fill senior management positions. Brenda Barnes made the point and it rings true.

Install the "No Penalty" Culture in Your Organization

Any one should feel free to try out a new idea or make a statement without fear of retribution. It may be different if the organization has firmly chosen and perhaps embarked on a different course of action but even then higher ups should listen.

Get Opposites Communicating

Meg Whitman got the engineers at eBay to communicate with the sales and marketing people. To get them talking, she had to resort to a seats on the train analogy. Her analogy, combined with the no penalty culture, fostered open communication.

Google, Inc., has 19 restaurants, including a 24-hour sushi bar, offering free food to 8,000 employees at its headquarters. It has countless on-site recreational facilities (volleyball courts, billiard tables, weight lifting, climbing walls, fitness facilities) not merely because it is a benevolent employer, which it is. Google has those things to foster employees communicating with each other, brainstorming and inventing.

In these and in other ways, an executive should try to get the downstream sales organization talking with the upstream production people, or the design team communicating with the wholesale and retail parts of the organization.

Avoid Trophy Director Status

Chapters 5 and 6 discussed Anne Mulcahy's and Paula Reynolds's trophy directorships and why trophy status is incompatible with good governance. This chapter adds two more: Brenda Barnes (seven directorships at one time) and Meg Whitman (directorships at five public companies as well as at Princeton University). The temptation to succumb to an excessive number of board membership invitations is particularly a problem for women who have reached significant levels of achievement, so prevalent that it has become the dark side of women's participation in corporate governance.

8 Five Who Leave Few Footprints

Angela F. Braly—Wellpoint, Inc., Christina A. Gold—Western Union Company, Carol Meyrowitz—TJX Companies, Indra K. Nooyi—PepsiCo, and Mary Sammons—Rite Aid, Inc.

ANGELA F. BRALY

Legal Career

Angela Braly, a native of Dallas and a Southern Methodist law graduate, is the only lawyer in the group of 21 women CEOs (15 active) this book features. She first surfaced in public databases, in 1995, in St. Louis. Already the mother of three boys, and 13 years out of law school, she joined Lewis, Rice & Fingersh, as a partner, doing healthcare law.[1]

She was in the right place at the right time. In 1994, Missouri's largest health insurer, the not-for-profit Blue Cross and Blue Shield of Missouri, had transferred much of its business to a for-profit subsidiary, Right Choice Managed Care, Inc. Blue Cross then caused Right Choice to do an initial public offering (IPO) of 20 percent of the Right Choice shares, establishing an initial $163 million market value for Right Choice as a whole and a $137 million value for the 80 percent of Right Choice stock Blue Cross held back.

The Missouri Attorney General, Jay Nixon, stepped forward. He brought suit on behalf of the state, which has power of oversight over not-for-profit corporations, lodged in the state attorney general's office. Attorney General Nixon protested the transfer of a charitable corporation's assets to a profit making one, without the state's or enrollees' approval. Blue Cross hired Angela Braly to defend.

Missouri's Cole County Circuit Court Judge Thomas Brown intervened to create a receivership (state control by an individual, the "receiver," whom the judge appoints and supervises) to take over Blue Cross's $137 million in shares and the right to elect directors that came with it. In turn, this state takeover threatened Blue Cross of Missouri with loss of its Blue Cross and Blue Shield trademarks. The national organization threatened fines up to $21 million, filing suit in Chicago to terminate the trademarks.[2] The judge's actions also disturbed a settlement Attorney General Nixon and Braly had negotiated. Braly caused Blue Cross to move for a finding that Judge Brown had exceeded his authority, got the settlement on track, got the national organization to dismiss its suit in Chicago, and arranged public hearings in various venues about the transfer.[3]

Angela Braly impressed everyone. In short order, she became interim general counsel, then general counsel, and then CEO of Blue Cross and Blue Shield of Missouri. The episode also highlighted the changing nature of health insurance: it has become potentially profitable, indeed, perhaps very profitable, and no longer the bailiwick of local physician-owed corporations, not-for-profits, and charities. It has become big business.

The Health Insurance Industry

Wellpoint, in Indianapolis, emerged from the 2005 merger of Wellpoint Health Networks of California and Anthem, Inc., of Indiana. Wellpoint operates for-profit Blue Cross and related entities in 14 states. Its 34.8 million enrollees and $62 billion in revenues make it the U.S.'s largest managed care company. Its shares are listed on the New York Stock Exchange.

Also with shares on the NYSE are the number two and three players: United Health Group of Minneapolis, and Aetna Insurance, of Hartford. Humana in Louisville and Cigna in Philadelphia are other large for-profit players.

In February 2007, Wellpoint named Angela Braly, a surprise choice who had arrived from Missouri only two years previously, to be its new CEO, effective June 1, 2007. She succeeded Larry Glasscock, the dealmaker who, through a series of mergers and other acquisitions, put Wellpoint together.[4]

Braly's appointment caused a stir in Indianapolis. She was a "relative unknown," and "not confrontational," described "as smart and smooth, 'very, very effective in dealing with people and in dealing with problems.' "[5] Wellpoint chose her over two other men in the company, including CFO David Colby, who had been Glasscock's heir apparent. She was also the opposite of Glasscock and Colby, who were aggressive male executives.

Healthcare, though, had changed yet again. Wellpoint, under Glasscock, and its competitors, had picked the low hanging fruit, making most of the acquisitions to be had. Between 2001 and 2007, healthcare insurance premiums had risen 78 percent while prices overall (inflation) rose 17 percent. Not much is to be gained, then, through further acquisitions and aggressive re-pricing.

On the other hand, 46 million of 300 million Americans have no health insurance at all. All political parties have pledged some form of remedy, none of which bases itself on the single payer model. Expansion of managed care and health insurance will come through enrollment with private companies, but funded pursuant to government initiative rather than private pocket books. "Braly's traits better fit the company's needs. [She] has an ability to navigate the halls of power where the health insurance industry's future will be determined, whether in Washington, D.C., or state capitals."[6] "She knows how to build coalitions around her."[7]

Her Tenure So Far

The day before Braly moved to the CEO suite, matters at Wellpoint went up for grabs. Wellpoint had to announce that the very capable CFO David Colby had resigned because credible allegations of "aggressive womanizing" by him had become public.[8] Luckily, Braly and the company received little negative publicity. Braly and her executive team spent their first months in office seeing to the reduction of general and administrative costs by $175 million, ending the year with a $3.3 billion profit, up 8 percent from the previous year. She prodded the company to go from 33 claims processing systems to 13, with three as the eventual goal.

The severe dislocations which hit businesses and the stock market through late summer and fall, 2008, hit the healthcare industry earlier, in spring, 2008, providing Braly with her first real crisis as CEO. In March, Wellpoint revised its earnings guidance downward, from $6.41 to $5.76–6.01 per share. Based upon the 6 percent downward revision, the market sent Wellpoint's share price down 25 percent, from $65.92 to $48.79, and then further to $47.00.[9] The share price had been as high as $90 in summer, 2007.[10]

Some analysts pinned part of the blame for the out-sized drop on Braly: "She was not really well known by the Street. Her background is more legal eagle and the Street more readily connects with financial or operational types."[11] Six weeks later Wellpoint took an even bigger hit, with first quarter profits off 25 percent, but the share price increased 7.3 percent, as all the health insurance stocks reported similar results.[12] Investors found positives in Wellpoint under Braly, with a 23 percent decline in the backlog of processing claims and projected elimination of 150,000 less desirable members, mostly because of elevated premium charges.[13]

Observations

We can learn three things from Angela Braly's career. First, she, Wellpoint and the healthcare industry have rocky roads ahead of them. Early in 2009, Wellpoint cut 1,500 jobs, as did competitors such as Aetna Inc. and Cigna Corp.[14] Braly forecast a "brutal year" for 2009, with $350 million in investment losses in late 2008, with extreme loss of health-plan members due to layoffs and job elimination, and with unemployment to peak above 10 percent in the 14 states in which Wellpoint does business.[15] Second, Ms. Braly exemplifies advice that this book suggests, namely, women in business should consider having children earlier in their careers. Before she became a partner in a St. Louis law firm, Angela Braly had three. Third, like some CEOs in this book, such as Marion Sandler, Andrea Jung, Susan Ivey, and Paula Reynolds, Angela Braly has an outspoken commitment to diversity not only at Wellpoint but also throughout her career:

> At Wellpoint we see diversity management as more than just a strategy; it's a fundamental part of the way we do business. . . . Strategic diversity management drives associate engagement and trust, which increases productivity and operational effectiveness.[16]

CHRISTINA A. GOLD

Canadian By Birth

Angela Braly may be the solo lawyer among all 21 female CEOs but Christina Gold is not the solo Canadian. Andrea Jung, Avon Products, was born and spent her early years in Toronto, and has retained her Canadian citizenship. Another background feature both have in common is that Andrea and Christina have significant connections to Avon Products, Inc.

Christine Gold majored in geography at Carleton University, Ottawa, Ontario, graduating in 1969.[17] Her first job was at a coupon clearinghouse, tallying cents off coupons. She soon jumped to Avon, for a short time in a marketing position and then in sales after Avon centralized marketing in New York. She could not follow marketing colleagues to New York because she was place bound. Her husband, Peter Gold, had a law practice in Ontario.

Ultimately, Christina Gold convinced her husband to follow her to New York, then back to Montreal as Avon's sales chief there, then to head of Avon's Canadian Division in 1989, and finally to president, Avon North America in 1993. The following year she left Avon, after 16 years, commencing a series of side steps that led her eventually to a CEO suite:

- 1994–1999: CEO of the Beaconsfield Group, a consulting firm specializing in selling and retail trade.
- 1999–2002: President and CEO of Excel Communications Co., a telecommunications entity.
- 2002–2006: Senior Vice-president of First Data, Inc., which had Western Union as a subsidiary.[18]

In September 2006, First Data spun off Western Union. Christina Gold became president and CEO at a newly independent Western Union.

Not Your Mother's Western Union

In old movies, important communications took the form of telegrams. Operators tapped out Morse code over wires. "Stop" and "Full Stop" punctuated pretend telegrams actors read out. Beginning 30 years ago, how-ever, fewer and fewer communicated by telegram. The facsimile (fax) and later email and long distance took the telegram's place. Western Union had to re-invent itself.

It did, morphing from a communications to a worldwide money transfer network. Consumers can transfer funds to other persons; from consumer to business (to pay utility bills, car payments, or mortgage obligations); and from business to business, wiring funds to other entities, in the United States or abroad. A Western Union customer can utilize walk-up services, visiting one of 14,000 Western Union locations. A customer with a credit or debit card can use an online money transfer service without visiting a physical location. The customer can use a telephone money transfer service, with which a customer can send or receive money by cellular telephone.[19]

It would put Christina Gold in a good light to be able to say that Western Union's remake had happened on her watch. It did not. Most of the trans-formation preceded her. The company has been around since 1851, known as Western Union since 1856. Christina Gold is one in a long line of CEOs.

Lessons From Her Career

Christina Gold has left few footprints (so far). Nonetheless, we can take three teachings from her career, as we did with Angela Braly. First is the side step. Many of the women (most) who have risen to the top made several career changes and moved from firm to firm several times, progressing upward as they did so. Christina Gold's career pattern exemplifies that.

Second, as with Angela Braly, Christina Gold exhibits a commitment to diversity and presides atop a trickle down, which at her company has resulted in promotions and career advancement by women below her. Five of the top officers at Western Union are women: Christina Gold, board chair, president, and CEO; Liz Alicea-Velez, vice-president Latin America, Mexico and the Caribbean; Gail Galuppo, executive vice-president and chief market-ing officer; Robin Heller, executive vice-president and chief of information technology; and Ann McCarthy, vice-president, corporate and governmental affairs.[20]

Third, as with many women CEOs and their spouses, early on in their marriage she and her husband prioritized their careers. Peter Gold continued to practice law for a few years after Christina moved to New York. They had a long distance marriage. Then Peter sublimated his career to Christina's. He closed his law practice, moved to New York, worked for a not-for-profit corporation for a while, and now lists himself as "retired attorney." They live in Colorado, where Western Union's headquarters are located, and have no children.

CAROL MEYROWITZ

Very Few Footprints

Of all the women this book profiles, Carol Meyrowitz leaves the fewest foot-prints, as does the company of which she has been CEO, since September 2006. TJX refuses to disclose even the most innocuous items, such as where Meyrowitz went to college or whether she has children.[21] TJX, of Framingham, Massachusetts, is a publicly held "off price" retailer, which operates 788 T.J. Maxx, 709 Marshall's, 238 HomeGoods, and 148 A.J. Wright stores in the United States.[22] Although by and large it flies "under the radar," TJX has been successful. Some analysts believe that TJX benefits when the economy slows, or enters a recession, while mid-line retailers such as Target, Kohl's and Macy's suffer.

Ms. Meyrowitz has been with the company, with one exception, continu-ously since 1983. From 2001 to 2004, she was CEO of the Marmaxx Group, TJX's biggest division. The exception was in January 2005, when she left TJX to become a consultant with Berkshire Partners "to pursue new opportunities and challenges."[23] Ten months later she was back at TJX, as CEO.[24]

One Crisis

The only ripple publicly known about Ms. Meyrowitz and TJX is a common one this day and age. Computer hackers gained entry into T.J. Maxx's computer network in January 2007. The hackers stole millions of credit and debit card numbers customers had given TJX stores.[25] Consumer protection lawyers brought a massive class action on behalf of card holders against TJX. Meyrowitz stayed on top of developments, quickly settling TJX's portion of the class action by $40.9 million payment into a recovery payment fund,[26] and the publication of a number of media statements aimed at affected TJX customers.[27] In 2008, federal officials apprehended 11 members of a ring which stole the TJX credit card numbers, storing their "digital booty" on servers in Latvia and the Ukraine.[28] The ramifications of the security breach have not become clear but CEO Meyrowitz continues to devote great attention to it.

Commitment to Diversity

We can find very little about Ms. Meyrowitz. We do not know where she went to college, whether she has advanced degrees, or who her spouse is.

The only items that come through are that she does have children and that both she and the TJX Companies have a strong commitment to diversity. The company has a "Supplier Diversity Program." The TJX website states that the company and its programs "support diversity in all aspects of our business and encourage the inclusion of minority and women-owned businesses in all sourcing opportunities."[29] The company has a Diversity Leadership Council, staffed by senior management of the company, which meets quarterly to review program goals and progress toward them. The company also is an active member in the National Minority Supplier Development Council, the New England Minority Supplier Development Council, the Women's Business Enterprise National Council, and the Center for Women and Enterprise.

INDRA K. NOOYI

Exotic Background

Indra Nooyi is the third of the 21 female CEOs, and the third of 15 sitting CEOs, to be foreign born (Jung and Gold are the others) but with roots more exotic than Canadian. She grew up in Madras, in southern India, the daughter of an accountant and a non-working mother. She earned a BS at Madras Christian College in 1976 and MBA at the Indian Institute of Management (Calcutta) in 1978. She spent short stints with Johnson & Johnson and Mattur Beardsell, Ltd. (textiles) in India. She then came to the United States, matriculating at the Yale School of Management, earning a Masters in Management in 1980.[30]

Then came a succession of jobs, with a succession of employers:

- 1980–86: director, International Corporate Strategy Projects, Boston Consulting Group.
- 1986–1990: vice-president and Director of Corporate Strategy, Motorola, Inc. (at which she remains a director).
- 1990–1994: senior vice-president of strategy, planning and strategic marketing, Asea Brown Boveri, Inc. (international engineering firm).

She joined PepsiCo, headquartered in Purchase, New York, in 1994, choosing a job there over a position at General Electric. PepsiCo soon promoted her to senior vice-president of corporate strategy, where she employed what has been called one of her greatest strengths, "strategic vision."

The Pepsi Generation

A decade ahead of her time, Indra Nooyi encouraged a healthier array of snack food options, which she helped to implement by overseeing PepsiCo's $13.8 billion acquisition of Quaker Oats Co. in 2001. With Quaker Oats came the Gatorade line of sports drinks, which has proven a success for PepsiCo. She spearheaded the acquisition of Tropicana, the fruit juice company.[31] She pushed the divestiture by PepsiCo of its fast food subsidiaries, Taco Bell,

Pizza Hut and Kentucky Fried Chicken, for three reasons.[32] One, she determined that the fast food industry had become saturated, meaning narrow profit margins in the future. Two, the PepsiCo food options offered through its franchise subsidiaries represented healthier choices than many competitors but not healthy enough for the new century. Three, divestiture permitted PepsiCo to focus on drinks and snack foods ("core competencies" in business jargon).

From 1999 onward, Nooyi marched upward at Pepsi: chief financial officer, chief financial officer and senior vice-president, president and chief financial officer, and member of the board of directors by May 2001. She assumed the CEO position on October 1, 2006, becoming the eleventh woman to become CEO of a *Fortune 500* company. She was only the fifth CEO in PepsiCo history, commanding a company with $33 billion in revenues.[33] Journalists called her "a 21st Century Everywoman,"[34] "A star," and "a true internationalist."[35] During her first full year as PepsiCo's CEO the share price increased 21.3 percent.

The Pepsi Challenge

One challenge is international, "to fill in the holes in Pepsi's international drinks and snacks business."[36] She seems the right person for the job: "I am a global thinker in everything I do."[37] "She has a good grasp of all the international opportunities and that is where the future of Pepsi lies," says a fellow Indian business person.[38] One of those holes is her native India, a nation of over a billion, with a rapidly rising standard of living. "India remains one of the world's best kept secrets," she sermonizes, "but we are too inward looking." She admonishes Indian leaders, "Don't let India become irrelevant."[39]

From India, though, comes a challenge, one that threatens to spread throughout East Asia. The New Delhi Center for Science and the Environment contends that Pepsi sodas contain unhealthy levels of pesticides. If the pesticide threat rises to the level of a campaign, Nooyi seems far-sighted enough to cause the corporation to take the action needed. A predecessor CEO describes her as "extremely visionary [who] challenges the status quo."[40]

As she took over, PepsiCo surpassed arch rival Coca-Cola in market capitalization, which exceed $115 billion each.[41] Of large publicly held companies with female CEOs, only Archer Daniels Midland, "Supermarket to the World," and Wellpoint exceed PepsiCo in annual revenues ($36 billion to $32.6 billion in 2007). Ironically, while Indra Nooyi rose to the top *Fortune*'s list of the 50 more powerful women, ADM CEO Patricia Woertz dropped significantly down the list: marketing soft drinks may have more importance to *Fortune* than agribusiness. Feeding the world, and by a company with greater annual revenue at that, has less importance than marketing snack foods and flavored water.

In 2008, Nooyi encountered management challenges as commodities prices rose (grain, vegetable oil, sugar) and, due to the housing crisis and general economic malaise, soft drink consumption fell. "We haven't seen this kind of a slow-down in 25 years," Nooyi said.[42] Domestic soft drink consumption fell (3 percent) for the first time ever.[43]

One Crisis

Indra Nooyi is known for breaking out into song. She is spontaneous, sometimes brash. These attributes may have gotten the best of her when she gave the commencement address at the Columbia University School of Business in May 2005. She analogized the five most populated of the world's seven continents to the fingers of one hand:

> Each of us in the US—the long middle finger—must be careful that when we extend our arm in either a business or political sense, we take pains to assure that we are giving a hand, not the finger. Unfortunately, I think that this is how the rest of the world looks at the US right now. Not as part of the hand—giving strength and purpose to the rest of the fingers—but instead scratching our nose and sending a signal.[44]

Nooyi's remarks at Columbia were on a slow news day: they set off a furor. PepsiCo felt compelled to post a Nooyi apology on the corporate website.

Commitment to Diversity and Management Style

In her college years, Indra Nooyi sang for an all-girl band. Since then, she has continued to pay attention to diversity and to women's achievements, in business as well as in music. On multiple occasions, she has talked about PepsiCo's strides in creating a more diverse workplace but cautions that "the full potential of diversity is not realized without an inclusive culture" at an organization.[45] Four of the most senior executives and three of the directors at PepsiCo are women. There has been a trickle down beneath that level as well. Indra Nooyi has a strong commitment to socially responsible corporate behavior, evidenced by her fostering the movement into healthier drinks and snack foods as well as promoting diversity:

> If all you want . . . is double-digit earning growth, and nothing else, then I'm the wrong person. Companies today are bigger than many economies. We are little republics. We are engines of efficiency. If companies don't do responsible things, who is going to? Why not start making change now?[46]

She shares also a characteristic of many other successful women: she and her husband prioritized their careers. He gave up a promising career at Hewlett-Packard so that Indra could pursue hers. He and Indra, together with their two daughters, live in Connecticut.

MARY SAMMONS

A Company In Trouble

Mary Sammons is the CEO of a company which reached the deepest depths of any. Enron, WorldCom, HealthSouth, and, arguably, Adelphia Communications—corporate governance train wrecks all, involved excessive greed, aided and assisted by senior managers and directors, willing to turn a blind eye to subordinates' fraudulent behavior, especially if the non-sanctioned behavior benefited the corporation. But wrongdoing at Enron or WorldCom did not involve intentional out-and-out theft and embezzlement, at least by those at the top. By contrast, Rite Aid's trouble emanated from intentional self-dealing of the worst sort, by senior managers, reaching up to the CEO, Martin Grass, whose behavior can be described not only as criminal but stupid.

Grass's father, Alex, had built up the drug and box retail chain into a publicly held company that became a favorite of Wall Street. Alex Grass remained humble: he wore lace up shoes, never loafers, for he believed that loafers signaled to others laziness on the wearer's part. He engineered his son Martin's succession as Rite Aid's CEO.

In the 1990s, Martin Grass, as well as other senior executives, began secretly to purchase store locations for their personal accounts. Then, at opportune times, they would arrange the conveyance of those real estate parcels to the company they controlled, at inflated prices, and without disclosure of the seller's identity. Grass used corporate funds to purchase an 83-acre headquarters site for his own account, ostensibly to re-convey to Rite Aid at a markup. Grass and other executives took millions in bonuses without board of director authorization. They backdated documents to increase rewards to themselves under the company's incentive plan. And they overstated Rite Aid profits by $1.6 billion.

Grass could have had any salary he wanted. He was, after all, CEO of a Wall Street high flyer and the founder's son. But he chose to defraud his own company through a series of secret manipulations. While he and others did this, they neglected Rite Aid business, which skidded badly. Five Rite Aid executives pleaded guilty to securities fraud, conspiracy to defraud shareholders, lying to grand juries, and otherwise obstructing justice. In May 2004, Federal Judge Sylvia Rambo fined CEO Martin Grass $500,000, ordered forfeiture of $3 million in ill-gotten gains, and sentenced him to eight years in prison.[47]

In 1999, when Rite Aid recruited Mary Sammons, along with several other executives, from Kroger, Rite Aid had truly skidded off the road: a 50.1 percent drop in annual income, to $158 million; a layoff of 300 employees at its home office in Camp Hill, Pennsylvania; and a consolidated securities law suit for billions of dollars, owing to Grass and others' wrongdoing (which CEO Robert Miller and Sammons settled for $200 million).[48] It was a company "with no cash flow, associates who weren't motivated, and suppliers who weren't doing business."[49] It had not only fallen far behind the number one and two companies in the business, Walgreen's and CVS, but Martin Grass had literally run it off the highway.

The Beaver State

Mary Sammons majored in French at Marylhurst College in the Portland, Oregon suburbs. She is one of two of female CEOs from a small Catholic women's college (Anne Mulcahy of Xerox Corp. is a graduate of Marymount in Tarrytown, New York).

In 1973, Sammons went to work for Portland-based Fred Meyer, Inc., after three years' teaching school. Fred Meyer is a Pacific Northwest institution, something similar to what Walmart would like to be, but of higher quality. A Fred Meyer is a grocery–wine shop–clothing–sporting goods–department store under one roof. Many families shop nowhere else. They have unbounded loyalty to Fred Meyer. To describe it merely as a "supermarket chain," as stock manuals used to do, does Fred Meyer a disservice.

Like Rite Aid, the eponymous Fred Meyer's had a humble man as its founder. Even after he had become a multi-millionaire, Fred Meyer would ride the public buses around Portland. Passengers reported Fred Meyer sightings.

Over 26 years, Mary Sammons worked her way up through Fred Meyer as a management trainee, buyer, store manager, regional manager, and, finally, president and chief executive officer. In 1999, Kroger, the nation's largest grocery chain company, acquired Fred Meyer. Nine months later Mary Sammons was gone. Along with three male executives (Robert G. Miller, David Jessick, and John Standley), she left Kroger for the desperately sinking Rite Aid to become president and chief operating officer.[50] A short time later she succeeded Miller as CEO.

Go East Young Woman

Ms. Sammons had some early successes but she has not been the tow truck to pull Rite Aid out of the ditch. A leading trade organization named her the "Drug Retailer of the Year 2001," citing the "dramatic metamorphosis" she had engineered by returning Rite Aid to profitability.[51] Rite Aid began a national television advertising campaign.[52] CEO Sammons caused the corporation's stores to put emphasis on service and pharmacists: "[t]his is a campaign about personal relationships, inspired by the kind of care we saw our pharmacists give as we visited Rite Aid stores across the country."[53]

Despite her efforts, Sammons failed to help the company gain any long-term traction. The share price slipped back into the single digit range, moving between $4 and $7 per share. The company experienced a modest loss in the second quarter of 2006, characteristic of its lackluster performance overall.

In summer, 2006, Sammons and her team engineered the $3.8 billion purchase of the Brooks and Eckerd drug store chains from private equity firm Jean Coutu Group, which earlier had purchased the Eckerd drug store chain from J.C. Penny. Sammons predicted great things from the acquisition: "Rite Aid will emerge as a stronger national drug chain [doing business in 31 states and the District of Columbia] with an increased presence through about 5,000 stores, some 56 percent bigger than its current store base," bringing it up from a distant third behind Walgreen's and CVS. "[E]verything we've built at Rite Aid over the last several years gives us the confidence to successfully complete the integration, and to withstand industry and competitive challenges."[54]

Sammons also has set out objectives for the Rite Aid organization:

- Building sales and growing the customer base at Rite Aid stores.
- Getting a deeper understanding of both the Rite Aid and the chain drug store customer.
- Differentiating Rite Aid from its competitors by effectively establishing itself as the premier health and wellness retailer.
- Increasing productivity while at the same time becoming an employer of choice.[55]

The Results?

None so far. Rite Aid lost $69.6 million in the second quarter of 2007, and $985.4 in the first quarter of 2008.[56] The Brooks Eckerd acquisition pushed Rite Aid's debt, which must be serviced (interest paid) out of cash flow, to $5.8 billion. The share price stood at $6.73 in June 2007, after the smoke from the acquisition cleared. By January 2008, the share price neared penny stock status (less than $1.00), at $1.91, when it had stood as high as $51.13 in January 1999.[57] Rite Aid's share price subsequently bounced up into the $2–3 range while Walgreen's and CVS (now CVS-Caremark) received the market's respect, trading at $36.37 (down from a high of $48.09) and $48.53 (an all-time high), respectively. Even amid the carnage of 2008–2009, CVS-Caremark and Walgreens stocks hover near $30.

On June 23, 2008, Rite Aid announced falling same store sales (a key measure of retail prowess), a $156.6 million loss in the second quarter (twice as large as predicted), and an inability to upgrade stores badly in need of it because the credit crunch and the overhang of debt from the Eckerd acquisition impeded further borrowing. The share price fell to $1.00 and then lower still, as low as $0.76.[58] Key executives, including the COO, the CFO, and the chief administrative officer left the company.[59]

No audible cries for Mary Sammons's ouster ring forth, even though in late 2008 the company had to begin engineering a reverse stock split (e.g., one for ten) to raise its share price and thus forestall delisting by the New York Stock Exchange.[60] Ms. Sammons receives good marks from industry analysts:

"[N]o senior executive at any pharmacy-based retailer is more experienced or well-grounded in pharmacy retailing ... [and] has learned her trade the hard way: by inheriting an impossible situation, by making mistakes, by being occasionally out-maneuvered, by being forever regarded as the senior executive at the No. 3 drug chain in a game that many believe that can support only Nos. 1 and 2. In the end, however, she has [always] won."[61] Sooner or later, though, probably sooner, given nine years at Rite Aid, and a share price as low as $0.20, she must produce, despite whatever praise is forthcoming.

Lessons Learned?

Few, or none. Mary Sammons is not, and expressly disclaims, being an advocate of any sort for women in business. She has not added women directors to Rite Aid's board of directors. Eight of the top 50 executives at Rite Aid are women but all of those women appear to be in staff, or so-called pink collar, positions: benefits and compensation, pubic relations, and manager of beauty product categories. These are not positions from which, historically, women step up into the circle of positions from which corporations chose senior executives and directors.

Sammons's career has involved a modicum of side stepping but 26 years at one corporation and nine at another hardly teaches anything to women who might follow in her path.

Like Jill Barad (Mattel), Ann Mulcahy (Xerox), Andrea Jung (Avon), Susan Ivey (Reynolds America), Brenda Barnes (Sara Lee), and Pat Russo (Alcatel Lucent), Mary Sammons's story lends credence to the glass cliff theory, which holds that companies are more likely or more open to naming a woman as CEO when they face particularly difficult challenges, as Rite Aid and its CEO did and still do. Board of directors and search committees faced with such situations are likely to reason, "Why not give a woman a chance?"[62]

Ms. Sammons has made no public pronouncements that could be of value to those who wish to learn from her experience, particularly women who aspire to higher ranks in business organizations. Sammons is another female CEO who leaves few footprints. The footprints she does leave are not particularly ones other women should seek to follow.

Tentative Teachings

Your Niche does not Necessarily Need to be Manufacturing

Contrary to the traditional viewpoint, many of the women in this book came up through marketing and sales (Barad, Jung, Fiorina, Russo, Ivey, Barnes, Gold, Meyrowitz, Nooyi, and Sammons) rather than line positions. A few did make their mark in production and distribution (Reynolds and Rosport). But marketing and sales does not exhaust the list of career patterns that may lead to a CEO suite. In healthcare, the needs have arisen for a government relations background, coupled with negotiation skills. Angela Braly had the right background to fit a large company's desires in a CEO.

Find your own niche. While some pursuits may be more promising than others, no one size or two sizes fit all. Do well in the job you have at the time.

Transition Jobs, Especially Early in a Career, do not Damage Future Prospects

Young people fresh out of school spend several years without knowing, and trying to decide, what they want to do. Today, many more young persons have the luxury to do that while, a generation ago, the expectation was for a much more linear progression (college, service perhaps, graduate school, marriage, career). Many of the women who have made it to the CEO suite had transition jobs in their twenties: Jill Barad (actress and Coty Cosmetics); Andrea Jung (Bloomingdale's); Marion Sandler (Bloomingdale's); Anne Mulcahy (Chase Manhattan Bank); Susan Ivey (Lanier Business Supplies); Mary Sammons (teaching French); and Brenda Barnes (US Postal Service) come to mind. Even Pat Woertz had a transition job, albeit it a more serious one (Ernst & Ernst). Spending two to three years doing "something else" does not damage a woman's prospects for a successful career in business.

Prioritize Careers with Your Partner?

Many two-career married couples pursue both careers for a time. Then, it seems, the very successful ones have a discussion and, based upon that discussion, consciously relegate one career to the other. Christina Gold, Indra Nooyi, Carleton Fiorina, Anne Mulcahy, and Susan Ivey and their husbands are examples. Marion and Herb Sandler chose to partner, but they could do so because they owned, or controlled, the business. Meg Whitman's husband had a parallel, successful career as a professional (a neurosurgeon). Only Brenda Barnes and her spouse attempted to pursue executive management careers simultaneously, both with PepsiCo. They divorced several years ago.

Bring a Global Attitude, if not Expertise, to the Table

Indra Nooyi best exemplifies this new requirement for any CEO. Large corporations today must be ready and able to market and sell products and services around the globe, to 6.2 billion persons. As recently as 1980, management experts thought it sufficient if a company was number one, two or perhaps three in a domestic market, such as the United States with 300 million, or the European Union with 490 million in population.

In many businesses, the economies of scale have become so great that, in order to maximize economies in manufacture and sale, companies have to grow rapidly, moving to larger and larger (potential) markets. With 1.4 billion, and 1 billion citizens respectively, the People's Republic of China and India have already become large markets. They may be the dominant economic players, worldwide, in our lifetime. Companies seeking candidates for director positions emphasize different skill sets from time to time. In recent years, at most companies the emphasis is to obtain directors with international outlook if not experience. The specifications for CEO candidates is becoming similar.

Those specifications are not "how to," strictly speaking, for the CEO and those who work for her will assemble the foreign legal, real estate, manu- facturing, marketing, and other experts needed. The "need to" and the "will to" are attributes companies are likely to seek. Thus, a modern CEO needs "how to" abilities not in narrow, technical senses but in a broader strategic sense. She needs to be able to lead a management team through the process of devising objectives and scale for the foreign outreach. She needs to help participate in understanding the tolerable levels of risk. Do we go it alone? Do we joint venture (e.g., partner) with an established foreign firm? Do we partner with a more marginal player? Do we seek to enter new markets only through distributorships or, on a lesser scale, with the foreign equivalent of a manufacturer's representative, who represents not only our products but also many others? What are the risks? What are the potential advantages of each? Any woman who aspires to a high management position must make evident her ability to implement the global thinking that the twenty-first century requires, as several of these women CEO biographies (Jung, Fiorina, Mulcahy, Ivey, and Nooyi) demonstrate.

9 CEO Additions of 2008–09

Lynn Laverty Elsenhans—Sunoco Inc., Carol Bartz—Yahoo! Inc., Ellen Jamison Kullman—El DuPont de Nemours & Co., Irene B. Rosenfeld—Kraft Foods Inc., and Laura J. Sen—BJ's Wholesale Club Inc.

The most recent period has signaled another breakthrough. Although one woman CEO (Pat Russo at Alcatel Lucent) resigned, and another sold her company out from underneath her (Paula Reynolds at Safeco Insurance), boards of directors appointed five other women CEOs at *Fortune 500* companies, bringing the number of women CEOs to 15.[1] Traditionally male-dominated companies in male-dominated industries (oil and gas, information technology, and paints and chemicals) appointed three of these women, reinforcing a tentative teaching of Chapter 6 ("Go Where They Aren't"). The two other women who have become CEOs in 2008–09 have done so in fields historically receptive to women in senior management, namely, food products and retailing.

LYNN LAVERTY ELSENHANS

The Oil Patch

Headquartered in Philadelphia, Sunoco has $42 billion in annual revenues, five domestic refineries, and 13,700 employees. Comparable numbers for Exxon, Shell, and British Petroleum are: $460 billion revenues and 104,700 employees (Exxon Mobil); $458 billion revenues and 102,000 employees (Royal Dutch Shell); and $361 billion and 92,000 employees (British Petroleum).[2] While not small in an absolute sense, Sunoco is tiny by comparison with the seven sisters (the major oil companies).

In fact, Sunoco reached out to one of those major oil companies, Shell, for its new CEO, who took office in August 2008. Lynn Elsenhans served as vice-president, Shell Downstream, LLC, from January 2005 to August 2008. As such she presided over 45,000 service stations, 40 plants producing petroleum and chemical products, and virtually all other operations downstream from exploration and production. Prior to those awesome responsibilities, she served as president, Shell Oil Products USA, Inc.[3]

Ms. Elsenhans became the first female to head a major oil company and the 13th female CEO in the *Fortune 500*.[4] She has had her work cut out for her. Sunoco's share price had fallen 52 percent in the months of 2008 before she took office.

Sunoco has to contend with tight profit margins because its refineries are capable of processing only light sweet, the most expensive crude oil, while the majors can process many forms of crude including high sulphur, which are cheaper and lead to greater profit margins. In addition, and unlike the household name oil companies such as those named above, Sunoco does no exploration and drilling. Thus, Sunoco is a wholly a downstream petroleum company. Ms. Elsenhans explains:

> [D]ownstream companies like Sunoco do refining but not drilling and don't benefit from the high price of oil. [B]ecause the economy is sluggish and product prices are high, people are changing their behavior in the way they drive and heat their homes. Product demand has been down dramatically . . . it [is] quite difficult to make money. That surprises people who think that oil companies are making tons of money. The companies that produce oil and gas are making a lot of money but the downstream companies aren't.[5]

Analysts continue to mention Sunoco as a possible takeover target.[6]

Another MBA

Born in 1956, Lynn Elsenhans grew up in New Jersey and Texas. Her father, a research and marketing executive for Humble Oil and then Exxon, did two tours of duty, with family in tow, in Houston. Thus Ms. Elsenhans had exposure to the oil patch from an early age. Her later jobs with Shell and Sunoco are less surprising when viewed in that light.

In high school she moved to Connecticut where she astounded classmates and guidance counselors by being the first student they knew to aspire to attend Rice University. Rice, of course, is a great school but no one, or a rare few, would know that on the East Coast. Lynn Elsenhans knew about Rice from having lived in Houston.

When she returned to Texas, she was caught up in a whirlwind of activities: campus politics, band ("The Marching Owls"), sports editor for the *Thresher* (school newspaper), and player on the women's varsity basketball team. She also found time to major in mathematical science.

After having graduated in 1978, like many other women CEOs in this book, Ms. Elsenhans went to business school. She received an MBA from Harvard Business School in 1980. She began her career in the petroleum industry and with Shell. Even though "opportunities for leadership . . . didn't exist" for women when Ms. Elsenhans began working in the energy industry in 1980, she began a career that would last 28 years with Shell and include many leadership positions.[7]

She is a director of International Paper Co. and a trustee of Rice University. She is married to John Elsenhans, also a graduate of Rice.

Elsenhans on Women in Business

Lynn Elsenhans believes that multiple opportunities exist for women to advance to management positions, even in industries such as energy in which those opportunities did not exist 25 years ago. She has promoted networks and promotions for women throughout her career.

> The numbers would suggest, however, that it's still difficult for women to get to the highest levels . . . [W]omen leaders tend to be competent or liked, but rarely both, and that's a double bind. People don't tend to trust people they don't like, and it's very hard to lead in business if there isn't mutual trust and respect. It's also difficult to go forward in a company if you're not considered competent. As society gets more comfortable with the notion that women can be tough when there's a reason to get tough . . . it will tend to make it easier for women to have top jobs and break that glass ceiling. There have been inroads, but I don't think we are there yet.[8]

CAROL BARTZ

Another Male-Dominated Field

One would think that the information technology (computer hardware, software, peripherals) would be one of the fields most receptive to the participation and advancement of women. Youth, west coast attitudes, and cutting-edge outlooks not only predominate but also characterize the industry. Yet the information technology industry's record in the hiring, advancement, and retention of women is atrocious:

- Women make up only 26 percent of the information technology industry's employment, compared with 47 percent of women in the total workforce at the time of the census (2006) and 50 percent plus today in industry overall.[9]
- "The worst industry in its treatment of women [as directors] is the computer industry. Nine corporations have six women directors out of seventy-eight, as follows: Dell Computer (28) [*Fortune 500* rank] (one of ten); Microsoft Corp. (41) (two of nine); Cisco (91) (two of twelve); Sun Microsystems (194) (one of nine); Oracle (220) (one of eleven); Apple

Computer (263) (zero of seven); Micron Technology (439) (zero of seven); Affiliated Computer Services (460) (zero of seven); and Gateway Computer (495) (zero of seven). Four large publicly held corporations . . . have no women directors at all. Apple Computer and Steve Jobs sell iPods and computers for purchase by women and mothers but, in this day and age, have no women on their board."[10]

- In information technology, not only are women under-represented in the employee and management ranks but women are also leaving employment at a rate faster than any other field.[11]

Carol Bartz's early jobs at Digital Equipment Corp. and Sun Microsystems, followed by 14 years as CEO of publicly held software company Autodesk, Inc., and then her appointment as CEO of *Fortune 500* company Yahoo! Inc. on January 13, 2009,[12] offers insights on how women might advance in male-dominated fields of endeavor.

Why So Few?

In the IT world, Carol Bartz is known for earthy, some say salty, language. One reason she believes men greatly outnumber women in IT is because "a mine's bigger than yours" mentality prevails, especially in the "hardware world," a game women are loathe to play, or do not play at all.[13] The industry has engaged in introspection about the paucity of diversity in IT, at least to the extent of posing various potential causes if not to the extent of doing anything about it. In addition to "mine's bigger" explanations, studies ascribe the paucity of women to these causes:

- *Machismo attitudes and outright sexual harassment.* Sylvia Ann Hewlett found that 63 percent of women in information technology report having experienced sexual harassment.[14] Women reported that IT culture is filled with off-color jokes, sexual innuendo, and male arrogance. Women in IT Forum, an industry group, reported a significant exit of females from the industry because they became "uncomfortable with the macho style of management" which is widespread.[15] Her penchant for salty language may have made it easier for Carol Bartz to adapt and be accepted in the IT industry.
- *Significantly greater aptitude among males.* Because computer use is much greater among males, males enter the IT field in much greater numbers.[16] With the advent of email, ipods and music downloads, texting, twitting, computer-based research, word processing, and the like, a gender difference in computer use no longer exists. A 2004 study of 430 college students found no appreciable difference in computer use by men and women. A 2005 study in Sweden reached the same conclusion. This reasoning, greater aptitude among males, lacks the explanatory power it may once have had.

- *Significantly greater motivation among males.* Men prefer working with tools and machines, which predominate in IT, while women prefer working with people—a form of labor which does not predominate.[17] Men were significantly more likely to identify love of technology and computers as a key motivator for entering the IT workforce. Women, on the other hand, were significantly more likely to list "job security, ease of entry, and flexible work hours" as primary motives for entering a particular field.[18]
- *Lack of support for women from educators in computer science and mathematics.* A noted educator was quoted as saying that "[s]omehow teachers or kids are pushing the idea that [information technology] is not a field for girls."[19] Women receive little or no encouragement either to enter the field or to continue after their studies have begun. A large percentage of the women who do work in IT do not have degrees in technology or mathematics. With a degree in computer science, from the University of Wisconsin, Carol Bartz is an exception to the norm which prevails in the industry.
- *Lack of mentors.* Advice books routinely advise women in business to seek out numbers of mentors, including several at your company and several others in your field. Mentors are like stocks: to put themselves in a position to advance, women should have a diversified portfolio. Many of these mentors should, or naturally will, be women. Because so few women are in higher level positions in information technology, however, fewer mentors, and almost no female mentors, are available to help women who aspire to advancement in the field.[20]

Exception: a Woman in Information Technology

After two years at William Woods, a women's college in Fulton, Missouri, Carol Bartz transferred to the University of Wisconsin. Her grandparents had raised her on a Wisconsin dairy farm. A course in computer science at William Woods had whetted Bartz's appetite, so she transferred to her home state's flagship university, where she could major in the subject.[21]

Her first jobs, however, were not in IT. She sold automated banking services to small banks throughout the upper Midwest, working for First Bank System, Inc., in St. Paul, Minnesota. She jumped to a sales position at Minnesota Mining and Manufacturing (3-M Corp.). There, in what one would assume would be an enlightened environment, she encountered a male-dominated world: "I first realized that this corporate thing against women really existed."[22] Being the sole woman in a 300 employee work group, "I was really singled out," recalls Bartz.

A 3-M manager sent Bartz, a new employee, to an out-of-town sales meeting. He booked Bartz into a double room she was to share with a male sales rep. When she arrived and found out, Bartz booked herself into a separate room. Nonetheless, the following morning the sales manager confronted her, and fired her on the spot for sleeping with a fellow employee. Bartz can laugh about it today: "I told them I didn't sleep with anybody last night . . . I didn't know anyone there. Even so, for the next several hours, I was fired."[23] When she applied for a transfer to corporate headquarters, 3-M managers bluntly told her that "[w]omen don't do those jobs."[24] After four years with 3-M she quit.

Bartz entered the IT field with Digital Equipment Corp., also in Minneapolis, where she stayed for six years. She jumped to Sun Microsystems in 1983, the manufacturer of complex, high-tech workstations and Java Script software. A fellow woman at Sun described Sun, then a company of 100 employees: "Sun was a culture of true opportunity. I don't feel at Sun the fact that I was a woman factored into whether I was advanced or not."[25] Bartz worked her way quickly up to the number two position, under founder and CEO Scott McNealy. McNealy described Bartz as "hardly a shrinking violet." She earned a "reputation as a direct and tough-as-nails manager who could soften her approach with humor and charm."[26] She spurned a great many offers to become CEO elsewhere, jokingly saying that she "lacked the male-dominated gene, the one that says you have to be CEO."[27]

She spent ten years at Sun Microsystems (sold to Oracle in 2009). While there she married, divorced, and remarried, to Bill Marr, Sun's vice-president for North America and Australia, by whom she had a son. She also has two children from her first marriage.

CEO at Autodesk

Autodesk was a company with a great product but in search of leadership. The company was the sixth largest in the software field, had existed for ten years, and had sales of $257 million.[28] But like eBay when Meg Whitman arrived, Autodesk remained "a classic Valley example of a successful company being run by an unwieldy group of innovators."[29] Most employees brought their dogs or cats with them to the office.[30] The flagship product, computer-assisted design (CAD) software had a "whopping 70 percent share" of the market. Architects, kitchen designers, boat builders, civil engineers, and all manner of other designers used Autodesk software.

One reviewer described Bartz's early days as playing "Wendy to the lost boys."[31] The Autodesk board brought her in to add structure to a chaotic environment. Not only did she insist that personnel be on time for meetings but she also insisted that they have meetings in the first place. She strongly disfavored the, until then, ubiquitous use of Blackberries and other hand-held personal assistants during meetings. Carl Bass, now Autodesk's CEO, recalls that "Bartz quickly sacked under performers, installing new lieutenants to help her manage," a performance she would reprise at Yahoo!: "[O]ne former exec was shown the door before the end of the first, all-day staff meeting" at Autodesk.[32] Bartz was "surprised at the level of disgruntlement" her practices engendered but "she felt under intense pressure to perform immediately at a very high level, not only because she was one of the first women to get the keys to a corner office in Silicon Valley, but because Autodesk was desperately in need of direction."[33]

Despite a rough beginning, Bartz's strategic moves enabled her to build up Autodesk "by spiffing up its bread-and-butter moneymaker, expanding the product line, and imposing adult management on a former wild child of a company."[34] In 14 years under Bartz, Autodesk stock increased ten-fold in value, annual revenues increased more than five-fold ($257 million to $1.5 billion), CAD decreased from 70 percent to 37 percent of sales, and the company added 50 new software products to its offerings.[35] She had "forged an effective leadership style out of her no-nonsense charm."[36]

She had also prevailed over personal adversity. In Bartz's second day at Autodesk, physicians diagnosed her with breast cancer. Bartz underwent a radical mastectomy, missing only one month of work. Asked why she returned to work so quickly, Bartz said "I didn't want people to make too big a deal of it. I didn't want people saying, 'There—women finally get to be CEOs and look what happens.' "[37]

CEO in the *Fortune 500*

Yahoo! was a dispirited company. Google, Inc. had stolen a march on Yahoo! in its businesses, internet advertising, and computerized search engines. In 2008, desirous of competing directly with Google, Microsoft made a $47 billion cash merger offer to Yahoo!. Jerry Yang, Yahoo!'s founder and CEO, and the Yahoo! board of directors rebuffed the Microsoft offer, despite Microsoft's characterization of its bid as a "first and final offer." Steve Ballmer, Microsoft's CEO, stood by his word. Microsoft withdrew its offer, never to return to the table.[38] Yahoo!'s share price fell from the high $20s to as low as $8.94 per share.

Yang and other senior managers stepped aside. The Yahoo! board then named Carol Bartz, who had retired the previous May at Autodesk,[39] as CEO of Yahoo!, in part based upon her reputation for a "direct management style." While the Yahoo! board trotted Bartz out like she was the winner of the Preakness or Kentucky Derby, analysts questioned whether management style was enough: "[T]here is a world of difference between the computer-aided design industry inhabited by Autodesk ... and the ad-supported Web-media business occupied by Yahoo!."[40] Bartz also stepped into a sea of red ink: Yahoo! announced a $303 million ($0.22 per share) loss for the fourth quarter of 2008, compared to a $206 million profit (0.15 per share) a year earlier.[41] Bartz began quickly, reversing Yahoo!'s decentralized organization, replacing it with a faster-acting top–down management structure and with new personnel in many management positions.[42] Whether Yahoo! will return to its beginning success, or merger or partner with Microsoft, remains unknown but Ms. Bartz has re-opened discussion between the companies.[43]

Women's Role on Corporate Management

What is known is Carol Bartz's no-nonsense attitude toward work–life issues. While she has made time for her husband and three children, she calls "the balanced life . . . a myth."[44] She believes that women have to quit obeisance to the myth.

> They beat themselves up for not doing it all . . . they get mad at everyone around them. That's nuts . . . They think, "I'm going to cook a great breakfast, wash up the dishes before I leave, take the kids to school, call my college roommate on the way to work, be a CEO all day, volunteer on the way home, do a little exercising, cook a wonderful dinner, help with homework, have sex." I don't think so.[45]

As a personal management tool for women in business, Bartz advocates rigid compartmentalization. Women can have it all, or mostly all, "but only by cutting life into compartments and then ruthlessly maintaining the boundaries" between compartments.[46]

In 1971, when Bartz graduated from Wisconsin, expectations for women in business were high. Despite the hoped-for opportunities at the time, Bartz realized "that male counterparts and supervisors shook the corporate ladder more fiercely with each rung that she and other pioneering women of her generation ascended."[47]

Today, even though Bartz has been extremely successful in the corporate world, she "sees the stubborn remnants of sexism in business." When she is in a group of CEOs and other high-level managers, executives from other industries frequently "assume I must be somebody's wife."[48] "I was in Washington, DC, with Bill Gates, Andy Grove, and some other executives . . . for a meeting with some senators. It was high-tech-CEOs come to town, and a senator turned to me and asked, 'So are we going to start the meeting?' He thought I was the moderator."[49]

Bartz believes that such treatments take their toll on women's ranks, contributing to the opt-out phenomenon. She thinks that many younger women "get the high-power degrees and then they drop back because they tell themselves that they're not going to get very far anyway. I think they look around and wonder whether the struggle is worth it or not." Although Bartz herself has achieved extraordinary success in business, "she believes that a lot of women take themselves out of the race to the c-suite even before it begins."[50] Carol Bartz also believes that women need to continue pressure on the glass ceiling, trying "to change the environment so that my daughter has a place" in the business world.[51]

ELLEN JAMISON KULLMAN

Chemicals and Coatings

French settlers built a gunpowder mill on Brandywine Creek, upstream from the Delaware River, and founded El DuPont de Nemours in 1802. Today, 207-plus years later, while the major business entity in Wilmington, and overall in the small state of Delaware, DuPont is a worldwide presence in chemicals, coatings, agri-business (seeds and fertilizers), safety and protection, and innovation. DuPont employs 60,000 persons who produce the Kelvar fabric in bullet-proof vests police officers wear, the Roundup herbicide gardeners use on weeds, the Tyvek house wrap builders employ to keep dwellings moisture free, and the Corian kitchen countertops households put in their homes, as well as countless other products.[52] Prior to 2009, 18 executives, many of them DuPonts, all male, led the company. In September 2009, the DuPont board of directors chose as the 19th CEO Ellen Kullman, who took office on January 1, 2009.[53] She became "one of the few women to rise to the top of the chemicals industry" and the sixth female CEO in the *Fortune 100*.[54]

How did she get there? One, she developed star power within the company. She began in 1988 as the business director for DuPont's x-ray film business. She rotated through various positions, becoming DuPont's first female business segment chief (chemicals) in 1995.[55] She then led DuPont's $2 billion titanium dioxide business when her predecessor CEO, Charles Holliday, came to her:

> [H]olliday asked Ellen Kullman to expand its service for training customers to use DuPont products safely. Kullman saw a larger opportunity and built a business to address the safety concerns of customers in such fields as food processing and aerospace. Then came 9/11 and risk prevention boomed. DuPont was way ahead; today Kullman's safety and protection division is the fast-growing DuPont unit, with some $5 billion in annual sales. Her domain includes bullet-resistant Kelvar and contamination-proof medical packaging. Kullman . . . [moved onto] the short list to replace Holliday when he retires.[56]

Kullman cobbled together disparate units that accounted for $3.5 billion in annual sales that account for $6 billion in revenue today, generating 63 percent of DuPont's profits in 2007.[57]

In 2006, she became DuPont's executive vice-president. In that capacity, she led a formal process planning for growth in emerging international markets, such as Latin America and Eastern Europe. She also led and thrived in DuPont's drive to transform itself from a chemicals and coatings to a market-driven science company. She recognizes that only by such means can DuPont safeguard itself against deteriorations in demand caused by the downturns construction, automotive, and textile industries periodically undergo. In the future, Kullman wants "to expand the company . . . into a high tech research business that also ventures into areas like bio-fuels and solar technology . . . [T]he strategy emphasizes developing useful products through scientific breakthroughs."[58]

She had great mentors along the way. Early in her career, she worked first at Westinghouse and then at General Electric. While at GE, she worked for legendary CEO Jack Welch, who taught her how to make trade-offs and about how constantly to make decisions as part of leadership. Later in her career, at DuPont she worked for Chad Holliday, who served a term as chairperson at Catalyst, and who, among other things, made creation and retention of diversity a prominent feature of DuPont annual executive reviews. Under Halliday, DuPont created an environment that fostered diversity instead of hindering it.[59]

Math, Science, and an MBA

Delaware is a cozy, somewhat in-bred place which takes care of its own. Not surprisingly, Ellen Jamison grew up in Wilmington, the youngest in a family of four (two brothers, one sister). She attended the exclusive Tower Hill School but went away for college, to Tufts University in Boston, where she majored in mechanical engineering, graduating in 1978. She took a Masters in Business Administration (MBA) from the Kellogg School at Northwestern University in 1983. As has been seen, she began her management career with Westinghouse, jumped to General Electric for several years, and joined DuPont in 1988. She is married to Mike Kullman, a senior DuPont marketing executive. They have three children: Maggie and twin boys, Stephen and David.

Ms. Kullman has not spoken out on women's lack of participation or advancement in business, in part perhaps because she became CEO at a difficult time in DuPont's history. In the fourth quarter of 2008, DuPont took a $500 million charge against earnings for restructuring. Four weeks after Kullman took the helm, DuPont announced a $0.70 per share loss for the fourth quarter ($0.60 per share profit a year earlier) and dim prospects for the ensuing several quarters.[60] The closest she has come is to credit her outgoing personality as an ingredient in her success in a male-dominated environment.[61]

She is a director of General Electric, was a director of General Motors (resigned December 2008), is a Trustee of Tufts University, and remains a member of the Board of Overseers for the Tufts School of Engineering.

IRENE B. ROSENFELD

Most Educated

Irene Rosenfeld has the most formal education of any woman in this book. She attended Cornell University, achieving her BA (psychology, 1975), her

MBA at the Johnson School (1977), and her PhD in marketing and statistics (1980). She is the only female CEO with a doctorate.

She began her career in advertising with a predecessor firm of Saatchi & Saatchi (Dancer Fitzgerald). After a short stint, she jumped to General Foods to do marketing research. Phillip Morris acquired General Foods in 1988 and merged it with another subsidiary, Kraft Foods. Along the way, Ms. Rosenfeld has been brand manager for Countrytime Lemonade, general manager of the General Foods Beverages Division, and general manager of Deserts and Snacks (1991–96). She got her first overall command when she headed up Kraft Foods Canada from 1996–2000. With the wordy title president of operations, technology, procurement, research and development, and information systems, Ms. Rosenfeld oversaw the integration of the newly acquired Nabisco into the Kraft Foods group, a $19 billion endeavor.

Like several other women in this book (Pat Russo at Lucent, for example), Irene Rosenfeld side stepped but at a very senior level. In 2004, she became the president and CEO of the PepsiCo subsidiary, Frito Lay, whose sales in 2005 alone were $9.6 billion. After two years, she returned in triumph, as CEO of Kraft Foods, Inc., then a subsidiary of Phillip Morris, which had changed its name to Altria Group, Ltd.

Altria decided to give Kraft Foods its freedom, as the market undervalued the company as long as it was affiliated with a cigarette company. Irene Rosenfeld was CEO of Kraft when it was privately held. The Kraft board retained her as CEO after Kraft became an independent publicly held company.

Consumer Focus

As befits her formal education (PhD in marketing and statistics), and her captaincy of a consumer products (food) company, Irene Rosenfeld is not only extremely consumer conscious but also consumer driven: "I've spent a lot of time getting everybody refocused on what really matters in the marketplace and working with my staff to rethink their role rather than being operators out of a corporate ivory tower."[62] She thinks about the role a food company should play: "[I]t really comes back to a fundamental understanding of how our products fit into the consumers' life."[63]

Within Kraft, Rosenfeld established a webpage on the corporate website entitled "Ideas for Irene." Employees may use the web to inform the CEO about ideas and thoughts on the company's processes and products. She also had caused the creation of a similar online forum for use by consumers. Analysts have suggested that these overtures are gimmicks, to which CEO Rosenfeld responds "They're gimmicks if you don't use them." Rosenfeld and her staff swear by their use of the feedback generated, being attuned to the needs of consumers and installing as a management strategy harvesting consumers' and employees' ideas for products to drive production.[64]

Apparently, the Rosenfeld strategy and the steps taken to implement it attract adherents. Warren Buffett and his Berkshire Hathaway have become the largest shareholder in Kraft, Inc.[65]

Irene Rosenfeld is married to Richard Illgen, a mergers and acquisitions specialist. They have two daughters. She is a trustee of Cornell University.

Few Opinions about Women in Business

One of Rosenfeld's criticisms of the institutional challenges women face in business organizations seemingly applies to men as well as women:

> The biggest institutional challenge is that in so many businesses there isn't enough discussion along the way as part of succession planning about the kind of experiences that one needs to reach the top jobs. A big part of Kraft's advancement-planning process is to talk about who our top talent is, what sort of experiences they need to have. . . . And then we spend a lot of time talking about what we need to do to give them those jobs.[66]

As Mary Sammons and Carleton Fiorina have stated (at least while Fiorina was in office) (Chapter 2), Irene Rosenfeld seems to believe that the glass ceiling either no longer exists, or is badly shattered: "There have been plenty of top women leaders, from Indira Gandhi to Margaret Thatcher to Angela Merkel." CEO Rosenfeld "would like to see the media get over their fascination with the subject."[67] When asked point blank about whether a glass ceiling exists, Rosenfeld dodged the question: as a woman, "I was most encouraged when I and a number of my colleagues moved into CEO roles, that there wasn't a lot of talk about the fact that we were women. There was a lot of discussion about the fact that we were very competent business people."[68]

Nevertheless, Ms. Rosenfeld professes a strong belief in diversity, at Kraft and in business. Although her public statements are sparse, she has spoken about work–life issues. She believes that flexibility coupled with an ability to multitask is the key. "I think that the issue of work–life balance is a critical issue for every company around the world." She advises women to "know what's important to you and make sure you're taking care of that. The rest will fall into place."[69]

LAURA J. SEN

The Newest Female CEO

On February 1, 2009, Laura Sen became CEO of a $10 billion company, BJ's Wholesale Club, headquartered in Natick, Massachusetts. BJ's has 178 warehouse-type discount outlets in 17 states. Ms. Sen majored in French at

Boston College, going from there to a career in retail. She began at Zayre Corp. (jewelry), progressed to Jordan Marsh Company (shoes), and joined BJ's when it was in its infancy. As with Patricia Russo or Irene Rosenfeld, Laura Sen performed a senior side step—but of the self-manufactured variety. In March 2003, Sen left BJ's to form Sen Retail Consulting. She returned to BJ's in December 2006, rising to the position of president and chief operating officer in January 2008.[70]

In a depressed economy, discount shopping clubs do well (Costco's sales were up 3 percent in 2008), and BJ's Wholesale Club were better than all the rest (sales up 8.5 percent).[71]

Ms. Sen's husband is the CEO of a Boston area bio pharmaceutical company. They have two children, both in college.[72]

There are readily available no public statements by CEO Laura Sen, either about business methods or the participation and advancement of women in business.

Tentative Teachings

Go Where They Aren't—Part III

The careers of Lynn Elsenhans, Carol Bartz, and Ellen Kullman add force to this strategic option for certain women (Chapter 6).

Side step

Several of these women (Carol Bartz, Laura Sen) switched employers several times as they rose upward in corporate ranks, as did, for instance, Andrea Jung (Chapter 3), Paula Rosport Reynolds (Chapter 5), Meg Whitman (Chapter 7), and other women on their way to the CEO suite.

The Senior Side Step

At a very senior level, Irene Rosenfeld left Kraft Foods, Inc., to become CEO at Frito Lay, the snack subsidiary of PepsiCo. Several years earlier, Patricia Russo left Lucent to become president and chief operating officer at Kodak, only to be lured back to Lucent to be CEO. The senior side step seems a risky strategy, especially if more than a chance exists that a career move at the senior level may burn bridges back to where you might wish to return. The latter would be especially true if one were to jump to a direct competitor. On the other hand, a senior side step might be just the "dynamite charge" that awakens senior managers at the company a woman has left and prove to them the market worth of what they had all along.

Self-Manufactured Senior Side Step

Laura Sen formed her own consulting firm. Carol Meyrowitz did something of the same. Nearly two years after Sen had left, BJ's Wholesale Club called her back to take a senior position which ultimately led to the CEO suite. Studies show, however, that entrepreneurial efforts are the worst route a woman can select to journey to the senior management realm or to the CEO position in a corporation.

The self-manufactured side step involves extensive investment of money, time, and effort and a high risk of failure, if success is defined as a return to the corporate setting and a high managerial position there. The strategy seems to be a risky one.

Value of Education

Three of the five women in Chapter 9 have MBAs (Elsenhans, Kullman and Rosenfeld). Of the 15 women who have ascended to *Fortune 500* CEO positions since 2000, including these five, 11 have MBAs and one has a law degree. If Ursula Burns (Xerox) substitutes for Anne Mulcahy, Burns has an MS (engineering) from Columbia. The number of women CEOs with graduate degrees then rises to 13 of 15 (11 MBAs, one JD, one MS).

Education in Math and Science

While the career patterns, and especially the failures, of women who have become CEOs in the past points to the near necessity of education in business subjects (managerial accounting, stocks and commodities, corporate finance, or an MBA), this chapter's profiles highlight the desirability, rather than the absolute necessity, of education in certain fields. Lynn Elsenhans majored in mathematics, Carol Bartz in computer science, Ellen Kullman in mechanical engineering, and Irene Rosenfeld in marketing and statistics. These are areas or fields into which women seldom go at the university or college level. Yet the best combination for women who aspire to business careers may be an undergraduate degree in computer science, math or engineering with an MBA layered on top. Lynn Elsenhans and Ellen Kullman have precisely those educational backgrounds. Such a pairing of fields may be the best insurance policy a young woman could have in difficult or any other economic times.

Part II

Why There Aren't More

10 Why Women?

The group of companies with the highest representation of women on their senior management teams had a 35-percent higher ROE [Return on Equity] and a 34-percent higher TRS [Total Return to Shareholders] than companies with the lowest women's representation. Consumer Discretionary, Consumer Staples, and Financial Services companies with the highest representation of women in senior management experienced a considerably higher ROE and TRS.[1]

> Catalyst, Inc., "Catalyst Study Reveals Financial Performance
> Is Higher for Companies with Women at the Top" (2004)

The weak empirical support of [diversity on] boards is mirrored by anecdotal evidence. Independent directors often turn out to be lapdogs rather than watchdogs. The majority independent board of General Motors did nothing for over a decade while GM floundered . . . The majority independent board of American Express fired former CEO James Robinson only when faced with open shareholder revolt, despite a decade of business problems, with a few scandals along the way. Many other companies—including IBM, Kodak, Chrysler, Sears, Westinghouse, and Borden—performed abysmally for years despite majority-independent boards.

> Sanjai Bhagat & Bernard Black, "The Uncertain Relationship
> Between Board Composition and Firm Performance" (1999)

Most studies find little correlation [between board diversity and financial performance] but a number of recent studies report evidence of a negative correlation between the proportion of independent directors and firm performance—the opposite of the conventional wisdom.[2]

> Professors Bhagat & Black

Catalyst publicizes its statistics that both corporations run by women, and those with numbers of female directors, have significantly higher returns on equity and on sales than those who do not.[3] Irene Lang, president of Catalyst, published in the *Wall Street Journal* correspondence highlighting these findings.

Over the last decade, scholars have published dozens of studies, the vast majority of which contradict Catalyst's conclusions. Board composition has no correlation with profitability. A widely circulated periodical, *Business Lawyer*, published a survey of surveys affirming the conclusion.[4]

No one is likely to publish such a study about women as corporate managers. Any such study would be viewed as atavistic, so politically incorrect as never to see the light of day, if it contained even a hint, or more, of a correlation with poor performance. The dismal performance of women CEOs, such as Brenda Barnes at Sara Lee, Pat Russo at Lucent and Mary Sammons at Rite Aid, along with the lackluster performance of Jill Barad at Mattel and Carleton Fiorina at Hewlett-Packard, gives reason to believe that a study would demonstrate such a correlation. The widely circulated studies as to the lack of any board composition effect on profitability also gives indirect support to questioning Catalyst's findings about women managers, particularly their robustness.[5]

Then, too, repetition of outlier studies such as Catalyst's, as well as a myriad of other studies, misapprehend the nature of a board of directors. Boards' highest calling is to monitor and, if necessary, replace the corporation's senior executive officers—most particularly, the CEO. Only as their third or fourth priority might directors engage in strategic planning, in conjunction with management, which generally is so theoretical and long term as not demonstrably linked to profitability. In the words of one grizzly corporate governance expert, Henry Bosch, "A board of directors is like fog lights on a car. You don't need it often but you are glad you have it when you do." A board directly consumed with short- and medium-term profitability has the wrong focus.

CEO Roles

But this book is about CEOs. They must focus on profitability. Beyond profitability, different CEOs fill different roles. Some are empathetic, while others have little regard for employees. Some CEOs are self-styled change agents. Some are quiet administrators, while others are productive narcissists, who boldly strike out in new directions.

Analogizing to the political arena, Barack Obama says "that the Presidency has little to do with running an efficient office: 'It involves having a vision for where the country needs to go . . . and then being able to mobilize and inspire the American people.' " As a contrasting view, Hillary Clinton likens "the job of President to that of a 'chief executive officer' who has 'to be able to manage and run the bureaucracy.' "[6]

Some CEOs are controlling, micro-managers, while others give subordinates wide latitude in the choice of approaches to problems. Some CEOs view themselves as cheerleaders, while others are hands on managers. Later chapters will discuss the differing roles which CEOs play. The contention here is that many women executives can play all of them, just as well as men, and also other roles, developed in the following sections.

Trickle-Down Effects

First is what commentators have labeled as the "trickle-down" effect, or the "talent rationale."[7] Having a woman CEO correlates well with an increase in number of female directors and senior managers. Women at the top signal to those below that the glass ceiling may not exist within a particular organization.

Sociologists and women's rights advocates have argued that not one, and not two (which in fact may be worse), but at least three is an important level of representation. The number three frees women, or other minority group members, from the legacy of tokenism, reversing a retreat to stereotypical behavior. The number three (or more) unlocks potential by aiding promotion of greater confidence of and freer discussion by women.[8] Whether in a peer group or job classification in the middle or the lower rungs of senior management, or on a board of directors, representation of at least that number is important.[9]

Corporations with CEOs who are women have greater female representation on their boards. Although the sample is small, the results are robust. Thus, at Avon Products, of which Andrea Jung is CEO, four women are directors. The same is true at Sara Lee, with Brenda Barnes as CEO and three women as directors, and Alcatel Lucent, with Pat Russo as CEO and three women directors. PepsiCo, with Indra Nooyi as CEO, has three women among ten directors. Marion Sandler, as CEO of Golden West Financial, presided over a board of directors with four women members.

The business case is that a trickle down would replicate itself among the ranks of executives should a woman become CEO.[10] Anecdotal evidence supports the claim that a trickle down exists for management positions when a woman is the CEO. For example, since Susan Ivey became the CEO at tobacco company Reynolds American, the company has appointed 19 women to officer positions and four of the top seven corporate officials are women.[11]

From time to time, women CEOs and senior managers might find solace in being what the advice books call the "Queen Bee."[12] Carly Fiorina seems to have been a Queen Bee at Hewlett-Packard, as has been Irene Rosenfeld at Kraft Foods, a woman who achieves a lofty position but takes undisclosed delight, or surcease, in being the only woman at a higher level.

In most cases, by virtue of the trickle down, having a woman CEO opens pathways for additional women in the ranks of upper management.[13] It can also signal a more beneficial environment to which talented women may return after having earlier opted out because of child bearing and child rearing responsibilities. A third result is eventually to enlarge the pool of women from which senior executives and directors might chose other directors and senior managers, helping solve the ancillary "pool problem," which incumbent directors and CEOs (males) say presently circumscribes the choices for diversity efforts.

There exists a large pool of females which remains untapped, whose knowledge and skills are being wasted. Women constituted nearly 30 percent of the law graduates and 20 percent of the MBA graduates as early as the 1970s. They constituted 48.2 percent of the law graduates and 40.7 percent of the MBAs in 2002.[14] Yet women are only 8 percent of the senior executives and "C-suite" officers in public corporations. Promotion of additional women to the CEO ranks will open more opportunities for aspiring women, keep additional numbers of women from "opting out," and facilitate the return to the workplace of those who have left.

What other effects could there be? Why diversity in corporate and business settings?

Market Reciprocity

A second role women as CEOs play lies in the area of greater sensitivity to consumers' needs, particularly in the area of brand name and consumer products. Corporations with women in management and on the board will more effectively market services and products in a manner that attracts women consumers. Those corporations will also be better equipped to develop new products that appeal to a wider array of interests and needs, more particularly those of women consumers. Enlightened self-interest, what management theorists term "market reciprocity," should inform corporate boards in staffing the ranks of senior management, including CEO selection.[15] If great numbers of women consume their products and services, corporations should make doubly certain that they have ample representation of women on the upper management level.[16]

Today, the market reciprocity phenomenon does not confine itself to consumer products. Management guru Tom Peters[17] states: "[W]omen have enormous market clout . . . [W]e would be a lot better off if we had people who understood the consumer in the positions of leadership. [That's] a simple hard-boiled economic argument."[18] Peters elaborates: "[W]omen buy everything . . . not just consumer goods . . . It's professional goods as well, because over 50 percent of purchasing officers now are women, over 50 percent of administrative officers . . . well over 50 percent of human resources people."

Gainsayers point out that corporations do not necessarily need women directors and managers to develop products. Corporations may achieve effectiveness by hiring specialist design or marketing firms. Then, too, overly targeted advertising and other marketing may produce backlash, quenching whatever enthusiasm may have existed for the product among women, or other targeted groups.

The market reciprocity rationale may have weaknesses as well as strengths. The symbolism of having members of the targeted group at or near the top, however, cannot be underestimated. For many years, Jill Kerr Conway, former president of Smith College, was the sole female director of Nike, even though Nike sold many pairs of shoes to women both as mothers to children and as athletes. It was Kerr herself, as a director, who pushed for the company's launch of a female sports-apparel division, which now accounts for 30 percent of Nike's revenue.[19]

Women as consumers may or may not know that women as managers have significant representation at a company with a woman CEO. Activist groups such as the National Association for the Advancement of Colored People or the National Organization of Women, however, will take note. Because of their awareness, such groups will refrain from actions they otherwise might take (boycotts, demonstrations, demands). They also will signal to their members and supporters which corporations are on the "A" list and which are on the "B" and "C" lists.

Avoidance of the Perils of Groupthink

A third reason for promotion of diversity within management is that diversity improves the quality of corporate governance. Most particularly, diversity aids materially in avoidance of groupthink groups of senior managers.

Diversity of viewpoints and perspectives results from a diversity of race and gender backgrounds. The opposite is groupthink, which can bring a host of perils to processes such as appointing persons to new vacant positions or strategic planning. Noted psychologist Irving Janis analyzed how groupthink led to Pearl Harbor, the Bay of Pigs, the Viet Nam War, and the Watergate cover up, as well as other foreign policy and political debacles.[20] Professor Marleen O'Connor has demonstrated how groupthink may dominate board-room decision-making, or the lack thereof, and did so at Enron.[21]

A prime determinate of groupthink is similarity of backgrounds and cohesiveness. The "we feeling" and clubiness that affects boards of directors and executive ranks within an organization is a starter for groupthink, caus-ing participants in the group to avoid hard questions and to avoid rocking the boat.[22]

Enron was the "perfect storm" of corporate governance. On the surface, Enron had acceptable governance. Its board of 14 directors consisted of 12 outside, independent directors, including one Asian-American, Wendy Gramm, spouse of ex-Texas Senator Phil Gramm; one Hispanic man; one Asian man; and one African-American man. Enron had a functioning board committee structure. The board and committees met the requisite number of times.

Yet the Enron board is an exemplary of groupthink. No director asked tough questions. Accounting statements revealed that at Enron cash dis-bursed far exceeded cash received for many months but no director raised the point. The CFO, Andrew Fastow, acted as the general partner of the LJM partnerships, and paid himself $46 million in compensation, while the partnerships furnished seed capital to many of Enron's 900-plus special purpose entities. No corporate director called attention to, or in any respect policed, this blatant conflict of interest while the transactions speeded Enron's death spiral.

Enron paid each director $350,000 per year (half in common stock), excessive in the extreme, constituting a moral hazard for directors who, by virtue of their positions, are not to become too complacent, even to rock the boat once in a while. Enron also paid to directors' accountancy or consulting firms, or donated in directors' names to pet charities, $100,000 and up per director, further corrupting them. The source of groupthink at Enron was the moral hazard of excessive financial benefits for directors, rather than a lack of diversity, but Enron graphically demonstrates groupthink and its perils.

On the surface, WorldCom, one of the other grand corporate imbroglios, had what appeared to be acceptable governance. Its board of directors consisted of 13: 11 of whom were independent and one of whom was a woman, Judith Areen, Dean of Georgetown University Law School. Groupthink predominated. No one asked questions about why WorldCom's line (local access) costs were so much lower than its competitors (55 percent for AT&T or Verizon but only 43 percent for WorldCom). Directors allowed the Compensation Committee to loan CEO Bernie Ebbers what came to be $405 million in corporate funds, greased by the below market rental ($60 per month) of a corporate jet to the Compensation Committee chair. No director raised an eyebrow.

Groupthink can render ineffective works groups and management ranks below the board level. In the afterword of her autobiography, Carleton Fiorina set out the common-sense case for diversity:

> A company's ability to look at new ideas and new solutions is linked directly with the homogeneity of its management team. If a management team is homogeneous . . . it means people are favoring consensus and conformity . . . rather than the creative tension that comes from differences in perspective, experience, and, yes, race and gender as well. This is why real diversity is in everyone's interests: better decisions come from understanding and hashing out the differences in people's points of view. If everyone thinks in the same ways and agrees quickly, decision making may be faster . . . and more pleasant, but it's not as effective.[23]

She adds: "We used to talk about diversity in the workplace as being a matter of 'equal opportunity.' . . . Today, however, diversity is no longer just about fairness, it's about winning or maybe even about surviving."[24]

Forward Thinking

A fourth reason for an increase of women in executive positions is simply that today the world, and the United States in particular, is much more diverse than it was 20 years ago. And it will be more diverse in the future. Demographers predict that white people will be a minority group in the United States by 2028.[25] Consumers of a corporation's products and services represent many more races and cultures than they did a short while ago. Lower level subordinate (employee) ranks are more than ever diverse. The world which the current tier of rising corporate managers will inherit will be a more diverse world. It is vitally important to have numbers of women in the management ranks, and in CEO positions, even if it cannot be demonstrated per se to lead to profitability. "A diverse organization will out-think, out-innovate, and out-perform a homogenous organization every time."[26]

11 How We Choose CEOs

My study of CEOs in the two hundred largest industrials in the country in 1917 showed [that] ... [t]he CEOs were disproportionately born in the Northeast and Midwest. They came from urban, economically advantaged backgrounds. They were all male Caucasians. Eighty-six percent were Republicans. Almost two thirds of them were either Episcopalians (34 percent) or Presbyterians (28 percent). Roman Catholics accounted for 7 percent. . . . [I]t was simply beyond the realm of consideration to have a woman or African-American running a corporation.[1]

Richard Tedlow, *Giants of Enterprise* (2001)

Since that time (1917), things haven't changed much:

[T]he most recent studies of the social backgrounds of top executives reveal that they are still . . . male, white, native-born Protestants from socially and economically advantaged families. [E]conomist Peter Temin has noted that while every study of the social composition of the executive class, ranging over several decades, has found this same homogeneity, most have predicted that this situation would not last. Researchers in the 1950s, 1960s, and 1970s "portray [the subjects of their study] as the last generation for which their observations would be true. Conditions have been changing . . . [b]ut the composition of the American business elite remains unchanged."[2]

Rakesh Khurana, *Searching for the Corporate Savior* (2002)

There has been change. In mid-2007, perhaps the near term peak overall, there were three African American and 12 women CEOs in the *Fortune 500*. Now two of the African Americans (Richard Parsons at Time Warner and Stan O'Neal at Merrill Lynch) are gone but a female African American (Ursula Burns at Xerox) has been chosen to be CEO (Ken Chenault at American Express is the surviving African American male CEO). Ten of 12 women CEOs from 2007 remain in office while five new ones have been added (see Chapter 9). So we have come some way since the time when "the Pennsylvania Railroad's directors stanchly opposed [a male's] promotion [to CEO in 1913] because [he] . . . had not pledged allegiance to Republican politics and . . . was not even an Episcopalian ([he] was a Presbyterian)."[3]

Expectations have been that while we do not expect parity, by this time we would have more persons of color and women as CEOs. One of the reasons reality lags behind the expectations is the highly scripted way in which large public corporations choose CEOs. This market limits access to those who, by and large, meet certain socially defined rather than skills-based or performance-based criteria. Because the system of CEO selection perpetuates itself, the system remains closed to other than late-middle-age white males.

The Search Committee

As universities, medical, law or business schools, foundations, charities, and many other institutions do, large publicly held corporations begin the process of finding a new CEO with formation of the search committee. When Hewlett-Packard began its search for a successor to Carleton Fiorina, HP's board named all nine directors to the search committee.[4] Usually, however, the board selects a subgroup from its own number, ranging from three to seven with four to five directors being typical. The most common method for determining composition "is asking for volunteers."

> The individuals who volunteer . . . are disproportionately directors who are retired executives or directors from non-business backgrounds such as nonprofits or education—essentially, directors who have more time than their peers to devote to the search. [O]n average, only one non-retired director serve[s] on the search.[5]

The result is a decidedly gray complexion to the search committee: on a board with a median age of, say, 59–60, the median and mean age on the search committee may be in the late sixties or seventies. Any heterogeneity on the full board is not apt to be well represented on the search committee. Because the directors with the ability to devote time to the search are the older directors, search committee members have a uniform appearance: white, male, older in age, Republican, and college educated.

Writing the Spec Sheet

Most search committee members use the first committee meeting to set out their personal theories of corporate leadership and ideas about the qualities a good leader should have. Sometimes there is, as there usually should be, a discussion of the strengths and the shortcomings of the previous CEO. This then should move on to an analysis of the problems the organization faces and possible skill sets which could face off with those problems. Often it does not.

Instead, the process deteriorates. Rather than a discussion of the situational context of the search and the corporation's needs, and concrete skills that could meet them, directors begin compiling a collection of personal traits that they (individually) consider important. The new CEO should be "aggressive." "The new CEO should be able to balance risk with reward." The new CEO should have an international (global) outlook. The prospect should have "line experience," that is, profit and loss responsibility. "Executive presence" is essential.

Nearly simultaneously, the search committee begins to draft a specifications sheet. This is a listing of the personal traits individual directors have identified. Rather than offend anyone, or argue about relative priorities, the specification sheet drafters include nearly every personal trait that committee members have mentioned: decisive, yes; intelligent, yes; charismatic, most definitely; aggressive, yes; energetic, certainly; change agent, yes; empathetic, surely; and so on. The document is so many things to so many people so as to render it useless.

Directors, or a subgroup of them, have thus missed an opportunity to distill in a meaningful way the organization's needs and to prioritize them. They have also produced a document of such breadth and generality that persons with widely differing skill sets and backgrounds (almost anyone?) can be viewed as meeting the list of specifications the committee has derived.[6] Or, worse yet, the "almost anyone" has one important caveat. The prospects for the CEO post will, because of the process and the list of specifications, tend very much to resemble the directors themselves.[7]

Role of Search Firms

Korn Ferry International, Russell Reynolds, Heidrick & Struggles, and Spencer Stuart dominate the executive search business.[8] There may also be local or regional firms which join the mix.[9] All the firms go by the not-too-complimentary appellation "headhunter."[10] The more dignified term is "executive search firm" (ESF).

The search committee may choose a particular search firm that has a past relationship with the company. Alternatively, the search committee will hear three or four firms' presentations in a "bakeoff," choosing one.

The services the firms provide are indistinguishable. They provide confidentiality, holding interviews in their local offices or at a neutral site (a hotel) away from corporate headquarters. Executives already employed at another corporation usually insist on confidentiality. ESFs provide it.

The ESF may also provide names of potential candidates, although the largest source of names traditionally is the directors themselves. ESFs will have available for use databanks containing several thousand names but in the typical search the ESF is the source of only a handful. An important exception is that the ESF will much more frequently be the source of women and other minority candidates' names than the directors will be.[11]

Candidates will initially interview with the search consultant, first by telephone, to be followed by live interviews for a smaller number. The ESF handles the logistics (coffee, food, telephones, hotel or other off-site space for interviews) of the search as well, then the search committee will interview three to five final prospects. A typical ESF search consultant will handle five to six searches simultaneously.

Veteran search consultants number successful searches almost as Native American warriors brag about numbers of scalps: Gerald Roche, senior Chair at Heidick & Struggles, has been involved in 185 CEO searches while Thomas Neff, chair at Spencer Stuart, counts 150 in a 29-year career.[12] The ESF receives one-third of the executive's first-year cash compensation plus reimbursement for its expenses.

Social Matching

Minority group members' names typically go right back out again, or move down the candidate list, as the search process goes forward. Many directors will quickly dwell on those candidates who look like the directors do: male, white, middle age, MBA from a quality school (but not necessarily Protestant any more). The profile of the typical search consultant reinforces social matching: "The typical headhunter is white, male, prep school, Protestant . . . Ivy Leaguers in neatly pressed pinstripes." Of 114 consultants at one large ESF, only one was black, 20 were women, and only seven were bald.[13] "There's no inner sanctum more controlled by elder white males than the world of CEO recruiting."[14]

Alternatively, "the social matching process is not so much one of consciously excluding candidates as it is one of creating expectations that can be fulfilled by only a small number of them."[15] The list narrows very quickly, as does the search committee members thinking about who the next CEO is likely to be.

Social matching also produces a list of safe choices: "a set of defensible candidates who, even if they fail, will obviate criticism to the effect that the board did not choose a candidate with the appropriate characteristics."[16]

Search committees and consultants today must pay more attention to the moral issues. In 2005, Boeing Company dismissed CEO Harry Stonecipher after company personnel discovered that Stonecipher had sent a sexually explicit email to a female Boeing employee with whom he was having an affair. This has been said to usher in "the post-Stonecipher era in executive searches."[17] The need to vet candidates on a host of moral issues has distracted search committees, including those who might otherwise be inclined to include women or blacks in the pool. The search apparatus must put in extensive time not only on issues such as driving records and personal bankruptcies but also personal use of company email or failures to withhold for household employees.

Derivative Prestige

Further constraining the choices of who can be in the CEO candidate pool is many directors' insistence that the finalist be, at a minimum, making a lateral move, or, better yet, coming from a firm or position thought to be a level or two higher in terms of reputation and prestige: "Prestige is particularly important in CEO searches . . . search committees see the status of the firm from which a CEO candidate comes as amplifying or reducing the status of their own organizations."[18]

One motivation behind such snobbery is that "matching up" will play well on Wall Street, producing an immediate upward movement in the share price, produced by who the new CEO is and where he or she is coming from, although the evidence that such a derivative effect exists is inconclusive. Importantly, though, directors likely to be on a search committee harbor strong beliefs: "the notion that CEOs have a status that can be transferred from one company to another has become deeply ingrained in directors' view of the role of the CEO."[19]

So no matter how wide a net a CEO search committee may initially cast, the candidate rooster dwindles rapidly, the focus centering on a very few prospects and then one candidate. Professor Rakesh Khurana includes a telling graphic early in his book *Searching for the Corporate Savior*. In 76 CEO searches, conducted with the aid of an ESF, no unsolicited resumes were considered while in 411 searches for vice-presidents marketing, by the same two firms, approximately 5,500, many unsolicited, resumes were reviewed. The CEO search firms initially contacted 8 to 19 candidates, interviewed five to seven candidates, and passed on to the corporate search committee three names for final interviews. By contrast, in open searches for marketing personnel, the ESFs contacted from 80 to 90 candidates, interviewed 14 to 17, and passed six names on to the client corporation.[20]

Necessarily, the closed nature of the search tends to exclude women and other minorities from CEO searches, much more than does a relatively open-ended search for a corporate manager.

A Closed Market

"The criteria employed in the social matching process that characterizes external CEO succession not only shed light on the closed nature of the CEO labor market, but also account, in particular, for the durable homogeneity we observe in the nation's CEO suites despite dramatic changes in the composition of the workforce."[21] Into this closed market, and highly scripted process, directors inject their personal predilection, not based upon deeds and performance but upon the leading candidate's personality traits. From the words directors most frequently use, "charisma" ("change agent" is a close second) has almost religious overtones—it does have a religious entomology—and directors regard themselves on a search no less than for "the corporate savior."[22] Other directors use similar words: "chemistry," "executive presence," and "stature." The choice of finalists for the CEO position thus depends on the eye of the beholder rather than a skill set and performance records. In the 1990s, "the whole business of CEO succession became about attracting a star . . . 'tall ships,' " as one well-known recruiter called them.[23]

Some directors substitute a current or former corporate savior for abstract qualities. Thus, a given candidate is "a lot like Jack Welch," or Steve Jobs, or Lou Gerstner.

Women can have charisma. Carleton Fiorina certainly did. But most persons, including corporate directors, associate the characteristic with males. Saviors, including corporate ones, tend to be males. All of the potential CEOs a director might hold up, or most often the one person identified early on as "the guy," as an example of "charisma," or "change agent" are males. The market for CEOs is thus not only a closed one, with strong tendencies quickly to focus on a very small number of finalists and to disregard candidates who do not have certain preordained and ephemeral characteristics. The way in which large public companies choose CEOs is heavily weighted against women. It explains in large part why women are underrepresented in the CEO suite as opposed to, say, political ranks, high education, or the non-profit sphere.

12 Glass Ceilings, Floors, Walls, and Cliffs

> It always happens at [conferences of business women]. I speak, I listen, I hear the same words over and over—"baffled," "angry," "lost," "trapped," "stuck," "overwhelmed"—as each woman tell me she feels that she's gotten only so far in business and can't get any further.[1]
>
> Gail Evans, *Play Like a Man, Win Like a Woman* (2000)

Feminists describe the glass ceiling as the transparent barrier "that allows women to see, but not to obtain, the most prestigious jobs" in Corporate America.[2] On her first day as Hewlett-Packard CEO, Carleton Fiorina proclaims that the glass ceiling no longer exists.[3] Mary Sammons, Rite Aid CEO, refuses interviews which might lead to an implication that she is in any way different because of her gender.[4] Three-fourths of male CEOs firmly state that the glass ceiling no longer exists.[5] Conservative economists go further: they maintain that in free markets corporations could not survive if they discriminated against women.[6] The Harvard Business School Press publishes *Through The Labyrinth*, by two women's rights scholars, which asserts that the glass ceiling concept no longer has validity.[7]

Does evidence exist as to whether the glass ceiling endures? Related concepts—glass floors, glass walls, glass cliffs—give support to the proposition that a glass ceiling does exist and begin the inquiry into why, blatant sexism aside, a glass ceiling remains in place.

Does the Glass Ceiling Exist?

The proof of something such as the glass ceiling at best turns on circumstantial evidence. It is not susceptible to direct proof. Yet the circumstantial proofs are persuasive. The first of these originate in corporations' selection of female directors.

Sixty-two percent of female directors "side step" onto corporate boards from positions in not-for-profits, government, academe, consulting, and law. They do not rise vertically, as it were, in corporate organizations, in the manner we would expect if the glass ceiling had shattered. In fact, attempting to rise vertically within the organization is the *worst* route a female executive can take in attempting to ascend to the boardroom: in 2001 only nine, and in 2006, only 11, of 460 and 568 women directors, respectively, had taken the inside route.[8] Corporations are forced to go outside of the organization because an insufficient number of women are rising into the pool of executives from which corporations might choose directors. Fifty percent of the middle managers are women while only eight percent of the executives are female. A cogent reason why is that in their ascension numbers of women bump into glass ceilings.

A second line of evidence is corporations' repeated selection of "serial," or "trophy," directors when it comes to women. Trophy directors serve on four or more corporate boards.[9] Of the women this book features, Brenda Barnes of Sara Lee Corp. had trophy director status while Ann Mulcahy, CEO of Xerox, Meg Whitman, ex-CEO at eBay, Paula Reynolds, ex-CEO at Safeco Insurance, and Pat Woertz, CEO at ADM, have had or come perilously close to trophy designation.[10] The number of women who have trophy director status is rapidly increasing while the number of male trophy directors is rapidly decreasing. Between 2001 and 2005, the number of women trophy directors in the *Fortune 500* increased from 29 to 80.[11] Simultaneously, many corporate boards forbade their CEOs (males) from serving on any outside board, or limited them to a single board engagement.[12] That among women large corporations choose the same people over and over again indicates that the pool from which corporations chose women executives, which is similar, is static. Again, the reason for such a trifling inflow is that numbers of women are bumping into the glass ceiling before they have risen high enough for corporations to consider them director or officer material.

Other Evidence

In her autobiography, an ardent public advocate that no glass ceiling exists, Carleton Fiorina reveals her private belief that she has had to confront a glass ceiling at every turn in her career. Early on a male district director called her a "token bimbo." Lower level managers at AT&T, of which she was one, described those the company was most likely to promote but who lacked substance as "42 longs" (male suit size). An aerospace executive with whom Fiorina dealt "could not talk to [a woman] without a constant leer on his face." A Boeing manager tells her that "some of you women can't take the pressure. . . . Don't you want to spend more time with your husband and have children?" Only one senior manager at AT&T Network Systems was female: "she was the head of Human Resources, an accepted position for a woman," recounts Fiorina. A manager told her after a promotion that she "was one of very few women and she would ruffle feathers." A fellow corporate officer tells Fiorina that "You're being emotional, not objective [because she was a woman]." Because she was a woman, men had tried to "pigeonhole me" for "my entire career."[13] In her book, Carleton Fiorina—the woman CEO celebrated for denying that the glass ceiling exists—gives as complete a picture as can be found of the attitudes and obstacles which make up a glass ceiling for women in business.[14]

But "[t]imes have changed and the glass ceiling metaphor is now more wrong than right. [T]here have been female chief executives, university presidents, state governors, and president of nations gives lie to the charge [that a glass ceiling exists]," reports a *Harvard Business Review* article.[15] That is the point: the very nub of the glass ceiling argument has been that women have not advanced in business while they have in academics, politics, and other spheres. Statistics give robust support to the argument: only 3 percent of corporate CEOs and 8 percent of the bylaw officers, are women, while 25 percent of university presidents, 17 percent of U.S. senators, 30 percent of parliament members, and so on, are female.

The *Harvard Business Review* depiction that the glass ceiling refers to "an absolute barrier at a specific high level in organizations" is not only overly literal, it is wrong. Women complain that they bump up against a barrier at various career stages, in various corporate organizations, and in few not at all. The glass ceiling is an abstract but representative idea, not an actual and uniform barrier, like the sneeze shield on a salad bar. All the better reasoned arguments, and the evidence, indicate that the glass ceiling exists in many business organizations and across the business sector generally.

The Glass Floor

A closely aligned concept is the "glass floor." When they fall out of favor, men in the ranks of higher management do not fall far. They rebound off the glass floor. Senior managers retain the under performing manager in some nook or cranny within the executive suite from which the fallen executive crawls back to respectability and another senior management position.

A glass floor also exist for, and protects, CEOs, at least male ones. Professor Rudiger Fahlenbrach at Ohio State University has studied 1,500 CEOs at large corporations during the period 1995–2002. He found that 65 of them are "boomerang CEOs," who had been CEO at the same or another publicly held corporation and returned to a second CEO tenure.[16] Needless to say, none of the boomerang CEOs has been a woman.

A common variant involves ex-CEOs who have caused themselves to be "kicked upstairs," relinquishing their CEO positions to become non-executive board chairs. When the corporation's share price falls, or revenue and profits lag, they take over the CEO suite once more. Examples include Michael Dell of Dell Computer and Howard Schultz at Starbucks.[17]

The boomerang CEO and glass floor are documented. Much like major league baseball managers who, no matter how badly they perform, seem always to re-surface as managers elsewhere, so, too, have male CEOs whose boards have forced them out found positions at other corporations. William Agree destroyed Bendix Corporation by making an ill-advised takeover bid for Martin Marietta. After the Bendix board deposed him, Agee found employment as CEO at Morrison Knudson, the international construction firm, which Agee proceeded to mismanage into bankruptcy. The labor unions and employee-owners of UAL, United Airlines' holding company, forced Stephen Wolf, formerly CEO of Flying Tiger, out as CEO. Wolf resurfaced as chairperson and CEO at U.S. Airways. Many other poorly performing CEOs rebound off the glass floor.

Pundits hypothesize that female CEOs who have lost their offices will bounce back up as well, but so far they have not. Although the numbers have been small, the deposed CEOs (Jill Barad at Mattel, Carleton Fiorina at Hewlett-Packard, Linda Wachner at Warnaco Group) have been high profile. They have yet to reappear in other organizations.

The group of deposed women senior executives is larger and perhaps more illustrative of what might be occurring. Women who fall from those lofty heights also seem to disappear, while many comparable male executives reappear in other senior positions, at the same or another public corporation. The difference may be that as she reaches toward the top, a woman is apt to be the only, or one of a very few, females, while a male surrounds himself with other male managers. When she falls from grace, then, a female senior executive does not have the same support group, or any support group at all, to retard or cushion her fall. When she falls from grace in a male-dominated management group, a deposed woman executive spirals into a black hole, never to be seen again.

The glass floor's existence, and the pronounced trend to replace CEOs with CEOs, of which it is a part, affects women in business if only because of the phenomenon of men rebounding within the clubby ranks of upper management results in fewer openings in which women could prove themselves.[18]

Glass Walls

According to Catalyst, 80 percent of the male CEOs they interviewed had an alternative explanation to the glass ceiling for why women have not advanced to the very top of their organizations, namely, women's lack of experience in line positions, that is, positions with profit-and-loss responsibility.[19] Of course, the CEOs themselves bear much of the responsibility for corporations not giving women line positions in which they could gain the requisite experience. Irene Rosenfeld, CEO of Kraft Foods (Chapter 9), is the opposite. She has spoken about how part of a CEO's responsibility is to ensure that promising subordinates, men as well as women, rotate through a number of worthwhile positions and experiences so that they are in positions for further advancement.

It can be worse for women in many businesses. Many CEOs and other male senior executives shunt women into staff positions, such as general counsel, head of human resources, public relations director, chief of the captive foundation, and the like. These positions are the antithesis of line positions, evoking a less than felicitous name ("pink collar jobs") in certain quarters, because women occupy a disproportionate number of them.

"Glass Walls" compound the problem. They "represent invisible barriers that prevent women from moving between functions and getting the experience of the variety of responsibilities that organizations require for upward movement."[20] Women who accept assignment to staff positions (many pink collar jobs) report that it becomes extremely difficult for them to "get back," resuming a mainline upward track. Similar to the imaginary barrier the glass ceiling represents, glass walls permit women in pink collar jobs to see, but not join, or re-join, their male counterparts as they scale the corporate ladder.

The Glass Cliff Phenomenon

The latest twist, which British theorists hypothesize, is the glass cliff theory.[21] They posit that corporations are more likely to turn to a female for an officer or CEO position when events magnify the risk of failure. Psychologists Michelle Ryan and Alexander Haslam found that businesses appoint women to corporate leadership positions "in problematic circumstances." Their appointments "[hence] were more precarious than men's appointments."[22] If she succeeds, of a woman CEO, directors and senior executive say "we expected nothing less." If she falls from grace, many will say "I told you so," leaving unstated that failure must have been due to gender.

The glass cliff theory seems to bear up under examination. Patricia Woertz became CEO after Archer Midland Daniels had reached a nadir, with the former CEO's son beginning a term in prison for price fixing on AMD's behalf. Susan Ivey became CEO at Reynolds American when the $346 billion settlement with 46 states and other adverse judicial outcomes had laid the tobacco industry low. Brenda Barnes got the reins at Sara Lee after overdiversification and lackluster returns had driven the company down. Ann Mulcahy got the top job at Xerox only after a sea of red ink flowed and the company's future was uncertain. Mary Sammons became the CEO of Rite Aid in the midst of deeply troubled times, with former CEO Martin Grass beginning a prison term and the share price reduced to a few dollars and cents. Patricia Russo became CEO of Lucent after it had laid off over 100,000 employees, while the shares price flirted with the $1.00 barrier. Carol Barz came to the CEIO suite at Yahoo! after a badly botched response to a takeover proposal, along with continuing losses, had caused previous management to resign. In fact, a near majority, 10 of 21, of the female CEOs this book portrays came to power only when the corporation faced very uncertain circumstances, or worse.[23] The glass cliff phenomenon has explanatory power in the United States as well as in Great Britain.

Why the Glass Ceiling?

The easiest approach, and one many militant feminists favor, is to ascribe the glass ceiling and its staying power to deep-seated sexism in our society and, most particularly, in business organizations. The evidence is persuasive that causes are much more subtle than deeply rooted sexism. Many males in business do detect a problem and have varying degrees of willingness to do something about it. Whether or not the militant view is accurate is also irrelevant in the sense that it does not lead to any proposal for a solution.

Many suspects exist, such as work–life, the price of motherhood, and opting out (Chapter 13), for the lack of women's ascension into the higher ranks of American business. The glass ceiling is only one. For this chapter's purposes, though, the glass walls and floors phenomenon indicate that the scarcity of women in senior management positions also is a critical mass problem. Women who do obtain promotions find that at their management level they are the token woman, or member of a skewed group (Chapter 15). They then find that they must walk a tightrope, as they have no support group, or a minimal one at best, should they falter. If they do falter, they fall completely from view. Conversely, they have little or no support group to push them up, helping them ascend through the glass ceiling, at whatever level it exists in that particular organization. Women writers urge women managers to "build networks," formal and informal, which will include male co-workers, advisers, and superiors, as an antidote to this lack of a support group. Most authors of advice books do not articulate that that is what they are doing, sensing it rather than spelling out an explanation for the advice they dispense.

Glass floors and glass walls have descriptive power. They tell us what goes on in many business organizations. They also have explanatory power. They give us insights into why the glass ceiling still exists and has such staying power.

13 Work–Life Issues and the Price of Motherhood

Men get a standing ovation if they miss a meeting because of parenting; women miss whole careers.[1]

Ann Crittenden, *The Price of Motherhood* (2001)

The most recent figures from the University of Wisconsin's National Survey of Families and Households show that the average wife does 31 hours of household work a week while the average husband does 14—a ratio of slightly more than two to one. [B]reak out the couples in which both husband and wife have full-time paying jobs. There the wife does 28 hours of housework and the husband, 16. Just shy of two to one . . . [the lopsided ratio] holds true however you construct or deconstruct a family. "Working class, middle class, upper class, it stays at two to one."[2]

Lisa Belkin, "Will Dad Ever Do His Share?" (2008)

The Issues

Issues working women face include:

- At home, women continue to bear a disproportionate share of the household and child rearing and all of the child-bearing responsibilities.
- At work, women face high employer expectations, including long hours, maximum face time in the office, 24/7 availability, and availability for travel on short notice, turbo capitalism features which do not mesh with child rearing.
- Unfavorable attitudes toward time off for parenting responsibilities prevail, as well as for part-time and flextime endeavor.

As a result of these factors, the following consequences result:

- Women receive lower wages than do comparable males for the same work and face the prospect of ever lower comparative wages as their careers progress.
- More women, especially those in management and professional ranks, are "opting out," leaving the workforce altogether, forever or for protracted periods of time.

- Fewer women remain to be eligible for promotions and progression into the pool from which senior executives will choose directors and senior managers, including CEOs. Women constitute 50 percent of the middle managers but only 8 percent of the upper level superiors.
- While they have improved, programs such as alumni/ae programs, welcome back programs, flextime initiatives, and reduced hours plans, which would benefit working women, remain deficient in many organizations and non-existent in others.

Women who have aspirations in business do not react adversely to child bearing; it is the disproportionate consequences of child bearing and child rearing that contribute to the perpetuation of results which lag far behind expectations.

Some Statistics

Over the three decades—1960s, 1970s, and 1980s—the proportion of married couple families with both spouses in the workforce doubled, from 28 percent in 1960 to 54 percent in 1990, reaching an apogee at 60 percent in the mid-1990s.[3] Yet "[i]f child care worries are increasingly shared by men and women, child care work is not. Women still do the bulk of all household tasks. Of the woman employed full time, 76 percent still do the majority of the housework."[4] Time diaries (similar to Nielsen television logs) other than the University of Wisconsin study show slightly better numbers now than they did in the 1950s. Yet persistent inequities remain. In 1960, the average working woman recorded 17 hours per week doing household work, compared to three hours for males. By 2006, the working woman recorded 11 hours while the working male recorded five.

This stressful tension for women, between work at work and work at home, takes its toll, as another statistical snapshot shows: employment among mothers of very small children has been falling. Over the five years 1998–2003, inclusive, employment among mothers with children younger than one year has fallen from 57.9 percent to 53.7 percent.[5] The trend is more pronounced among upwardly mobile women. They are departing the workforce, including the ranks of the professions and upper middle management, to bear children, then to postpone or forego altogether a return to professional or management positions. In her penetrating *New York Times* piece, Lisa Belkin described the "Opt-Out Revolution."[6]

Many other working women are making a different choice, one to forego children altogether. In the United States, the number of women over 40 who have no children has doubled, to one-fifth of that age group.[7]

The One Child Alternative

Women who seek to rise to the higher levels of corporate organizations can do so while at the same time having and raising children. They often, however, limit their child bearing to one child, as, for example, exemplars such as Andrea Jung, CEO at Avon Products (who also has an adopted son), or Paula Rosport Reynolds, ex-CEO at SafeCo Insurance have done.

Even with one child, aspiring women managers and professionals must have excellent day care available 60 or more hours per week to be able to work after hours, on weekends, and on out-of-town trips. They must limit themselves to the maternity leave their employers provide, and no more, going on a severely truncated "mummy track" of only two or three months' duration.[8]

If women executives follow that child-bearing prescription, at age 39 their income will be 99 percent of the income of their male counterparts.

Even then bosses and co-workers may subject them to criticism. Toward the end of her three month maternity leave, one female physician overheard a male co-worker say: "She's sure milking the system for all it's worth."[9]

More Children More Time Off

Women who do " more" in the way of child rearing pay a price. The "more" may be an extension of maternity leave beyond what the employer allows. The "more" may be the birth of a second child, with a second maternity leave and a concomitant increase in child-rearing responsibilities. The "more" that may prove fatal to career aspirations may be a leave of absence to attend to children who are beginning school, or a refusal to travel out-of-town, or work after hours or on weekends. At age 39, career women who have in any of those ways pursued the mummy track will earn only 60 cents for every dollar their male counterparts take home in pay. On average, over her lifetime, a college-educated mother who goes on to the mummy track will earn $1 million less than an equally educated and capable male.

In one area, part-time work, the "more" is less for many women who desire to stay in management ranks, at least until children reach school or high school age. Sixty percent of work women say that working part time would be ideal. Only 24 percent of women who work actually do work part time. Along with opting out, the desire to work part time "is a reaction [against] the 50 or 60 hour work week and the insanity of the work schedule and inflexibility of employers," says Professor Ellen Bravo of the University of Wisconsin-Milwaukee.[10] In a study of CPAs at Deloitte Touche, women reported that asking for a flextime schedule was akin to committing professional "hari-kari." A majority of female CPAs in the study reported that they believed part-time or flextime work would damage their careers.[11]

Male Leadership Attitudes

Pronouncements on these issues feature a significant amount of hypocrisy. Typical is a statement by Lawrence Summers, former secretary of the treasury, president of Harvard University, and Economic Advisor to President Obama, who stated that "Raising children . . . is the most important job in the world," but opined that women academicians were not achieving tenure in fields such as math and science because "women with children are reluctant to work the 80-hour weeks that are required to succeed in those fields." He suggested the possibility that differences in men and women long attributed to socialization might be "innate."[12] These (oft-times contradictory) statements by men caused one woman observer to note: "[L]ip service to motherhood still floats in the air, insubstantial as angel dust."[13]

"Raising children may be the most important job in the world, but you can't put it on your resume." Not only is child rearing not rewarded but in many sectors, corporate America also penalizes it. Superiors consider child rearing and household management to have no economic or job enabling value: "[T]he United States is a society at war with itself . . . We talk endlessly about the importance of family, yet the work it takes to make a family is utterly disregarded."[14]

Due to male attitudes, a stigma attaches to leaves of absence or part-time endeavor which may be necessary to accommodate child bearing and child rearing by women managers or professionals and other female employees. Some employers do realize that the corporate organization benefits in the long run when the organization permits a maternity leave and two to three years part-time work but retains the employee for a 35-year career. When an employee leaves, the corporation loses institutional memory associated with that employee; loses customer or client relationships; loses productivity while the departing employee's position remains unfilled; and suffers a loss in collegiality and in morale of those left behind. The corporation also incurs significant costs in replacing the employee which personnel experts peg at 150 percent, or more, of the departing employee's annual salary.[15]

Employers and their managers know these things. Despite the common sense of it, however, male supervisors tend to see not the long but the short-run view: "Part-time work is highly stigmatized in many departments . . . Part-time [employees] report isolation, loss of status within their departments, negative comments from supervisors, colleagues and clients, loss of desirable assignments, elimination of advancement opportunities, and relegation to sub-par office space." Law Professor Joan Williams heads the Project for Attorney Retention (PAR) and the Center for the Study of Work–Life Issues at the University of California's Hastings Law School. In a series of reports, PAR examines reasons for the lack of opportunities for women in law firms. PAR concludes that "[l]ong hours, macho attitudes, competition for limited advancement, and a management that is not itself in a position of [doing the needed] juggling . . . combine to create a culture that rejects or undermines part-time policies."[16]

Reduced Legal Redress

In 2007 term, the conservative Bush Supreme Court set equal pay advocates back decades by its decision in *Ledbetter v. Goodyear Tire & Rubber Co.*[17] About to retire, Ms. Ledbetter found that for years Goodyear had been paying men more than to women at its Alabama plant. She had good proofs so she went to court. The Court held that she had to make her complaint within 180 days of the injury, which in her case had been years before. She, and others like her, had to have sent a letter of complaint to the Equal Employment Opportunities Commission, necessary to have a right to sue, soon after a material disparity opened up between men and women doing comparable jobs. Obviously, the case ended most chances for legal redress for pay differentials in the workplace. Most women will discover that they receive less only some time afterward. The few who do learn that more is in males' pay envelopes will adopt a wait-and-see attitude, at least if they have not yet consulted an employment lawyer. Early in 2009, the House of Representatives entertained the *Lily Ledbetter Fair Pay Act* reversing the Supreme Court.[18] The episode highlights unequal pay for equal work issues.

Opting Out

So what happens? Because of the economic loss they suffer, the hypocrisy they see, and the difficulty of coordinating job and family they encounter, most women penalize themselves. They take time out to rear children, the cost be damned, returning to the workforce when the children reach high school. Or they may stay in the workforce with a part-time position. Or they may retain their position but place severe restrictions (articulated to others or only mental) on their participation (no out-of-town travel, home by 6:00 pm every day), which often is fatal to their chances for subsequent advancement.

As one woman executive recounted:

> My erratic work schedule worked well for me and my son, but it was hard on everyone else at my office. I missed meetings; I bowed out of last-minute crises; I won't travel; I couldn't stay late. In short, I was not the kind of employee who could be counted on in a crunch. Dependable, yes, hardworking and competent, yes, but highly restricted. I was passed over for projects I would have liked.[19]

A recent study disputes that women leave the workforce to have or to rear children: "Since the 2001 recession women have lost jobs and withdrawn from the workplace at the same rate as men. More to the point, they've remained out for the same reasons as men: layoff, downsizing, outsourcing, and wage stagnation."[20] The study's findings purport to "debunk" the opting out rationale as a "myth."

The frustration of career plans may occur in the same proportions and for similar reasons, among men and women, at the lower ranks, up to and including portions of middle management. In contrast, among women with graduate degrees, in the professions, and among the higher ranks of middle management, the opting out phenomenon is demonstrable and has great explanatory power. Otherwise how is it that the pipeline is so leaky? Women have obtained 40 percent of the law degrees and 30 percent of the MBAs since the late 1970s (50 percent and 40 percent for the last 20 years) yet are only 8 percent of the senior managers and 3 percent of the CEOs. The biggest leaks in the pipeline leading to the corner office are the opt-out detour and the opt-out exit that affect women.

Mummy Tracks

The company will pass over for promotions, as well as projects, the woman who can't, or won't, travel or stay late, according to career women who go on that particular form of what experts term the mummy track.

In a paean to family values, women who have chosen one of the alternatives face another reality. They subordinate themselves to their husband's careers. If their husbands accept a transfer, they follow, abandoning altogether whatever chance they had for promotion. The late opera diva Beverly Sills left New York and the Metropolitan Opera to follow her husband to Cleveland, Ohio. She felt that "my only alternative was to ask Peter to scuttle the goal he'd been working toward for most of 25 years. If I did that, I didn't deserve to be his wife."[21] No "good wife" wishes to rob her husband of the masculinity men associate with the primacy of their careers within the family unit.

In successful female careers, the opposite may be true. Susan Ivey's husband Trevor and Carleton Fiorina's husband Frank took early retirements to enable their partners better to advance in corporate organizations. ADM CEO Pat Woertz's husband expressly agreed to subordinate his career entirely to hers. Peter Gold, the spouse of Christina Gold, CEO of Western Union, gave up a law practice career in Ontario so that Christina could accept a position with Avon Products in New York. Evidence exists that the husbands of Angela Braly (Wellpoint), Indra Nooyi (PepsiCo) and Mary Sammons (Rite Aid) relegated their careers to a second position.

For most educated women who begin in business, however, at some point it becomes not "family then career" but "family—no more career." Knowing the odds they face in seeking promotion, or survival in their current position, women with children simply quit fighting. They opt out completely, at a high cost both to society and to themselves. The number of children being cared for by stay-at-home mothers increased 13 percent in the 1990s.[22] Many women who look up at the top in their organizations are increasingly deciding that they do not want to do what it takes to get there. In fact, this phenomenon affects even the top: *Fortune*'s examination of 108 business women who in recent years had appeared on its annual list of "The 50 Most Powerful Women in Business" revealed that 20 of those women had voluntarily relinquished their positions.[23]

The Leaky Pipe

Richard Parsons, the African American chair and, until December 2007, CEO of Time Warner, appeared on CNBC in 2006. The interviewer asked Parsons when he foresaw numbers of women and minorities in senior corporate positions. "It's just a matter of time," Parson predicted, "they have been in the pipeline for some time."

He failed to note that the pipe has numerous holes in it. Women have been pursuing and receiving MBAs, law and other advanced degrees in numbers for 30 years. In unprecedented numbers, they then enter the workforce. But it is a leaky pipe, with a torrent at the supply end but a tickle at the tap end. The "tap end" of course consists of the ranks of upper middle and upper management from which women could spring upward into positions as corporate directors and CEOs. The Harvard Business School survey of women MBAs from the classes of 1981, 1985, and 1991 found that 15 or more years later only 38 percent of them were working full time.[24] The leaks in that pipeline, and the resulting losses, both societal and personal, are the "price of motherhood," the title of an excellent book by Ann Crittenden: "[A] 70s feminist peering in the window would be very confused at best and depressed at worst." A Princeton and Duke law graduate who left her law firm to rear two small children states: "This is what I was meant to do . . . I know its very un-p.c., but I like life's rhythms when I'm nurturing a child."

"One of the misleading impressions [of] the women's movement is that it swept away women's traditional lives, like a sandstorm burying the artifacts of an ancient civilization. The media constantly remind us that women have become doctors, lawyers, merchants."[25] Yet, of married women with school-age children, 28.4 percent are not in the labor force, at all. An additional 20 percent work only part time. Only about half of all women with school age children, numbering 18 million strong, work full time.[26]

Children and families have not suffered because of women's entry in great numbers into the working world, despite what conservative politicians and religious leaders maintain. Instead, women fulfill multiple roles. It is "career and family," not "career over family." They do so by employing a number of artifices. They delay having their children. They have fewer children.

Work Versus Life

What gets squeezed? Between career and child rearing, the first thing to go is housework. One child of a career woman thought that everybody got dressed in the morning in front of the clothes dryer.

The second thing to go is cooking. In the 1960s the average meal took 2.5 hours to prepare. Now it's ready in 15 minutes.[27] Some families may go a week without sitting down together for dinner. A career woman has her teenage son put the empty pizza boxes in the alley garbage cans only on pickup day so that the neighbors won't know just how dependent her family has become on takeout pizza.

The third thing to go is leisure. There is no longer any time for long walks or bridge games for the career woman with children. One woman executive would combine leisure and face time with her children by having her teacher husband bring the children to a city park near corporate headquarters. In fair weather the family would eat lunch at a picnic table and spend an hour together.

And the squeeze gets more severe. Through the 1990s to 2000s, U.S. style "turbo capitalism" has steadily lengthened the work day and the work week for white collar employees and managers. We now have the most productive managers in the world, who have the heaviest workload in the industrialized world, exceeding those of even Germany and Japan. For all workers, the average number of hours worked per year climbed to 1,980 in 1995, from a post World War II total of 1800 in 1982. For higher paid managers, the increase has been more dramatic.

Despite the women's movement, and the increased entry of women into professions and business, "one thing has stayed the same: it is still women who adjust their lives to accommodate the needs of children, who do what is necessary to make a home, who forgo status, income, advancement, and independence" by having children.[28] That fact alone has great power in explaining the paucity of women in senior management and in CEO suites.

A large subset of women who have opted out cite not the gravitational pull of bearing and rearing children but the more burdensome nature of work: "[I]t was not a change I made only because my children needed me. It's more accurate to say that I was no longer willing to work as hard—commuting, navigating office politics, having my schedule be at the whim [of someone else], balancing all that with the needs of my family."[29]

Of the three factors behind the opt-out phenomenon (unfair treatment in the workplace, gravitational or genetic pull toward rearing children, and the changing nature of work itself), a surprisingly high percentage of opt-outs "talk not about how the workplace is unfair to women, but about how the relationship between work and life is different for women than men,"[30]—a seeming combination of the second and third factors.

The result is a "quiet exodus" of highly trained women from corporations, consulting, accounting, and law firms. Today young women finish college, go to MBA or law school, acquire skills, develop seniority, accept transfers in order to climb the ladder, work endless hours, make partner, get promoted to the ranks of senior management, and postpone children until their biological clock is winding down. When they do give birth, "they are expected to treat the event like an appendectomy."[31] Despite it all, ultimately they still opt out, exiting corporate America, or becoming a part-time "consultant," or finally resigning themselves to the less demanding staff or "pink collar" job.

The Studies

The 1970s and 1980s produced young women who were determined to "have it all": meaningful careers and promotions, family and children, athletic fitness, travel and luxurious vacations. How successful have they been?

The answer is not very, at least by objective criteria. One study followed 1,200 college educated women from 1969 until the mid-1990s, when they had reached the ages of from 37 to 47.[32] Fewer than 20 percent had managed to maintain both career and family by their late thirties or early forties. The percentage of women who had been graduated from college between 1966 and 1979 and who reached mid-life with career intact and children was between 13 and 17 percent of the sample. The women who did not have children were twice as successful in achieving a career as were the women with children.

Another study queried 902 women who had obtained law, MBA, and other professional degrees from Harvard between 1971 and 1981.[33] Fully 25 percent of the Harvard MBAs had left the workforce entirely by the early 1990s. Although 82 percent of the mothers had taken a minimum maternity leave of four months or less, ultimately 70 percent cut back on their careers anyway as their first child grew or after a second child was born.

Subjectively, these talented women felt "blind sided," in that they never had imagined the difficulty of combining career with family. Many said they had been forced out of the best jobs after they had become mothers. They lamented a corporate culture in which employers are not content with "a dedicated high performing employee. They want your soul." The emphasis on "face time" in the office and the 24/7 work culture prevalent throughout corporate America are workplace realities that cause well-educated, highly talented women who elect also to have children ultimately to throw up their hands and to opt out.

Women have numbered in excess of the 40 percent mark (50 percent in the 2000s) of law school graduates since the mid-1980s. Normal partnership tracks require seven or so years as an associate before consideration for partner. Yet only 13 percent of the partners, and 7 percent of the equity partners (owners), in the nation's 1,160 largest law firms, are women.

A principal reason is the "female brain drain." Workplace demands, the need for face time, the 24/7 culture, the lack of acceptance for flextime work exist in those settings as well, causing women with children at some point to abandon the partnership track or to quit "the big time" of law or accountancy altogether.

The Economic Value of Child Rearing

The flip side of the 24/7 workplace culture and the demand for face time is the lack of economic value accorded motherhood. As long ago as 1870 it became official, when Francis Walker, an economist who headed the U.S. Census Bureau, solemnly pontificated: "We may assume that speaking broadly [a wife] does not produce as much as she consumes."[34] Ergo, house holding and child rearing would not be considered when in the 1930s economists began calculating gross national product.

One hundred and thirty years after Francis Walker that remains true. The notion of the "unproductive housewife" persists. Domestic labor is accorded no recognition in economic calculations. Those realities have negative consequences for women who take time off or a "time out" to attend to children.

Economists in other countries have calculated the additions to gross domestic product unpaid work represents, even though most of that work occurs in the home and may only be partly visible. In 1994, the Australian Bureau of Statistics calculated the value at 48 percent of GDP. Other studies have found the percentages to be as high as 55 percent in Germany, 40 percent in Canada, and 46 percent in Finland. In the United States, Nobel Prize-winning economist Gary Becker is the only prominent advocate of treating parenting as economic production.[35]

The official U.S. position, and the position adopted by most male law firm partners, senior accountants, economists, and corporate higher ups, is that child rearing and other forms of domestic labor have no economic value.

Not only is child rearing unrecognized but career women who do it often also suffer penalties in the workplace. Not only do they suffer penalties but those penalties are also disproportionate, revealing the discrepancy between what we say we value (families and child rearing) and what we actually value, in terms of pay, promotions, and flexibility in the workplace.

Return to the Career Track

A development yet to play out is the return of opt-out mothers to the workplace and how co-workers will receive them there. For many women, absences to rear children are not permanent: "It's not black and white: it's gray. You're working. Then you're not working. Then maybe you're working part time or consulting. Then you go back." Child bearing and child rearing are merely chapters; they're not whole books.[36]

This is a hot button issue in the work–life debate: how liberal will employers be in permitting women to return to the workforce and under what conditions will they permit returns. One legacy of the high-tech and dot.com boom has been that non-linear career tracks have become more acceptable. Resumes with gaps and zigzags are less off-putting to many employers.

Related issues arise as women revert back to full-time labor not only from leaves of absence or part-time work but also from job sharing, compressed or unconventional work schedules, and other flexible arrangements certain employers provide: "Returning to full time would mean either firing the job share partner or increasing the . . . department's personnel budget—neither of which is likely to be feasible."[37] Those are difficult "crunch type" questions for even the most enlightened employers.

There is also an equity issue. How will women returning to the profession or other workplace after a three- or five-year hiatus be integrated with those who did pursue a linear career path? Part of the answer is in the team production and collaborative nature of work in the modern world. In many companies, managers and professionals move from team to team with higher ups assembling ad hoc teams suited to the task at hand. The upward linear progression in the workplace is a thing of the past: "Now the logic of corporate careers is less likely to resemble the bureaucratic pattern of an orderly progression of ever-higher level and more remunerative jobs. Instead, people are more likely to move from project, rewarded for each accomplishment, like professionals."[38]

An irony of the modern workplace is that while some features (the 24/7 culture, high overhead to support) may drive women and mothers from it, other features (team production, other collaborative work environments) may ease the return of women to the workplace after children have reached a degree of independence.

Persistent Pay Disparities between Men and Women

In Leviticus, God instructs Moses to tell the Israelites that women, for purposes of tithing, are worth 30 shekels while men are worth 50—a 60 percent ratio.[39] From 1930 to 1980, "the value of women in the workplace eerily reflected the biblical ratio: [t]he earnings of full-time working women were only 60 percent of men's earnings." In the 1980s this condition began to change. "By 1993 women . . . were earning an average of seventy-seven cents for every dollar men earned" but by 1997 the gap had widened again, with women's earnings falling to 75 percent of men's.

Yet those statistics are for women who work in job classifications that contain both women and men, undoubtedly influenced by Title VII's proscription of discrimination on the basis of sex.

When pay for women who work in exclusively female occupations is lumped with women's pay in joint occupations, the average earnings of all female workers in 1999 was 59 percent that of men, right at the biblical ratio.[40]

A survey of Stanford Business School MBAs, class of 1982, who were still employed, found that women earned on average $81,300 while men earned $139,100, a ratio of 58 percent. By the late 1980s, 1974 women graduates of the University of Michigan Law School earned 61 percent of what their male counterparts did.[41]

Still another survey of 200 female MBAs focused on a group who had made only slight detours down the "mummy track." These women had, on average, taken 8.8 months off for child-related activities. They were, however, less likely to receive promotions and earned 17 percent less than their female counterparts who had no gap in employment.[42]

The Attitude that Motherhood does not Matter

The penalties women suffer for slight deviations from the career track are "strikingly harsh." The question that arises is "why?"

Many career women report that bosses, male and female, believe that mothers who work part time or take time out for child rearing responsibilities have a "recreational" attitude toward work. They also report that "face time" matters more than actual productivity in many companies, so women who leave promptly at the end of the work day or who have taken "time outs" suffer.

Many more women in business are choosing not to have children. Of female college graduates, 28 percent are childless by age 40. The Catalyst, Inc. female MBA study found that only 20 percent of the female MBAs had children while 70 percent of the male MBAs did.[43] The percentage of all women who remain childless is also rising, from 8 percent in the 1950s, to 10 percent in 1976, to approximately 20 percent today.[44]

Why Motherhood does Matter

Corporate America seems to regard child bearing and child rearing as just a lifestyle choice that some women may make, just as other women dedicate leisure time to improving their tennis game or to training for a marathon. Bearing children and raising them well, however, is not just another lifestyle choice. It is the source of human capital, a sufficient supply of which is critical to the society as a whole. No corporate executive, male or female, should tolerate the attitude that "Well, it's their choice" when women in the organization take time off or "time out" for child rearing.

By contrast, the timing of child bearing may have an element of lifestyle choice to it. Anne-Kathrin Deutrich, of Freiburg Im Breslau, is an exceedingly rare commodity. She rose to become CEO of a publicly held German company, SICK GmbH. She is of the opinion that women would progress more smoothly in their careers if they had children earlier, even before they began their careers, as she did, rather than interrupting their careers later. She believes that women who have children at a younger age regard the birth of a child certainly as a special and blessed event, but they take it more in their stride. Women who have children later, say, in their early to mid-thirties, regard child bearing as episodic, working a dramatic change in their ambitions and outlook on life.[45]

Today, elite MBA schools not only advocate but also require that applicants have three, four or five years' work experience after college or university, no exceptions allowed, before applying to business school. For a woman oriented toward business, she will be 26 or 27 when she matriculates at "B" school and 28 or 29 when she obtains her degree. If she works three to four years before she contemplates having children, she may be 33 or 34 when she has her first baby. She may well regard that event as not only special but exceedingly so, opting out, for a significant period of time, from job and career.

Corporations as well as universities, including MBA schools, should treat men and women fairly and alike, except when a demonstrable biological difference requires variation in treatment. Perhaps imposing a work prerequisite is one area in which MBA schools should treat men and women differently.

Prescriptions

In business organizations, as opposed to business schools, what other sorts of solutions will lower or eliminate altogether the price of motherhood? What kinds of things can corporations do to eliminate the "built-in headwinds" that mothers face on the career track?[46]

Consider the recommendations contained in Ann Crittenden's book *The Price of Motherhood* for a comprehensive proposal:[47]

1.   Give every parent the right to a year's paid leave.
2.   Provide equal pay and benefits for equal part-time work.
3.   Eliminate discrimination against parents in the workplace.
4.   Facilitate women's return to the workplace [alumni/ae and welcome back programs] and to the promotion ladder under conditions equitable to all.

After analyzing work–life issues in law firms,[48] Professor Joan Williams offers more detailed recommendations:

1.   *Individualized flexibility.* Best practices employers allow many different types of flexible schedules, including leaves of absence, part-time work, job sharing, sabbaticals, telecommuting, and the ability to "buy" time off through acceptance of less pay for periods of time. They maintain websites which outline what may be available to employees.
2.   *Have the attitude that any job can be done flexibly.* Ms. Williams group found corporations in which personnel on flexible schedules were doing every job previously thought of as suitable only for traditional full time endeavor.
3.   *Fairness: make alternatives available to everyone.* This avoids the appearance even of favoritism. It also recognizes that, although they may not have children, single, gay and lesbian, and other employees have parents, siblings, and partners who may make demands on the employee's time.
4.   *Employ part-time parity: proportionality.* Employees in flexible arrangements should have, insofar as is possible, pay, benefits, bonuses and opportunities for advancement but some of these benefits will differ for them in

that they will be distributed only on a proportionate basis. They will not
be denied altogether.

5. *Equal advancement opportunities.* The pervasive notion is that employees
cannot advance as managers or supervisors unless they adhere to a
standard schedule. Enlightened companies may slow the part-time
employee's progress along the advancement track but they do not derail
it altogether.

6. *Equal job security.* Those employees in flexible job schedules should not
necessarily be the first the employer lays off.

7. *Measure and reward quality performance.* An old saw states that "you manage what you measure." If evaluation processes measure face time and
24/7 availability, those are the quantities employees will produce and the
quality of output will be left to chance. Effective evaluations measure
"effectiveness, judgement and quality of work so that the amount of time
spent in the office becomes less meaningful." Professor Williams, along
with countless human resources managers, finds that 360 degree reviews
in which superiors, peers, subordinates, customers, and others evaluate
employees are a more accurate gauge of what most employers actually
wish to manage.[49]

Tentative Conclusions

Have Children Sooner Rather Than Later?

For women themselves, besides the alternatives of postponing child bearing,
or foregoing having children altogether, Frau Deutrich's analysis suggests a
third possibility: *having children early*, before a woman begins her career in
earnest. Among the 21 women CEOs this book profiles, several of them had
children before their careers began in earnest, namely, Jill Barad (Mattel),
Marion Sandler (Golden West Financial), Ann Mulcahy (Xerox), Pat Woertz
(Archer Daniels Midland), Angela Braly (Wellpoint), Brenda Barnes (Sara
Lee), and Meg Whitman (eBay).

Prioritize Careers As You Come Within Site of the Top

Women have long sublimated their career aspirations to those of an ambitious
spouse, including one with eyes for the corner suite. This study, albeit of a
small number, shows that many husbands of successful women have done the
same thing. Moreover, they have reached that choice through a conscious
process. Spouses of Susan Ivey, Carleton Fiorina, Christina Gold, Angela
Braly, Indra Nooyi, Mary Sammons, and Carol Bartz sat down with their
partners to *prioritize careers*, promotions, geographical relocations and the like,
before they occurred.

Have Children If You Want Them

Jayne Barnard, a well-known corporate governance scholar, finds that, at the time she wrote, eight female CEOs in the *Fortune 500* had no natural children. Beware then of what you wish for because it (a senior management position) may come with significant deprivations, Professor Barnard concludes.

I find the opposite. Of 21 female CEOs, 19 of those women collectively have 36 children.[50] The statistic includes adopted children as well as natural born: Susan Ivey, Pat Russo, and Carly Fiorina became mothers to their husbands' children, while Andrea Jung has one of each. The responsibilities of rearing an adopted child do not differ from those of rearing a natural born one.

Eighty percent of working women over 40 have children; 20 percent do not.[51] Ninety-one percent of women CEOs (19 of 21) have children. Women who have made it to the CEO suite thus have not had to sacrifice having a family any more, and perhaps less, than the population of working women at large. Do not hesitate: *have children if you want them.*

14 In a Different Register

Few elements of our identities come as close to our sense of who we are as gender. . . . Perhaps it is because our sense of gender is so deeply rooted that people are inclined to hear descriptions of gender patterns as statements about gender identity—in other words, as absolute differences rather than a matter of degree and percentages, [as] universal rather than [cultural]. . . . Men, whose oppositional strategies (joking, teasing, playful putdowns) are interpreted literally may be seen as hostile when they're not . . . When women use conversational strategies to avoid appearing boastful and to take the other person's feelings into account, they may seen as less confident and competent than they really are.[1]

> Deborah Tannen, *Talking from 9 to 5 —Women and Men in the Workplace: Language, Sex and Power* (1994)

Are these differences biological or cultural? [The] patterns I describe are characteristic of female and male styles in a particular time and place. There is no inherent, biological reason for them.[2]

> Deborah Tannen

Many men perceive women as lacking the requisite boldness and rugged individualism to function well as senior managers. They perceive women to be "intuitive rather than analytical" and "too emotional." Men base these assertions on what they have observed in their own lives and careers: women speak and act differently than men. Linguists, lead by Professor Robin Lakoff at the University of California Berkeley, and Professor Deborah Tannen at Georgetown University, have agreed that it is true. In our society, women speak "in a different register," but the baggage that men allege to come with those female behaviors is non-existent, as Lakoff and Tannen demonstrate. Nevertheless, male managers' perceptions prevent women from migrating upwards into the pool from which boards of directors and search consultants chose CEOs and other senior corporate managers.

An early analysis of attorneys' trial practice techniques by Messrs. Conley, O'Barr and Lind, which finds "that women's language is really powerless language," is illustrative.[3] "[W]omen's tendency to be indirect is taken as evidence that women don't feel entitled to make demands," according to linguist Tannen.[4]

Because many women speak with rising intonation in their declaratory speech, men perceive women as more emotional, less dispassionate than men, even though, again, that may not be the case. The "how to books" advise women in business to "lower the pitch of your voice" and not to "show emotion."[5] University of California at Berkeley Law Professor Mary Ann Mason, a leading women's rights scholar, echoes them: "Speak lowly and slowly but smile" she advises women.

[W]omen must adhere to a narrow band of behavior in order to be effective in mostly male settings. Women who speak too fast, or in too shrill a tone, are overlooked. Women who act in a highly assertive manner are attended to but are not invited back. Women must be friendly, but they cannot be too friendly, or a sexual connotation may be inferred.[6]

Early on, linguist Erving Goffman demonstrated that women smile more and do so more expansively than men.[7] This fact places women in a double bind: "[W]omen are expected to smile more than men are. [W]omen are seen as severe and lacking in humor if they rarely smile."[8] But men perceive women who smile too much as "frivolous" and "hare-brained."

This chapter raises the question of whether a "disconnect" exists between business organizations and the speech and actions of women within them.

Early Linguistic Research

In 1975, linguist Lakoff made the claim that there is a distinctive "women's language" that differs from male speech.[9] She argued that women who use this mode of speech appear less assertive and confident than those who use male speech patterns. Lakoff went on to assert that this "women's language" not only reflects women's subordinate position in society but also reinforces that subordination, including what feminists term "economic subordination," much of which occurs in the workplace and in the corporate management hierarchy.[10]

Lakoff's pupil, Deborah Tannen, theorized "that systematic differences in women's and men's characteristic styles often put women in a subordinate position in interactions with men."[11] Tannen, however, had reservations. She thought that context (the "framing") often was as important as gender in the speakers' use of linguistic strategies. For example, asking for directions or to pass the salt may be relatively neutral while arguing about a business proposition may be framing of a different sort. In other cases, other facets of the situation, such as body language or cultural traits, trump what examination of linguistics alone reveals.[12]

Lakoff's and Tannen's contentions sent many researchers off on the trail to test the theories. Researchers contrasted speech of women of different age groups.[13] Others examined speech of a generation or two gone by.[14] Another conducted empirical studies on the effect of women's speech in the courtroom.[15] A professor of criminal law, Janet Ainsworth, applied linguists' theories to the subject of custodial interrogation of women by the police.[16]

Speech Patterns and Context

In English, men and women do not speak different dialects, as they do in some other languages, but gender does correlate with the use of different linguistic registers. A register is a characteristic way of speaking that certain members of a speech community adopt under specific circumstances.

Use of a particular register depends on the context of the speech (the "framing"). A register may be associated with certain settings or situations, or may be correlated to social role or relationship. Not all women share the speech characteristics of the register; some men will exhibit that register of speech. But researchers have shown that a particular register is gender linked. Sociolinguistic research on gender and language supports the disproportionate use of a characteristic speech register by women.

Some contexts will maximize gender differences in language. One relevant to the corporate setting is when there exists a power disparity between the speaker and the hearer, as in female subordinate to CEO, or rising woman executive to a member of the board of directors.

Other contexts minimize gender difference. An example linguists use is of an impersonal, formulaic interaction, such as making an inquiry at a public information booth.[17] A linguist with blinders on may record "pass the food" as an interruption at the dinner table. Many linguists think interruptions to be more the province of male speakers and attempts to dominate conversations. All present at the dinner table, however, would regard "pass the food" as an aside or overlapping bite of language.[18]

The Female Register

Characteristics of the female speech register that have application to women's role in corporate governance include: avoidance of imperatives and the use of indirect interrogatories instead; increased use of modal verbs; use of hedges; rising intonation in declaratory statements; and silence or quiescence versus adversariness or aggression.

Avoidance of Imperatives

Users of the female register avoid using the imperative, substituting interrogative forms. As Lakoff states: "An overt order . . . expresses the (often impolite) assumption of the speaker's superior position to the addressee, carrying with it the right to enforce compliance, whereas with a request the decision on the face of it is left up to the addressee."[19]

The imperative is the most starkly assertive of grammatical forms. In adult speech it may seem to be the prerogative of the male:

- Place the order (male).
- Hire X as a consultant (male).

- Should we hire X as a consultant? (female).
- Get it done this week (male).
- Can you get it done this week? (female).

Demands which speakers phrase in the interrogative form sound less presumptive, more tactfully deferential than baldly stated imperatives (commands). Modern interpersonal relations allow for less use of imperatives by either males or females but, because the exercise of power represented even in the occasional use of imperatives is considered "unfeminine," "women are socialized from earliest childhood to avoid directly ordering other people to do things." In corporate settings, bosses may perceive reticence as a deficiency most women exhibit.

The widespread American assumption to associate indirectness in conversation with female style is "not universal." In Japanese and other Asian cultures, the indirect manner is more nearly universal. A European aristocrat communicates with servants and subordinates only in an indirect manner. "Indirectness, then, is not itself a strategy of subordination. Rather it can be used by either the powerful or the powerless."[20] In American business, however, the tendency is to associate indirectness in conversation with subordination.

Increased Use of Modal Verbs

Users of the female register make far more frequent use of modal verbs such as "may," "might," "could," "ought," "should," and "must."[21] Those verbs hedge the pragmatic impact of a sentence, making the speaker appear perhaps less confident or assertive when that may not be the case at all:

- You might hire X as a consultant.
- You should meet with me Friday at 10:00 am.
- The audit committee ought to discuss that.
- You could travel to Phoenix next week.

Strong modal verbs "such as 'should,' 'ought,' or 'must' carry the implication that the statement is the product of surmise, deduction, or process of elimination rather than an unmediated statement of fact."[22] Again, penultimate perceptions that a subordinate or co-worker lacks confidence or acts upon surmise, while having their foundation solely in speech patterns, may lead to ultimate perceptions of women that put them at a disadvantage in management settings.

More Frequent Use of Verbal Hedges

Qualifiers, called hedges, are expressions that function to attenuate the emphasis that otherwise the statement might carry. Speakers use hedges such as "about" or "around" with respect to numerical quantity to render the statement less precise, thereby less contestable. Hedges such as "kind of" or "to some extent" soften the assertion by qualifying the application of the idea expressed, thus undercutting assertiveness.

Other hedges, such as beginning expression with the qualifier "I think" or "I suppose," or using "maybe" or "perhaps," convey the sense that the speaker is uncertain about the statement. Alternatively, those hedges convey the notion that the speaker prefers not to confront addressees with bald assertions.[23] A similar hedge out of the "how to" books for women is "I'm sorry," as in "I'm sorry to interrupt you" or "I'm sorry that our profits forecasts have been revised." "The word *sorry* is a female addiction. We use it so often, to express so much, and in many contexts it has virtually no meaning. It's just something we say, the iceberg lettuce of conversation, a kind of verbal filler."[24]

Lakoff demonstrated that women use hedges more frequently than men.[25] Frequent use of hedges "arise[s] out of a fear of seeming too masculine by being assertive and saying things directly." Some male managers misinterpret hedged speech as a sign that the speaker (often a female) is lacking in confidence.

Rising Intonation in Declaratory Statements

Females may exhibit a further "paralinguistic characteristic: its speakers use rising inflection in making declarative statements."[26] Ordinarily, English speakers use rising intonation to signal a question or to express incredulity.[27]

The use of rising intonation in ordinary declaratives when the speaker does not intend to express uncertainty or incredulity is a gender-linked trait.[28] American men tend to pronounce their sentence endings at the lowest level of intonation that they customarily use whereas women frequently adopt a rising "sentence terminal." Women also exhibit a much greater dynamic range of intonation—four or five separate levels of intonation, while men seldom use more than three.

Rising intonation at the end of declarative sentences and use of a greater range of levels of intonation indicate emotion, or extreme emotion, in male speech. Male addressees may assume that the same is true in female speech when that is not the case at all. Men in boardroom or corporate positions hearing female speech with rising or slightly rising intonation may be reinforced in preconceived and sexist notions that "all women are emotional" or that women bring to business decisions an inappropriate level of emotion.

Silence or Quiescence Versus Adversariness or Aggression

Overall, Deborah Tannen finds that "male speakers tend to be competitive and more likely to engage in conflict (for example, by arguing, issuing commands, and taking opposing stands) and females tend to be more cooperative (for example, by agreeing, supporting, and making suggestions)."[29]

Importance of Apparent Differences

The differences that males associate with a different register are more than trivial. As one advice volume for women, by Catalyst's Sheila Wellington, puts it:

> *Eschew emotion.* Certain behaviors work against you in the workplace . . . Emoting about anything, be it your own screw up, frustration at yet another photocopier jam, work poorly presented by your staff . . . is one sure way to make others uncomfortable in the workplace. Keep your cool; emotionalism makes you look unreliable and unsteady and reinforces the stereo types about women that men already hold.[30]

Silicon Valley pundits ascribe at least part of Carol Bartz's rise to become CEO of Yahoo! (Chapter 9) to her ability to use earthly and salty language, a trait more usually associated with male rather than female managers.

Professor Ainsworth concludes that "[t]he overall pragmatic effect of the female register is the substitution of indirect and tentative locutions for strong and assertive modes of expressions."[31] Speakers utilize the female register to convey uncertainty, soften the presumptiveness of direct speech, or to preempt opposition from the addressee. Pioneer Robin Lakoff finds that:

> Men's language is the language of the powerful. It is meant to be direct, clear, succinct, as would be expected of those who need not fear giving offense, who need not worry about the risks of responsibility . . . Women's language developed as a way of surviving . . . without control over economic, physical or social reality. [To survive under those conditions] it is necessary to listen more than speak, agree more than confront, be delicate, be indirect.[32]

Cognitive psychologists tell us that we tend to hear what a speaker says to us as though we had said it and to hear what we think the speaker said rather than what she actually may have said. Men in positions of power hear emotion in the female register when there is none; they detect lack of confidence or assertiveness when the reality is that there is not.

In its doctrine and its models, business management presumes that actors will utilize assertive speech—a mode of expression characteristic of men. Gender bias results in the treatment of prototypically male behavior (confident, assertive, powerful) as a synonym for *all* human behavior, at least on the rarified level upon which corporate executives act and on the pathways to get there.

Implications of the Theory

The unwitting incorporation of a male normative standard in business may be nearly invisible but it is not inconsequential. Women whose behavior fails to conform to the behavioral norms encoded within the management model are penalized on the route to the upper rungs of the corporate ladder, reaching the destination far less frequently than would be predicted based upon the demographics.

Drawing a broader conclusion yet, the characteristically male preference for assertive speech, rather than suggestion, innuendo, implication or inference, may be seen as but one instance of a more generalized male preference for assertive behavior in corporate and business settings which goes back 150 years. Sociologist turned historian Stephanie Coontz observed that:

> In eighteenth-century Europe and early nineteenth-century America . . . [t]o men were assigned all the character traits associated with competition: ambition, authority, power, vigor, calculation, instrumentalism, logic, and single-mindedness. To women were assigned all the traits associated with cooperation: gentleness, sensitivity, expressivism, altruism, empathy, personalism, and tenderness.[33]

Men assign women those traits whether they possess them or not. Then the unstated but real preference for the assertiveness and competitiveness men are presumed to possess by those in executive suites hamstrings women in many areas of corporate life.

Prescriptions

Women rising in businesses should not necessarily change, wearing power suits and becoming "bully broads" in the lexicon of one popular work.[34] Male directors, directors on nominating committees, CEOs, and others who evaluate women in business settings should become aware that they may be evaluating though a lens colored in a manner that creates inaccurate perceptions of female behavior, often putting women at a distinct disadvantage.

The changes necessary may be subtle. One firm found that hiring of qualified women MBAs increased when the company lengthened interview times from 30 minutes to an hour. Women were much more likely to speak out about their talents and accomplishments in the longer interviews.[35]

Another prescription may be to refrain from sidetracking women into the "soft" side, or "pink collared" sector, of business, where a different register and qualities such as less assertiveness or competitiveness are perceived by male superiors as advantages, or at least not disadvantages.

Combination with Other Realities

When one blends in what has been discussed in an earlier chapter, "Work–Life Issues and the Price of Motherhood," with "A Different Register," the gauntlet women must run to the CEO suite lengthens. The ideal worker takes little time off and certainly none for child rearing and household management. Though this ideal worker paradigm does not define all jobs in the corporate setting, it does define the good ones.[36] The good jobs will be positions that require 60 to 70 hours work per week in the office, out-of-town travel, and profit and loss responsibilities. They will not be on the soft side of business into which organizations are far more likely to shunt women.

Women may be ideal workers but they may be constrained by the field they occupy (soft side of business), the register they use (different), the traits they are assigned (not assertive, emotional, not analytical, intuitive) and the other roles they are required to play (mother, household manager).

15   Legacies of Tokenism: Retreats into Stereotypes

Alice Garratt (not her real name) was consistently placed second, third or fourth in her work group of 15 representatives in her region, selling complex, top-of-the-line information processing systems. She was the only female in the group. Alice helped other salesmen with their paperwork, in addition to her own. She also was the "go to" person in the work group when seemingly intractable problems arose (for example, what combination of less expensive items could the salesman recommend to achieve all, or almost all, of the client's objectives, at lower cost?).

At the annual awards dinner, and at other functions, Alice voluntarily went last. She always received an award, and praise, but arranged to receive them at the end of the line. Higher ups featured her when time had become shorter, praise less effusive, and other attendees less apt to pay attention, often because they had had a drink, or two, or three.

Over a 12–15 year period, other salesmen graduated to regional sales manager and headquarters marketing positions as well as onward to vice presidencies. Competitors recruited several of Alice's cohorts away. Alice remained in the same work group, at the same job, and roughly at the same pay.

Anonymous (2007)

This story illustrates both the benefits and the burdens of token, or skewed group (see), status:

- Token status lends itself to a retreat into stereotypes (mascot, class clown, iron maiden), or as here (mother figure, queen bee), or the imposition of token status, whether the recipient wants it or not.
- Stereotypes limit downside risk (demotion, dismissal, layoff, transfer).
- Simultaneously, stereotypes mask from view real achievement, capping or limiting upside potential.

Women often are tokens (the only, or one of two) in their job classification, work center, or employment rank. They retreat into stereotypes, or permit the majority to visit stereotypes upon them. They thus limit, severely, their chances for migration into the pool from which boards of directors and senior executives will choose senior managers and candidates for promotion generally.

These observations about token status and its ramifications come from the work of sociologists. They help explain why the number of female CEOs and other senior managers lags far behind expectations we have had for over 30 years.

Token Status

Within an organization, members may treat a single minority group member (woman, black, Hispanic) as a token. She may have to bear the brunt of jokes, practical and otherwise, at her expense. Tokens draw attention, much more so than any of the group's dominants. Even if she does not retreat into a stereotype, the token will suffer by application by co-workers of a stereotype to her.

The dominants will apply to token women many of the stereotypical attributes thought applicable to their type ("emotional," "intuitive," "not rational"). As the token's type increases in number in a work center or group, her visibility and attribution to her of various characteristics hopefully will decrease "because each individual becomes less surprising, unique or noteworthy."[1]

A second perceptual phenomenon, however, is that, among themselves, with a token in their midst, the dominants become more aware and expressive about their common characteristics (enjoy professional football, talk about cars and women, smoke cigars). They emphasize differences they perceive their kind having from the token (males are rational while women are not; men are unemotional in matters of business while women are not). To preserve their commonality, the dominants keep the token at arm's length, outside the dominant group. They offer a boundary to themselves, as dominants, within which their commonality can flourish. This is the process sociologists term "boundary heightening."

Skewed Groups

As another person with the same characteristics (a woman, a black, a Jew, a Muslim) enters the group, intuition might spark a tentative conclusion that stereotyping and boundary heightening decrease. Often the outcome is counterintuitive, the opposite of what an onlooker might surmise. The dominants now perceive a threat rather than an irritant. They increase boundary heightening. They pursue strategies such as divide and conquer, attempting to turn one skewed group member against the other.

Skewed groups are those in which a significant preponderance of one type (the dominants) within the job classification or work center prevail over the next most represented type by a ratio of up to 85 to 15. In skewed groups, the dominants control the group and its culture. They set the tone, often pointedly so.

Performance Pressures on a Token

In meetings at Rosabeth Moss Kanter's mythical corporation, Indsco, male dominants would consistently ask the token woman for "the woman's point of view." They expected a response for all women, not just from the token's personal perspective. A result was heightened self-consciousness on the part of the woman, about her presentation, personal appearance, and decisions. Insignificant decisions about what to wear, where to sit at meetings, or whether to have lunch and where were no longer inconsequential.

These treatments eclipsed the token's true skills and achievements. "The token does not have to work hard to have her presence noted, but she does have to work hard to have her achievements noted," Professor Kanter concludes.[2] Aspects of her femininity hid from view actual job performance.

A second performance pressure may be paradoxical. While a token woman may feel that she has to do better than everyone else to be noticed or to win promotion, she cannot show up the dominants in her group. If the dominants perceive her as doing so, they will regard her as aggressive, pushy, and overly ambitious. Because she is the token, she has difficulty keeping her actual job performance a secret because, as the token, she has many eyes upon her. She may have to play down her accomplishments, or not speak of them at all. If she does not, she risks the dominants' retaliation. At best, she walks a tightrope between those extremes, staying invisible or trumpeting her achievements.

Coping Strategies

Tokens may respond to performance pressures in several ways. A solo woman may over achieve but construct a facade that minimizes peer concerns. She may adopt a plain appearance. She will wait patiently in line to receive kudos or a promotion, as in the hypothetical above, standing at the end of the line when bosses hand out praise or rewards.

A second and opposite strategy is to revel in the notoriety of token status. The reveler may undercut possible new woman hires and excessively criticize potential woman peers. She enjoys the advantage in being the only woman so she intends to keep it that way, pulling up the rope ladder after her. This is the Queen Bee syndrome (see *infra*) the advice books describe.[3] In sociological terms, Queen Bees retard the creation of skewed groups because a token will find it easier to manage to her advantage a token as opposed to a skewed group situation.

A third strategy tokens adopt is, as best they can, to make themselves invisible. Previous generations of women often pursued this strategy. They hid their sexuality by adopting mannish forms of dress, from overalls to power suits, and wore little or no makeup. Many avoided work-related social functions or even meetings at work. They sat on the periphery of the meeting room or remained silent at meetings they did attend.

Observers of these coping strategies may think of them as gender linked but, as Rosabeth Kanter feels, they "can be better understood as situational responses, true of any person in a token role."[4] Just as Hispanics, African Americans, Jews, or Catholics did while trying to succeed in culturally alien environments, women may fear visibility because of retaliation costs and performance pressures token status creates for them.

Boundary Heightening

As has been seen, the presence of a woman may make the dominants in a work group more aware of what they perceive themselves as having in common. The males may also feel uncomfortable, or uncertain, in the token's presence. The result is that the majority group members take steps further to cement themselves together, emphasizing their sameness and highlighting the token's differences. Again, this process is boundary heightening.

The dominants, then, exaggerate their culture: "Ironically, tokens, unlike people represented in greater proportions, are thus instruments for *underlining* rather than *undermining* majority culture."[5] The men increase camaraderie among themselves, with tales of sexual adventure, sports talk, bragging of work prowess, and telling of off-color jokes. In fact, when the token woman is not present, the dominant males' discussion returns to more prosaic topics such as child rearing, schooling, and household tasks.

The men may engage in creation of more formal boundaries by purposefully isolating the token. They may not attend meetings the token attempts to convene, or they may RSVP "Yes" but conspire not to attend the actual meeting.[6] At Indsco, Professor Kanter observed that dominant males:

> [m]oved the locus of some activities from public settings to which tokens had access to more private settings from which they could be excluded. [Another] result was sometimes "quarantine"—keeping tokens away from some occasions. Informal pre-meeting meetings were sometimes held. Some topics of discussion seemed rarely raised in the presence of women peers.[7]

Responses to Boundary Heightening

Tokens may act out disloyalty to the minority group of which they are a part. A price of being "one of the boys" may be to be catty, to turn against women, even to backstab other women in the organization. The token may attempt to portray herself as exceptional to the male dominants who respond, "You're not a typical woman."

Humor may become central. The token allows herself to become the object of the dominants' humor, laughing with them to signal acceptance of their dominant culture. In contrast, if the token objects to being the brunt of joke telling, the dominants deny any hostility, accusing the token of lacking a sense of humor. The token woman may go drinking with the men, take part in male evaluations of other women's physical attributes, and otherwise attempt to become one of the boys.

In order to cope, the token may allow the males to encapsulate her into a stereotype to which the majority is receptive. The token assimilates the characteristics associated with that stereotype. For example, the dominants set the token woman up as the mother figure. The stereotype is that all women are sympathetic and good listeners. The males seek her counsel and bring their troubles to her.

The downsides to encapsulation as the mother figure are several. The males value the token not for her independent job performance but for her counseling and other solace she provides. The males expect her to be a non-critical, accepting mother figure. While the mother role may give her a place in the group as its emotional specialist, the role may come back to haunt her. One of the stereotypical characteristics attributed to women, and one that holds them back from advancement, is that males regard women as excessively emotional. By accepting a role as the mother figure, the token woman plays into that stereotype of feminine characteristics.

A token may also permit the majority to encapsulate her in the role of the group's pet, the mascot. The males expect her to be of constant good cheer. She expresses unvarying appreciation of the males' humorous displays but does not enter into it herself. In turn, the males may compliment her but on form rather than substance. They tell her "You speak so fluently" after she has given a presentation while, after a presentation by a male, they comment on substance, giving content-oriented feedback.

Tokens pay a price for pursuing a coping strategy, whether it involves becoming invisible or being encapsulated in a stereotypical role. The coping strategies mask or diminish recognition by others in the organization of the productive activity and achievements the token has accomplished. Token status forestalls recognition, and fewer women rise to the level at which they are entrants into the pool from which boards of directors and senior executives choose future senior managers.

Further, many dominant group behaviors, and the coping strategies thought necessary to counteract them, are distasteful to women. They may leave a particular corporation altogether rather than put up with them. While we have known for some time that token and skewed group status forestalls many women's entry into corporate governance realms, it may be only the tip of the iceberg. Minority status and its unseemly effects may account for many more tokens who leave organizations altogether, never becoming prospective players at all, similar to the opt-out phenomenon observed among promising women who turn to child bearing. We have known about the legacies of tokenism for a long time but we have never thought much about the legacy's effects on corporate governance.

Other Stereotypes—The Iron Maiden

We have seen the mascot, one of the boys, the mother figure, the queen bee, and the iron maiden. A reaction to token treatment pressures is resistance. The dominants often perceive such behavior as tough. Sociologists term this perception of women as the "Iron Maiden".[8] If a token woman insists on full rights in a group, displays her competence in a forthright manner, cuts off sexual innuendo, refuses to be one of the boys, and so on, the male dominants will regard her with suspicion and distance themselves from her. They will stereotype her as more militant and aggressive than she really is.

Male co-workers will leave the Iron Maiden to flounder on her own when she encounters difficulties. Within her work group, she will find no peers sympathetic to her plight when she encounters problems. Coworkers and higher ups may abandon her.

The Bully Broad Hypothesis

The existent how to succeed books counsel women to be assertive and, indeed, aggressive. Those behaviors may indeed procure a first or second promotion for a woman. Thereafter, more likely than not, over aggressiveness will result in an aspiring woman's career being sidetracked. Jean Hollands, a behavioral psychologist who has consulted with Cisco, Intel, Wells Fargo, Netscape, and other major corporations, has termed this phenomenon, somewhat infelicitously, the "Bully Broad" stereotype.[9]

The Women's National Basketball Association started out in the 1990s with women coaches. Very quickly, owners and general managers weeded out women coaches, replacing them with men. One of the principal reasons, Hollands reports, is that the first generation coaches were Bully Broads. What had caused those women to succeed in their careers as players, and in coaching in the lower ranks of the game, did them in when they reached coaching's upper echelons: "Why have . . . the women washed out as coaches? For the same reason they have washed out in the corporate world . . . Women can't get away with the harsh command-and-control style that many male managers and coaches can."[10] Although it is doubtful that anyone, man or woman, can succeed today with such a management style, it certainly holds true for women.

In promotion tournaments and other evaluative rituals, candidates for higher management positions must go through as they ascend, superiors regard overly aggressive women as accomplished but deficient. They perceive "Bully Broads" as lacking in the diplomatic and strategic skills that higher ups deem essential to be able to represent the organization anywhere, at any time, and necessary to reach the upper rungs of the corporate ladder.

The Queen Bee Stereotype

The "Queen Bee" syndrome occurs when the first woman to reach a job classification or management level tries to exclude other women who follow from the same classification, level, or status. Queen Bees treat other women coldly. "Once some managerial women get a taste of power, they may be afraid to share it or delegate it, because they fear they are going to lose it. So they hold on. They stay aloof," author Carol Gallagher posits.[11]

Queen Bee behaviors represent aspects of "women's cruelty to women." The behaviors rise up out of insecurity and, often, out of a warped sense of competition. Organizational psychologists observe that some women compete not just to best but to conquer or crucify their opponents. Men and women "who have been involved in healthy competition (such as participation on sports teams) typically know how to compete more effectively than those who did not."[12]

The Ice Queen

Women who remain largely silent but appear judgmental and who tend to be rigid, feeling that their way is the only way to accomplish a given task, fit under this stereotype, as Jean Hollands describes it: "[The Ice Queen] is reserved and steely. People shy away from her because they expect her to judge them [harshly]." These women remain silent, "afraid of revealing their true feelings because they are often perceived as being negative" as well as judgmental.[13] They frequently "turn their frustration on to other people. They always look to the other person as being the source of the problem."[14]

The advice books for women (*How to Succeed in Business*; *Smash the Glass Ceiling*; *Play Like a Man, Win Like a Woman*; *Hardball for Women*; *How To Get the Corner Office*; *The New Success Rules for Women in Business*), are filled with colorful descriptions of stereotypes women should avoid.[15] The six or seven this chapter reviews capture the substance of the descriptions and advice.

More on Skewed Groups

Tokenism is difficult for the solo representative. As Professor Kanter portrays it, when an additional minority or two join the work group, "the temperature rises": " 'Xs' realize that circumstances are changing and they could be replaced by 'O's' competing for 'X's' slots. A trickle of 'O's' can thus create a backlash and a taste for discrimination to accompany the 'X' group's greater awareness of a greater threat to its dominance—to its monopoly over opportunity and power, its ability to define the culture and the values."[16]

When a second token joins the team, the dominant males may attempt to play one token off against the other. The males may set up one token as the superior performer. The dominants may attempt to insert a layer of hierarchy between two women who have started out at the same level, as for example making one the boss of the other.

As game theory teaches, an appropriate response is for the two women to develop a close alliance and refuse to be turned against each other.[17] Another response is prevent a skewed group situation ever from occurring. Feminist scholars who have surveyed studies and digested the analyses have formulated the cry that "Three Is the Magic Number." Their prescription is that whether it be at the board of directors level, among senior managers, or in middle management ranks, three or more women managers or directors are necessary before women believe themselves to have the ability to speak freely and to demonstrate to peers or to subordinates what they are capable of achieving.[18]

These then are the legacies of tokenism which have shielded from view the achievements and capabilities of women in many business organizations. They help explain why fewer women than would have been expected have migrated upward to the point at which they may sight the senior most positions, including that of CEO, in major corporations, and why until 1997 there were no female CEOs. These behaviors also highlight the added difficulties women have had in reaching toward the top, factors board governance committee and sitting CEOs should consider in evaluating women's and other minorities' candidacies for upper level positions.

Part III

How to Get There

16 Narcissists, Malignant Narcissists, and Productive Narcissists

[N]arcissus . . . fell in love with his own reflection in a pool, could not tear himself away for food or drink, and from sheer frustration at length died.[1]

Richard Hathorn, *Greek Mythology* (1977)

In the territory of the Thespians is a place called Donacon. Here is the spring of Narcissus. They say that Narcissus looked into this water, and not understanding that he saw his own reflection, unconsciously fell in love with himself, and died of love.[2]

Jan Bremmer, *Interpretations of Greek Mythology* (1987)

Sigmund Freud identified three personality (libidinal) types: the erotic, the obsessive, and the narcissistic.[3] "Narcissism" equates with "exaggerated concern with the self" and "excessive self love." "Narcissistic Character" represents "a personality pattern characterized by excessive self-concern and over-evaluation of the self." When these traits predominate, a "Narcissistic Personality Disorder" eventuates, leading to "[a] clinical diagnosis of a disorder characterized by grandiose ideas of self importance, need for attention and admiration, feeling entitled to special favors, and exploitation of others."[4]

Narcissists and Women CEOs

Narcissists make the best CEOs, according to noted psychologist Michael Maccoby, who published his idea in the *Harvard Business Review*,[5] and then in a best-selling book, *The Productive Narcissist—The Promise and Peril of Visionary Leadership*,[6] and now in a second book, *Narcissistic Leaders: Who Succeeds and Who Fails*.[7] The narcissist CEO also is the celebrity CEO who purposefully puts himself at the organization's forefront:

[C]ompare them with the executives who ran large companies in the 1950s through the 1980s. Those executives shunned the press and had their comments carefully crafted by the press. . . . Today's CEO's—Bill Gates, Andy Grove, Steve Jobs, Jeff Bezos, and Jack Welch—hire their own publicists, write books, grant spontaneous interviews, actively promote personal philosophies. Their faces adorn magazines like *Business Week, Time* and *The Economist*.[8]

In analyzing over 100 CEOs, Maccoby identifies only one women as a narcissist, Martha Stewart, the domestic diva.[9] If the narcissistic personality type is rare among women, and if the belief that narcissists make the best CEOs holds water, then the low incidence of this personality type among women may explain why so few women have risen to lead business organizations. Does this fact help explain why relatively few women have reached the corner office, or why numbers of women are unlikely to get there in the future?

Narcissist CEOs

Different CEOs have different goals for the organizations they lead: satisfy customers, build better widgets, build cutting-edge products, cut costs, increase revenues, keep shareholders content, grow the company, or contribute to the social good. In addition, the narcissistic CEO brings a vision, "a sense of mission and a crusade." The period 1990–2002 saw a plethora of celebrity CEOs—Jeff Bezos at Amazon, Jim Clark at Netscape, Bill Gates at Microsoft, Steve Jobs at Apple, George Soros at Soros, Jurgen Schremp at Daimler-Chrysler, Robert Shapiro at Monsanto, Ross Perot at EDS, Larry Ellison at Oracle (who compares himself to Galileo), Andy Grove at Intel, Jack Welch at General Electric, even Bernie Ebbers at WorldCom and Jeff Skilling at Enron. All of these have narcissistic personalities: "The difference between God and Larry Ellison is that God does not believe he is Larry."[10]

A narcissist "(1) doesn't listen to someone else when he believes in doing something and (2) has precise vision of how things should be. A narcissistic possess this dual combination of traits . . . It is the *combination* of a rejection of the status quo, along with a compelling vision, that defines the narcissist."[11]

> Because narcissistic adults cannot provide themselves with sufficient self-approval or with a sense of strength through their own inner resources, they are forever compelled to satisfy these needs through external sources: by extracting praise from or exercising dominance over others . . . Lacking a *stable cohesive self* . . . they suffer from a fundamental deficiency in the center of their personality. They may harbor feelings of greatness side by side with low self-esteem. They may respond to the frustration of their exhibitionist impulses and to the failure of their grandiose ambitions with shame.[12]

Narcissists exhibit "hypersensitivity to slights," "radical shifts in self perception and self esteem," "overt rage," "intense loneliness," "subjective emptiness," and a host of other unpleasant personality traits: "[T]hey are compelled to endlessly enact the same primitive, fixated behavior in their frustrated search for the whole being."

Freud's Other Personality Types

Personality is the way we habitually relate to the world around us, shape and deploy our talents, and control our passions and instincts. Psychologists sort patients by personality type, basing the treatments they choose on personality. Career choices and performance in a chosen career vary according to personality type as well: "There is no one-size fits all career advice. It depends on personality type."[13]

An erotic (not a sexual term) is "a person for whom loving and being loved are the most important thing. At best, he is caring; at worst he is dependent" (Maccoby never uses female pronouns to illustrate points). Erotics dominate the social service fields—"teaching, nursing, social work, mental health, and therapy—and service industries, careers that involve personal management, nurturing creativity and growth . . . and emotional hand holding." They do not become CEOs. "I have never worked with an erotic CEO," at least "of an innovative or high tech company. . . . They just don't exist. When erotics run organizations [which is rarely] it's usually in the caring fields."[14]

Freud's other personality type, the obsessive, may well become a CEO. "The obsessive is a person who lives by the rules, [believes that] the rules are set by some higher authority," and regards those rules as binding on everyone in the same circumstance. Maccoby types Benjamin Franklin as a productive obsessive, "filled with [respect for] self-regulating maxims for systematic living like 'Early to bed, early to rise, makes a man healthy, wealthy and wise.' "[15] George Washington as well was a productive obsessive, "a successful farmer and businessperson who kept detailed records." The most creative and productive obsessive in the business world today, according to Maccoby? "Warren E. Buffett, whose analytic, stick-to-his-guns approach to investing has keep him on top for decades"[16] and made him the world's second richest person.

"An obsessive may make it to the top of a corporation and take on a leadership role, but only in a company that is itself obsessive—conservative, value-based, focused on the bottom line, where the goals are to cut costs and improve quality and profits. . . . I don't know of any obsessives running innovative companies."[17] Everyone has had to deal with an obsessive. Their "most annoying work habit is that they always want to be right":

> There is a well-known checklist of obsessive pitfalls: [they] can become mired in details and rules, losing sight of overall goals; they become more concerned with doing things in the right way than in doing the right thing; they turn into control freaks, paper-pushing, bean-counting bureaucrats; they resist change to the point of obsolescence; they are

rigid, judgmental, stubborn, and cheap. [T]hey are "anal" in exactly the way Freud described.[18]

Most of the generic business best sellers aim at obsessives. They include *Who Moved My Cheese: An Amazing Way to Deal With Change in Your Work and Life*, which has been on the best seller lists for a decade; *The Seven Habits of Highly Effective People*, and *The One Minute Manager*.[19] Newer works on best seller lists include *The Five Disfunctions of a Team* and *The Six Disciplines Execution Revolution*.[20] These books give obsessives more rules, rigid guidelines around which they can organize their lives.

The Narcissist

For other types of personality, their quest is "to do the right thing." Different personality types define the right thing in differing ways. "For an obsessive, it's doing things the way his father did, or teachers told him . . . For an erotic, doing the right thing means holding on to the love and the interest of significant others." By contrast, "[t]he narcissist has very little or no psychic demands to do the right thing. [He] doesn't care about getting good grades, impressing the teacher [and] doesn't necessarily want to follow in his father's footsteps or take over the family business."[21]

A narcissist marches to her own drummer. She has her own world view, her own vision. She recruits others to join her in that vision, thus overcoming her isolation and sense of a lack of security. It's not enough for the recruits to mix the Kool-aid: they must drink it. To get recruits to join, and to drink the Kool-aid, the narcissist "is driven to be captivating, inspirational, and seductive."[22] Freud depicted this personality type, expatiating on it at length.[23]

"Narcissists *need* to get others to buy into their vision, to create a world that they populate with devoted followers. [They do] wildly creative acts, in which the narcissist envisions an entire world and draws others into it."[24] Bill Gates envisioned a world built around personal computing and networks, drawing others into the world which became Microsoft. A thousand miles south of Seattle, Steve Jobs envisioned another world, created Apple Computer, and recruited brilliant young programmers to his fledgling company, which had little or nothing. Over two hundred years ago Napoleon twice had in his mind his own vision, his world view. Both times he was able to recruit generals, officers, and soldiers to his vision, following his lead to the death if need be.[25] Productive narcissists have always peopled the ranks of corporate CEOs, from Henry Ford, Andrew Carnegie, John D. Rockefeller, and Thomas Edison, to Jim Clark (who with Netscape mass marketed the first web browser),[26] Bill Gates and Steve Jobs.

There are drawbacks: "The most successful narcissistic business leaders aren't interested in talking to their employees because they're not interested in talking to *anyone*. There's not a lot of gray in the narcissistic world—you are either a friend or a foe, either for the vision or against it." For the narcissist, it is my way or the highway. You have to drink the Kool-aid.

The Productive Narcissist

Being a stand-alone narcissistic personality type can be a detriment in business. The overweening ego, the lack of empathy, retreats into insecurity and even paranoia can easily outweigh whatever positive attributes a narcissist brings to the table. So Dr. Maccoby makes a distinction. It is the *productive narcissist* who makes a great difference in businesses and makes the best type of CEO.

The attributes (good) a narcissist brings to a business leadership position:

- *Independence and risk taking*. These traits originate in a narcissist's willingness to take extraordinary risks to achieve their world view. As a byproduct, they do not follow trends or listen to what others may say. They are "not resisting, they're ignoring."
- *Passion*. "[T]hey go after their vision with an overabundance of energy and determination. Nothing seems to stand in their way." This constant and passionate devotion to their mission can be brutal on subordinates, advisers and colleagues, who must be available, by office phone, home phone, cell phone, email, and pager, starting at 7 am every day or, indeed, 24/7.
- *Charisma*. The charm they exhibit and the ability to recruit and hold others to their passion and their vision is essential for the productive narcissist CEO.
- *Perseverance*. Winston Churchill is Maccoby's paradigm. Churchill's finest hours came after the massive retreat at Dunkirk, during the Battle for Britain in England's skies. "It's how a person reacts to failure that differentiates the productive narcissist from the unproductive one. . . . Productive narcissists retain the ability to ignore any and all obstacles."[27]

The attributes (bad) a narcissist also brings:

- *Not listening and over-sensitivity to criticism*. Narcissists tend to be "hard of hearing" when it comes to criticism. "When Henry Ford started to lose market share in the mid-1920s, he refused to listen to his staff. [AT&T CEO] Mike Armstrong didn't let a VP finish a sentence, much less listen; he knew everything, Jurgen Schremp [at Daimler-Chrysler] boasted . . . 'the operational issues have nothing to do with what I term the absolutely perfect strategy [which I devised].' "[28]
- *Anger and put downs*. The narcissist has an urge to get things done. She thus deals harshly with subordinates whom she perceives as underperforming. She is known "for outbursts and eruptions." The narcissist's impatience and aggression are always just below the surface. Microsoft

employees tell tale after tale of Bill Gates's rude, even sadistic treatment of coworkers.[29] Apple Computer workers tell similar tales of Steve Jobs.

- *Over-competitiveness and over-control.* At its worse, this attribute can lead a narcissistic leader to surround herself with "yes men." Narcissists have to overcome an inherent distrust of lieutenants who disagree with them.

- *Exaggeration and lying.* Narcissists tend to ignore any obstacle that may stand in the way of accomplishment of their vision. They may treat the vision as though it already has become a reality. According to Maccoby, this accounts for vaporware in high-tech fields: narcissistic CEOs claim to have products that do not exist and may never materialize. Exaggeration can lead to lying and "cooking the books" to manipulate revenue and make costs appear lower than they really are, as Chainsaw Al Dunlap did at Sunbeam or Bernie Ebbers at WorldCom.[30]

- *Grandiosity.* At the extreme, the unchecked narcissistic CEO "feel themselves entitled to live in the grand manner. They build palaces and buy yachts. They begin to put themselves before the interests of the company, expanding their empires."[31] Dennis Kozlowski used corporate funds to buy Renoir paintings and a $6,000 shower curtain for his Central Park West apartment, and to travel to Sardinia to host a multi-million dollar birthday party for his wife. At Adelphia Communications, the Rigas's bought a National Hockey League team and built a championship golf course adjacent to their mansions. Their success at the company is "intoxicating. [They] start to think. 'Yeah, I can do anything.' "

Strategic Intelligence

What separates the productive narcissist from the malignant one, and tends to damp down the negative attributes outlined above, is what Dr. Maccoby terms "strategic intelligence." Several years ago Daniel Goleman's business leadership book, *Emotional Intelligence*, became a best seller.[32] Goleman exhorted business leaders to demonstrate such qualities as empathy, sensitivity to others' feelings, and understanding of one's own emotions. To succeed as leaders, managers should be self-aware, in control of their impatience, anger, and other base emotions. Maccoby trashes all of this.

The best leaders are just the opposite: "Productive narcissists . . . are insensitive to feelings and have almost no awareness of how their emotional outbursts affect people." "The model of an empathetic, understanding humble leader is not necessarily suited to head up [a company in] a competitive change oriented industry."[33]

The productive narcissist who makes the best corporate CEO exhibits five traits, in nearly equal parts. These traits elevate her among co-workers and fellow managers:

1. *Foresight.* "A strategist anticipates how current movements, ideas, forces, will play out in the future, driving changes in technology, global

markets, competitors, customer needs and values."[34] Bill Gates became the chief architect of strategy, leaving management to COO Steve Ballmer. Often extrapolation masquerades as foresight. If a CEO takes the dot.com business method from, say, the sale of financial products, replicating in the sale of steel or of widgets, she has moved the company further onto the information highway and made inroads into the world of B to B and B to C commerce. But it is extrapolation, re-applying an existing idea, rather than evolving new methods or techniques themselves.

2. *Systems thinking.* The ability to visualize and direct the weaving together of various strands, some seemingly disparate, into a coordinated whole is an ability many otherwise competent managers lack. The person with strategic intelligence can visualize not only how systems may combine but also how the whole will be greater than the sum of the parts.

3. *Visioning.* The latter ability, combining foresight and systems thinking into a holistic vision, is visioning. When Jack Welch became CEO of General Electric, he could have regarded GE as a light bulb and white goods (appliances) company. Instead, he envisioned the "boundaryless organization" in which both formerly separate businesses and new endeavors all fed into a well-oiled, holistic enterprise.[35]

4. *Motivating.* As CEO, the productive narcissist must demonstrate "an ability to get people—a social system—to embrace and implement your system."[36] This real-world skill (the previous three are abstract) is often lacking. AT&T CEO Michael Armstrong "has never taken the problem of creating a corporate culture seriously: management does not cooperate with him, nor is it motivated towards his goal. . . . He is known for delegating problem tasks and barking out orders . . . [offering] little in the way of incentive or motivation to implement his massive reorganization. He does not persuade: he blames."[37] Maccoby singles out James Wolfensohn, World Bank 1995–2005, as another narcissist CEO who lacked this essential ingredient:

> [W]olfensohn is not a leader who can make it happen. [He has] many of the strengths—especially vision, passion, and energy—but also all of the weaknesses . . . He's capable of uncontrolled rages, ranting and raving at his managers and blaming them for his mistakes, taking everything personally [and] overreacting to criticism . . . Wolfensohn is 'quick to rebuke and humiliate managers, often in open meetings' and 'He does not welcome criticism or tolerate dissent.' "[38]

By contrast, CEOs Jack Welch at General Electric and Herb Kelleher at Southwest Airlines had superior motivating skills. They were both able to win over entire organizations to implement overarching business plans and grand pronouncements.

5. *Partnering.* "Someone with emotional intelligence makes friends; a person with strategic intelligence makes allies." Every productive narcissist who

has headed a major business organization has had an obsessive personality to attend to details and to back her up, often as second-in-command. Bill Gates has had a COO, now CEO, Steve Ballmer at Microsoft. Andy Grove headed Intel while Craig Barrett served below him. Larry Ellison, CEO and emperor at Oracle, had Roy Lane in the background. Herb Kelleher was assisted by Colleen Barrett at Southwest Airlines. Even Bernie Ebbers at WorldCom had CFO Scott Sullivan, and Ken Lay at Enron had Jeffery Skilling. The single exception was Carleton Fiorina (Chapter 2), the only woman CEO who could be termed a productive narcissist. She did not have an obsessive number two. Her refusal to have a number two at all, obsessive or otherwise, led to numerous failures to execute on business plans which, in turn, led the board of directors to demand that she hire a chief operating officer (COO) and to fire her when she refused.

Women as Productive Narcissists

Of the 21 women CEOs this book profiles, only one, Carleton Fiorina, seems to come close to being Michael Maccoby's productive narcissist. Jill Barad at Mattel was an obsessive, whose obsession with Barbie, the doll, got her to the CEO suite. Most women CEOs tend to be what author Jim Collins (Chapter 17) labels "the plowhorse," the antithesis of the productive narcissist.

Carleton Fiorina reached the apogee of grandiosity as her Gulfstream jet whisked her around the world. She demonstrated foresight, systems thinking, and visioning as she re-organized Hewlett-Packard from 83 to four departments. She began to fall down on motivating. She never was able to win over HP engineers and other employees in Oregon and Idaho, who never did accept her vision, including the notion of a grand merger with Compaq Computer. Her resistance to partnering gave an unhappy board of directors the pretext to remove her from office. But her penchant for surrounding herself with absolutely loyal young staff, who did drink the Kool-aid, is reminiscent of a narcissist.

Throughout his book, Michael Maccoby is relentlessly sexist. All pronouns are male ("he," "him," never "she," "her"). "Fathers' " (not mothers') visions loom large. "Helms*men*," "chair*men*," COO "him[s]" populate his pages. Productive narcissists, all men, have strong mother figures. Maccoby never set out purposely to exclude women from his discussion of the productive narcissist. It just happened, which may be the real lesson.

Is it highly likely that few women in business will often rise to the top because so few are productive narcissists? Is it that productive narcissists are born, and not made, and that accidents of birth or rearing in the formative years produces far fewer female than male productive narcissists? Is there another personality type or business literature which better describes women's progress in business and to what they might aspire?

17 Good-to-Great Companies and Plowhorse CEOs

No matter how dramatic the result, good-to-great transformations never happened in one fell swoop. There was no defining action, no grand program, no one killer innovation, no solitary lucky break . . . Good to great comes about by a cumulative process—step by step, action by action, decision by decision, turn by turn. . . . We expected good-to-great leaders would begin by setting a new vision and strategy [as the productive narcissist would]. We found instead that they *first* got the right people on the bus, got the wrong people off the bus, and the right people in the right seats—and *then* they figured out where to drive it. All great companies have a culture of discipline. When you have disciplined people, you don't need hierarchy.[1]

Jim Collins, *Good to Great: Why Some Companies Make the Leap and Others Don't* (2001)

Management theorists spew out CEO models:

- Celebrity CEO
- Change Agent
- Change Warrior
- Productive Narcissist
- Strategically Intelligent
- Empire Builder
- Political Astute
- Ms. Fix-It
- Salvage Artist
- Team Builder
- Coach
- Cheerleader
- Possessor of Emotional Intelligence.

Good-to-great folds the coach, team leader, cheerleader, and fix-it models into one, using the appellation "Plowhorse," and then touches again, briefly, on other models and lists of CEO specifications.

Good-to-great Companies

In 2001, author Jim Collins poured over research his team had done over previous years, publishing a best-selling book (still a business best seller almost a decade later) *Good to Great—Why Some Companies Make the Leap and Others Don't*. Copycat books, such as Keith R. McFarland's *The Breakthrough Company: How Every Day Companies Become Extraordinary*, also deal with how leadership style and corporate culture can make smaller companies excel.[2]

In Collins's research, he began with 1,500 publicly held companies, which his staff whittled down to good companies, and then to 11 "good-to-great" companies by application of various screens.[3] Overall, the metric used was that in the stock market these were the companies whose shares had outperformed the market by a factor of three for 15 consecutive years: "Great companies are easy to find but *good-to-great* companies are much more rare."[4] He listed the 11 companies: Abbott Laboratories, Circuit City, Fannie Mae, Gillette, Kimberly Clark, Kroger, Nucor, Phillip Morris, Pitney Bowes, Walgreens, and Wells Fargo.[5] His staff also selected comparison companies—firms with very similar businesses that had fared poorly over the same period (Silo to Circuit City, Bethlehem Steel to Nucor, Addressograph to Pitney Bowes).

For example, Pitney Bowes and Addressograph were equals in 1973 when the government ended the monopoly on postage meters: "[T]hey had similar revenues, profits, numbers of employees, and stock charts." Addressograph then bought in as CEO Roy Ash, who had earlier built the conglomerate Litton Industries. As of the time Collins wrote, 2000, Pitney Bowes had over $4 billion in revenue and 30,000 employees while Addressograph had faded, dramatically, with revenues of less than $100 million and fewer than 700 employees.[6]

The mention of Roy Ash (a productive narcissist) gives a hint of what Collins analyzed. What kind of CEO makeup, or makeups, make companies go from good to great? As a corollary, what are some CEO attributes which might leave a company (the comparison companies) standing still over the same period of time?[7]

Good-to-great CEOs

Below are some of Collins's conclusions:

- "Larger-than-life celebrity leaders who ride in from the outside are *negatively* correlated with taking a company from good to great."[8] Yet, as Chapter 11 demonstrates, public companies not only continue to revel in external CEO searches but they also continue to quest for "corporate saviors," and change agents oozing with "charisma"—an essentially undefinable quality.[9]
- "The good-to-great companies did not focus on what to *do* to become great; they focused on what *not* to do and what to *stop* doing."[10] By

contrast, advocates for celebrity CEOs, change agents, or productive narcissists focus largely on CEOs with ideas for new initiatives, vision, and "strategic intelligence," which will lead to new products, new business plans, and new personnel.[11]

- "Mergers and acquisitions play virtually no role in igniting a transformation from good to great."[12] Among women CEOs, Carleton Fiorina at Hewlett-Packard staked her career on an acquisition (of Compaq Computer). Mary Sammons at Rite Aid (the Brooks-Eckerd chain), Jill Barad at Mattel (Computer Leaning), and Pat Russo at Lucent ("merger of equals" with Alcatel) have "bet the farm" on a major combination or acquisition. By contrast, with one notable exception (Skype, an internet calling firm), Meg Whitman has been successful in building eBay through acquisitions.[13]

- "Greatness is not a function of circumstance. Greatness, it turns out, is largely a matter of conscious choice."[14] On this point, all management theorists agree, including those who ballyhoo the change agent and the productive narcissist. The will to achieve, both for one's self and for the organization simultaneously, cannot be overstated.

The Progression

Of particular interest to a woman who aspires to rise in business is the question of how to get there. From his research, Collins identifies five stages through which managers, men and women, pass in their progression at good-to-great companies.[15]

At entry, the future business leader should have attributes Collins labels as "Level 1, Highly Capable Individual." These are "talent, knowledge, skills, and work habits." A motivated person with an MBA would certainly possess these attributes, as would a number of other persons from other backgrounds.

"Level 2, Contributing Team Member" sounds very much like an erstwhile manager on the cusp of her first promotion. Her superiors find that she "contributes individual capabilities" she possesses "to the achievement of team objectives and works effectively with others."

Moving well into middle management, Collins's hypothetical manager assumes control of a large work center, an important corporate function, or an entire plant or facility. She has reached "Level 3, Competent Manager." She "organizes people and resources toward the effective and efficient pursuit of predetermined objectives." She may or may not have participated in the formulation of those objectives. In common parlance, she "makes her numbers," or in the rare cases in which her group does not reach objectives, she has a very good reason why that is so and a plan to remedy the situation.

"The Effective Leader [Level 4]" might command an entire subsidiary or division. She "catalyzes [subordinates'] commitment to and vigorous pursuit of a clear and compelling vision," for the subsidiary and perhaps for the whole company, which "stimulat[es] higher performance standards."

Finally, after a decade or more, a rising manager may become CEO material. Only these persons, whom Collins terms "Level 5 leaders," have the potential to become leaders of corporations capable of making the good-to-great transformation. They "build enduring greatness through a paradoxical blend of humility and professional will." Noticeably absent from the description are the terms executive search firms and board of director CEO search committees use: "charisma," "change agent," and "star power."

CEO Material

Collins describes at length what he found in Level 5 leaders. One size, apparently, does fit all: "All the good-to-great executives were cut from the same cloth. It didn't matter whether the company was consumer or industrial, in crisis or steady state, offered services or products. It didn't matter . . . how big the company. All the good-to-great companies had Level 5 leadership."[16]

In contrast to Dr. Michael Maccoby, and his heavy reliance on the narcissist model, Collins weighs in heavily on the modesty and humility side" "[G]ood-to-great leaders don't talk about themselves. During interviews . . . they would talk about the company and the contributions of other executives." Level 5 CEOs say "I hope I'm not sounding like a big shot," "I don't think that I can take much of the credit," or "There are plenty of people in the company who could do a better job than I do." In direct contrast to narcissist CEOs, good-to-great company CEOs "never aspired to be put on a pedestal."[17] In fact, "[a] trait of Level 5 leaders [is] ambition first and foremost for their companies . . . [T]heir ambition is first and foremost for the institution and not themselves."[18] Collins use as examples CEOs Coleman Mockler at Gillette, David Maxwell at Fannie Mae, and Darwin Smith at Kimberly Clark Co.

He goes into great detail with counter examples, concluding that "[i]n over two-thirds of the comparison cases [companies that fared poorly], we noted the presence of a gargantuan personal ego," or, in other words, a narcissist.[19] While posing as the CEO who rescued Chrysler in the 1980s, Lee Iacocca wrote a widely publicized autobiography, appeared live on national television, and talked openly of running for president.[20] "Running Chrysler has been a bigger job than running the country," CEO Iacocca said with a straight face.[21]

CEO Al Dunlap reveled in nicknames such as Rambo in Pinstripes, Mean Al, and Chainsaw Al, which daily press coverage bestowed upon him. He was another who fitted the narcissist model. Dunlap set impossible high sales and earnings targets for subordinates, summarily firing them when they failed, no matter what the explanation. At Scott Paper, Dunlap slashed the workforce, cut the R&D budget in half, and put the company on growth steroids in preparation for sale. He earned $100 million for 603 days of work but put 11,200 people, 34 percent of Scott's employees, out of work.[22] Only later, in egomaniacal stint as CEO of Sunbeam, did the press finally discover that his bluster was a front for accounting manipulation, including widespread improper revenue recognition, and the resulting fraud.[23]

Collins uses as an illustration of the narcissist as CEO, Stanley Gault, who became CEO of Rubbermaid, at the time one of America's ten most admired companies. Gault was a hard driving, egotistical executive who left behind him a company which quickly slipped and was forced to enter a merger with Newell merely to survive. Did Rubbermaid's failure only after Gault had left prove his worth while he was there? Not according to Collins: it proves that Gault was a "tremendous Level 4 leader but not a Level 5 leader."[24]

Level 5 Leadership

The raw material necessary for the achievement of Level 5 leadership includes ability for self-reflection, a pattern of personal development, a mentor, great teachers [for women including formal education and advanced degrees, see *infra*], significant real-life experience, and a Level 5 boss in their past.

- "Level 5 leaders display a compelling modesty, [and] are self-effacing and understated."
- "Level 5 leaders display a workman-like diligence—more plowhorse than showhorse."
- "One of the most damaging trends in recent history is the tendency [by boards and board committees] to select dazzling, celebrity leaders and to de-select Level 5 leaders."[25]

The Hedgehog Concept and the Kiss Principle

"Foxes pursue many ends at the same time and see the world in all its complexity. . . . Hedgehogs . . . simplify the world into a single organizing thing, a basic principle or concept that unifies and guides everything."[26] Collins labels this the hedgehog concept. Good leaders build their organization around one.

Warren Buffett, termed by many as the world's most successful investor, is a subscriber. He tries to stick with what he understands, and let his abilities, not his ego, determine what he attempts.[27] So wrote Warren Buffett when he caused Berkshire Hathaway to make an initial $20 million in Wells Fargo, despite serious reservations about the banking industry overall.[28]

Internally, a CEO might keep the product list short and ensure that every employee in the organization knows and can discuss with customers the details of each product. By contrast, one recent study found the opposite of the hedgehog keep-it-simple cultures: in all of the organizations studied, senior managers were unable to name "their companies' five biggest customers, five biggest competitors, five top products or services in revenues."[29] Collins illustrates the hedgehog concept by drawing three overlapping circles: *circle one* is what you can be the best in the world at; *circle two* is what drives the organization's economic engine; and *circle three* is what you as a potential CEO are deeply passionate about. The hedgehog concept will be in the triangle formed by the three circles as they overlap.

"The hedgehog concept is not necessarily the same as a core competence. You can have competence at something but not necessarily the potential to be the best in the world at it." Similarly, you can have competence in a line or calling but not be passionate about it.

Great leaders build a culture of discipline. A great portion of the discipline necessary is for subordinate leaders and other managers to stick with the hedgehog concept. They have to construct, and periodically revise, a "stop doing" as well as a "to do" list. Another description for, or a corollary to, the culture of discipline is the well-known KISS principle, as in "Keep It Simple Stupid."

The opposite, what not to do, is to replace an egalitarian, "flat" organizational chart with hierarchy. "Chains of command appear. Reporting relationships [arise] . . . an executive class with special perks begins to appear. 'We' and 'They' segmentations appear . . . [P]rofessional managers . . . create order out of chaos but they also kill the entrepreneurial spirit" that got the organization going in the first place.[30]

Why do many managers do what they do? They "build their bureaucratic rules to manage the small percentage of wrong people on the bus, which in turn drives away the right people [for] the bus, which in turn increases the number of wrong people on the bus."[31] A culture of discipline begins with disciplined people. The transition from a good to a great company begins not by trying to discipline the wrong people into the right behaviors but by getting self-disciplined people in the first place. The organizational choice highlights the personal necessity of an aspiring woman manager to appear controlled and disciplined, not shooting from the hip.

Examples of the wrong direction include Patricia Dunn at Hewlett-Packard, who invested her efforts in compliance with the then new Sarbanes–Oxley Act and plugging inconsequential boardroom leaks, rather than encouraging the technological innovation (what you can be best in the world at, what drives your economic engine) and engaging in the strategic planning that made Hewlett-Packard great.[32] Another example of a business leader who lacked discipline, or who had the wrong kind, is Lee Iacocca, who actually discussed taking Chrysler into the aerospace business, as well as running for president. From an organizational standpoint, excessive hierarchy and perks played a part in dooming Bethlehem Steel. Bethlehem had a fleet of corporate aircraft, which were used to take executives' children to prep school, executive dining rooms, corporate financed country club memberships, and a hilltop corporate lair.[33] By contrast, Nucor, a good-to-great company, locates steel mills in farm towns, where it can recruit a capable and disciplined workforce (farmers), keeps bureaucracy to a minimum, has a flat organizational structure, and allows no perks to speak of for its managers.[34]

"The good-to-great companies at their best followed a simple mantra: *Anything that does not fit within our hedgehog concept, we will not do.* We will not launch unrelated businesses. We will not make unrelated acquisitions. We will not do unrelated joint ventures. It if doesn't fit, we don't do it. Period."[35]

The Flywheel

Once a company on the move has gotten the right people on the bus, and once its leaders have centered on their hedgehog concept, greatness does not immediately follow. It builds, slowly at first and only over time. Collins's metaphor for this process is a flywheel, with which he assumes his readers have familiarity (but many readers do not).

A flywheel is a large wheel with weights on the circumference. When drivers (a diesel or electric motor, water power) cause the wheel to turn, because of the weights, the wheel turns slowly. It is heavy as well as large. As it gathers speed, however, it runs faster and faster, as the weights and centrifugal forces magnify the force applied to the center of the wheel and accelerate its revolution.

An organization headed for greatness is like a flywheel. Nucor Steel, founded in 1978, was in business for 14 years before the first story about it appeared in *Business Week* and for 16 years before a story appeared in *Fortune*. Afterwards, however, came 96 major periodical pieces about Nucor, 40 of them major profiles of the company and its business method.[36] Once the company's ascent achieved a certain pace, turning more and more rapidly like a flywheel, Nucor shares became Wall Street darlings. Its organization and management methods became the subject of strategy courses in every business school.

A Digression

The flywheel concept is about companies, though, not about managers and not about women managers, at least not in any obvious way. So discussion of Collins's flywheel concept is a digression. There are lessons for individual development to be learned about being controlled and disciplined. A less obvious lesson is that the transition from good to great usually is a long one for leaders as well as for organizations.

It is a continuum. It takes 20 or more years to get the flywheel up to speed, that is, to build a great company. Sam Walton stuck to his hedgehog concept ("stack it high and sell it cheap") in building Walmart over 25 years. Dave Packard and Bill Hewlett did the same at Hewlett-Packard ("manage and encourage innovation by walking around"). A plowhorse manager needs to know that she is not going to get it done, either for herself or for the organization, in one to two jobs alone, on just one watch, or even on the next one, or the one after that. She has to have core values, and stick to them. She has to put the organization first. She has to be patient as the flywheel starts to turn.

18 The Plowhorse Versus the Showhorse

> The CEO as an American icon [the celebrity CEO] is a cyclical thing. It was up in the 1920s—think Henry Ford and Alfred P. Sloan—down in the 50s and way up again in the 90s. Now the cycle seems to be on its way down again . . . "This is a tenuous time for CEOs—big risks, big bets to make and a lot to lose and you really have to pay attention to what you're doing every minute of the day."
>
> Ellen Pollack, "Twilight of the Gods: CEO as an American Icon Slips Into a Down Cycle" (1999)

> [W]e sell short any company whose CEO appears in Town & Country.[1]
>
> Unidentified Mutual Fund Manager, idem.

Bill Gates at Microsoft, Sanford Weill at Citigroup, Gerald Levin at Time Warner, Lee Iacocca at Chrysler, Jeff Bezos at Amazon, Larry Ellison at Oracle, Steve Jobs at Apple, Jack Welsh at General Electric, Michael Eisner at Walt Disney, and Carleton Fiorina at Hewlett-Packard exemplified the celebrity CEO. Prominent magazines' covers pictured them; television programs featured them; their accomplishments, their movements and their comments appeared in daily newspapers. *Architecture Digest* took us into their homes. Celebrity CEOs were as big at the box office as movie stars and professional athletes.

During the bear market of 2000–2002, "a newer cadre moved in: the Fix-it *Men* . . . lower key leaders like Charles O. Prince at Citigroup and Richard D. Parsons at Time-Warner, whose job it was to repair the excesses and mistakes of their predecessors."[2] Fix-it *women* included Pat Russo at Lucent, Ann Mulcahy at Xerox, Susan Ivey at Reynolds America, Mary Sammons at Rite Aid, and Brenda Barnes at Sara Lee Corp.[3] Women CEOs, although few in number, better exemplified the fix-it breed and its most salient characteristics than did the men. Later still, the edifices that certain celebrity CEOs had built crumbled, including Citicorp under Sandford Weill and General Electric under Jack Welsh.

Just as the average tenure of a CEO has gone from ten to four years,[4] the life of the CEO model in vogue has decreased from a decade or so to a few years as well: "[T]he current environment demands, and is attracting, yet another kind of chief executive: the team builder."[5] The team builder insures that the top 100 people in their organization know that they are all in this together and that their fates are connected. Management gurus hold up A.G. Lafley at Proctor & Gamble and W. James McNerney Jr. at Boeing as examples: "[T]hey possess the vision of the empire builders without their overpowering egos."

A recent iteration of the team builder CEO "views himself more as coach and cheerleader," "focusing on the proper way to treat people and the rewards that can come from doing so intelligently."[6] A popular business best seller espouses the mode: "[M]otivate with praise, 'You can never underestimate the power of telling someone he's doing a good job.'" "Always be on the lookout for reasons to celebrate the achievements of others." Be "ever vigilant to other people's point of view," writes Yum Brands CEO David Novack.[7]

During their tenure, the Mr. Fix-its were still in the shadow of the celebrity, empire building CEOs they followed. The Fix-its were not able to build their own teams. According to the management experts, the follow-on CEOs, the current crop, are able to do so. But the current crop (coaches, team builders, cheerleaders), the Mr. Fix-its before them, and, most importantly, the enduring crop who have lasted through two, three, or four CEO fads, may all be what Jim Collins labels "plowhorse CEOs" in the best selling *Good to Great*. The celebrity CEO, the change agent with "vision" and "charisma," the empire builder, all appellations for the same CEO model, one that re-appears through time, is Collins's "showhorse," Michael Maccoby's "productive narcissist."

Resurgence of the Productive Narcissist CEO?

Michael Maccoby sees the stage set for the return of the celebrity CEO, just as the stage had been set for the rise of the Mr. Fix-it and the team builder: "The lack of understanding of narcissistic CEOs . . . led to a backlash, a pendulum swing to the conservative, value-based bottom-line CEOs, the ones who are suited to their companies but cannot lead in innovative or change-based industries."[8]

The background for the 1990s rise of the narcissistic CEO was the tech revolution and the transition from the old to the new economy, including to the new economy CEO (Bill Gates, Larry Ellison, Jim Clark, Jeff Bezos, Steve Jobs). Old economy companies such as Westinghouse disappeared altogether while newer entities (Microsoft, Intel, Cisco, Oracle) blossomed overnight. It seems very difficult to predict that a sea change similar to the tech revolution will come again, so soon into the twenty-first-century. But Maccoby makes that prediction: "Contrary to proclamations in the business pages that there is an end to arrogance [and] a return to the self-effacing humbler CEOs . . . productive narcissists seem to be all around us."[9] While Maccoby premises part of this resurgence on the enduring qualities and necessity for productive narcissists as CEOs, he premises another part on the ineptitude, or lack of suitability, which inheres in the plowhorse.

The Case Against the Plowhorse CEO Model

"Jack Welsh has few of the traits that Collins attributes to 'great' company CEOs." He is "arrogant," has lots of "aggressiveness," "overreacts to criticism," and is not seen as a "company man."[10] In fact, author Maccoby heavily criticizes the formulas for effective leadership in the business literature today, with special excoriation reserved for Jim Collins and his plowhorse model.

"[In *Good to Great*], Collins asked: What do great companies have in common? [T]he most crucial and provocative thread [Collins and his researchers identify] is what they call 'Level 5 Leadership.' The Level 5 leaders, Collins claims, are not celebrity CEOs, larger than life personalities . . . instead, they are *'quiet, humble, modest, reserved, shy, gracious, mild-mannered, self-effacing, understated.' "*[11] Collins's ideal leaders are diametrically opposed to Maccoby's productive narcissists.

"[T]he model of an empathetic, understanding, humble leader is not suited to head up [a company in] a competitive, change oriented industry."[12] Who is? Maccoby's narcissist, or at least one with strategic intelligence (foresight, systems thinking, visioning, motivating and partnering).

Then it gets personal. Somewhat anecdotally, Maccoby presents Bill Gates and Jack Welsh as successful CEOs who score highly on all five elements of strategic intelligence and as successful productive narcissists. It is Collins, however, whom Maccoby accuses of being anecdotal. Moreover, "Collins has a clear ideological agenda."[13]

The evidence is the opposite. Collins describes in detail how his researchers culled the good-to-great companies from a large sample. They applied various screens, neutrally, to shift through 1,500 companies to come up with 11 which met their criteria. There is no evidence of anything anecdotal, let alone "ideological," about it.

The Plowhorse Case

"Many of the comparison companies," companies which Collins singled out as moving from good to oblivion while the select 11 moved from good to great, "followed a genius with a thousand helpers model. In this model, the company is a platform for the talents of [one] extraordinary individual," who fits Maccoby's productive narcissist specification to a "t." "[A principal difficulty is that] when the genius leaves, the helpers are often lost. Or, worse, they try to mimic their predecessor."[14] That is certainly true at many of Maccoby's narcissistic CEOs. Jeffrey Immelt took over from Jack Welch and GE's financial and stock market performance have been on a downward arc ever since. Steve Ballmer succeeded Bill Gates; Microsoft's stock market performance has been worse than lackluster ever since, now going on a half dozen years.

The plowhorse concentrates on getting the "right people on the bus" while the showhorse concentrates on himself and his "vision." The showhorse does not altogether neglect important personnel considerations but leaves them to his chief subordinate whom he will have "partnered" with, another key ingredient in strategic intelligence. Both schools of leadership recognize that "[n]o company can grow revenues consistently faster than its ability to get enough of the right people"[15] but the showhorse school accords such a task a much lower priority than the plowhorse one does.

Obtaining the best people pays dividends: "The best people don't need to be managed. Guided, taught, yes. But not tightly managed."[16] In fact, if an aspiring manager feels that her bosses attempt too tightly to govern her and her peer group, it may be time for her to think of moving on to greener pastures.

Another benefit of plowhorse priorities is that visions, objectives and goals can emanate from dozens of sources, and they will, because of the emphasis on the quality of people hired and promoted and the freedom given them. By contrast, the productive narcissist regards himself as the only source from which visions can come. When an idea, an ideal, or a new business plan comes from elsewhere, the showhorse will plagiarize it, making it his own.

Another feature that Collins observed in the good-to-great companies is that "they made a habit of putting their best people on their best opportunities, not their biggest problems. The comparison companies had a penchant for doing just the opposite, failing to grasp that managing your problems can only make you good, while building opportunities is the only way to become great."[17] The danger with the productive narcissist is that he will put himself on the best opportunities, leaving those he regards as inferiors to wrestle with more intractable issues, their morale be damned.

"The moment a leader allows himself to become the primary reality people worry about," which the narcissist leader will do, "rather than reality being the primary reality, you have a recipe for mediocrity. This is one of the key reasons why less charismatic leaders produce better long term results."[18] Don't companies need a "compelling vision" to supply motivation and make their managers and workers take the company toward greatness? "The answer, surprisingly, is 'no.' Not because vision is not important but because trying to motivate people [another key element of the Maccoby strategic intelligence formula] is a waste of time . . . If you have the right people on the bus, they will be self-motivated."[19]

Confronting real-world reality seems to have helped forge good companies into great ones. Kimberly Clark faced the reality that Proctor & Gamble, the 800-pound gorilla, was entering the consumer paper products business. Gillette faced a series of attempted hostile takeovers. Nucor and its mini mills faced imports of German and then Korean steel. Pitney Bowes faced the loss of its government-granted monopoly on postage meters. Abbott Laboratories faced numerous product recalls and Kroger confronted the need to replace 100 percent of its existing supermarkets. "In every case, the management team responded with a powerful management duality. On the one hand, they stoically accepted the brutal facts of reality. On the other hand, they maintained an unwavering faith in the endgame, and a commitment to prevail as a great company despite the brutal facts."[20]

Plowhorse or Showhorse? How to Advance a Career

Of course, the alternatives may not always be mutually exclusive, even though the choice seems a binary one. For example, new CEO paradigms which overlap both alternatives emerge. University of Chicago business school professors studied 313 CEO candidates, 225 of whom became CEOs of public companies, evolving the "tough CEO" model. They found that the five traits most closely associated with CEO success were "persistence, attention to detail, efficiency, analytical skill, and setting high standards," a bit show-horse and a bit plowhorse. The five traits on their menu with the lowest correlation to CEO success were "strong oral communication, teamwork, flexibility, enthusiasm, and listening skills," most closely associated with Collins's plowhorse model.[21] Yet the peers of the woman manager who attempts to adhere to the "tough CEO" model will accuse her of "shoulder pad feminism," or worse.[22] The tough CEO model does not seem promising for many women.

Moreover, there is no correct choice, among plowhorse, showhorse, or some other model, which does not neatly fit in one of the broader categories. It may well be that the showhorse model better suits the innovative, technology-oriented company while the plowhorse specification better suits companies that replicate the same or similar products or services thousands or, indeed, millions of times.

Yet the plowhorse model comes from observation of companies which Collins's team selected only after close empirical scrutiny. The 11 corporations Collins screened out had outperformed 1,500 other companies over 15 years. They did so where it counts the most, in the share markets. And, most convincingly, they all had the same types of leadership for all of that period. It is not serendipitous, or coincidental, or the product of ideology.

It is instead the productive narcissist argument which relies on anecdotal observations, rather than empirical research, recounted from the author's personal observation, albeit with a trained eye. None of the companies productive narcissists have led, however, have achieved enduring greatness. None made the final list in Collins's carefully crafted elimination process. Microsoft, General Electric, Citicorp, Oracle, and other companies Maccoby featured reached high heights for periods of time, to be sure, but all declined or plateaued, and pronouncedly so, eventually.

From a woman's personal perspective, it may be that the plowhorse model is the better one to emulate because it is the model women are more capable of emulating. The evidence is that of the 21 women CEOs this book portrays only one arguably fits the showhorse (productive narcissist) model. The rest answer to the call of team builder, cheerleader, coach, or plowhorse.

Then too it perhaps is that narcissists, including productive ones, are born and not made. It would not avail any manager, man or woman, to attempt to remake themselves in the productive narcissist mode. At least in this respect, you are what you are; nature rather than nurture controls. But that's a question for a psychologist, not for a corporate governance expert.

19 Education, Mentoring, and Networking

Of the Elite Eight [women CEOs 2004], only three—Carly Fiorina, Susan Ivey, and Meg Whitman—have an MBA. . . . Andrea Jung studied English literature; Anne Mulcahy studied math and journalism; Pat Russo studied political science; and Mary Sammons majored in French.[1]

Professor Jayne Barnard, "At the Top of the Pyramid: Lessons from the Alpha Woman and the Elite Eight" (2006)

Bill Gates, founder of Microsoft, dropped out after his sophomore year, albeit at Harvard College. Larry Ellison, CEO of Oracle, went to a large, impersonal state university (Illinois). Michael Capellas, CEO first at Compaq Computer and later at MCI, graduated from Kent State, a regional school. Paul O'Neill, CEO of Alcoa and Secretary of the Treasury in the Bush administration, went part-time to Fresno State.[2]

To management theorists, where you went to school, what your major is, or how well you did are irrelevant. Psychologist Michael Maccoby finds "little correlation between long-term CEO success and the criteria that have been used . . . Take, for example, appointments based upon stellar resumes. Too often, corporate boards look to someone who has succeeded in the past."[3] To make his case, Maccoby continues: "When you take a look at success stories, the common thread is not emotional intelligence, IQ [or] proven track record . . . Instead, long term [CEO] success is measured by a set of interrelated skills that I call strategic intelligence."[4]

I find exactly the opposite of what Professor Barnard finds and Dr. Maccoby theorizes. For women who aspire to higher positions in business organizations, it is very different. *Education matters.* Of the 21 women CEOs in this book, all 21 were graduated from college or university. More than a few of these women attended elite colleges (Princeton (2), Wellesley (2), Stanford, Georgetown, Tufts, Cornell).

Ten of the 14 sitting women CEOs about whom we have information (TJX refuses to divulge information about Carol Meyrowitz) completed graduate school (nine MBAs, one JD), again many at elite universities (Northwestern NYU, MIT, Columbia, Yale, Harvard (2)). If we replace Anne Mulcahy with Ursula Burns, who succeeds Mulcahy on July 1, 2009, 11 of 14 women CEOs have graduate degrees (nine MBAs, one MS in mechanical engineering (Columbia), one JD). Two who obtained MBAs at regional universities have done well (Susan Ivey (Reynolds America) at Bellarmine in Louisville and Brenda Barnes (Sara Lee Corp.) at Loyola in Chicago).

Currently, applications to graduate schools of business are flat, or declining. Experts attribute the statistics to commonly held perceptions that an MBA does not lead to rapid promotions the way it once did. Whatever truth the proposition might have for males, the female CEO career tracks this book profiles contradict completely the truth of any such proposition for women. Education matters—an MBA from a reputable school of business matters most.

Overall, 13 of 20 female CEOs (again excluding Meyrowitz) have graduate degrees (12 MBAs, one JD). Again substituting Burns for Mulcahy, over two-thirds (14 of 20) have graduate degrees. Two (Nooyi with two MBAs, Rosenfeld with an MBA and a PhD) have multiple graduate degrees.

The results of a CEO survey are clear, even given the sample's small size.[5] Education does matter, more for women than it does for men. The next question is, what kind of education?

Financial Literacy

Case studies such as those about Jill Barad as CEO at Mattel and Carleton Fiorina at Hewlett-Packard demonstrate that lack of knowledge and feel about how to make revenue and earnings projections, the way in which financial analysts operate, and the way in which markets react when a company does not "make its numbers" are fatal to a CEO, perhaps particularly a female CEO. In addition, prevalent seems to be an impression that what a woman should know about finance is different from what a man should know.

Currently popular is celebrity Suze Orman who specializes in finance for women.[6] Her centrality in media outlets (she seems to be on television every night) might mislead women into believing that what Susie Orman dispenses is sufficient, or is what I am talking about. It is not. Ms. Orman teaches about *personal* finance: how to shop for a mortgage, pension and 401(k) plans, choices available for investment, and so on. For a career in business, an aspiring woman needs additional knowledge, grouped loosely under the heading of *corporate* finance, the rudiments of which would be garnered in an MBA school through courses in corporate finance, stocks and commodities, managerial accounting, and corporate strategy.

The career patterns of women who have succeeded in business demonstrate the worth of an MBA degree, from quality regional schools or elite universities. In fact, 86 of the 200-plus accredited business schools in the United States have women deans.[7] MBA programs are user friendly for women.

Full-time attendance at an MBA school may not be a viable choice for those who have careers, families, or simply a need to put bread on the table. An alternative is the executive MBA program. An enrollee attends Friday and Saturday MBA classes every other weekend for two years. She usually has to arrive, many times in a distant city, on Thursday evening. She returns home on Sunday. Many schools have residential facilities, with dorm rooms, meals, and recreational facilities, for students. A student need not give up their day job in order to do an executive MBA program (that's the point of having such programs). Attendance does, however, still entail hardship, including separation from spouse, partner, or children, and surrender of free time over a long period (two years).[8]

College

Should women lament that they did not major in business as undergraduates? Should women who are younger rush to switch college majors or choose a business major in the first place? Resoundingly, no. First, most students are too young to make those choices when our university system requires students to make them. Second, a college major in history, art, philosophy, or any other of the liberal arts has great value in itself. It instills a sense of perspective and wider vision in a way few pursuits do. Those college majors also teach reading, writing, speaking, and other communication skills necessary for whatever the student eventually does. They inculcate in students a curiosity and a general knowledge quotient that make their lives richer by far, both inside their careers and outside their trade or calling as well. As has been seen, Andrea Jung (Avon) studied English literature; Anne Mulcahy (Xerox) studied math and journalism; Pat Russo (Lucent) studied political science; and both Mary Sammons (Rite Aid) and Laura Sen (BJ's Wholesale Clubs) majored in French.

Third, a student, man or woman, who stands a chance of a career in business, and many do, even though they may not be CEO aspirants, can take a few elective courses that would prepare them for that eventuality even as they major in one of the liberal arts (history, English, communications, theater). A course in managerial accounting would not deal with debits and credits but instead paint with a broad brush, familiarizing students with balance sheets, profit and loss statements, and cash flow analyses, teaching the student what those statements can tell and, more importantly, what they do not say. A corporate finance course introduces students to the manner and means whereby businesses raise money. Economics 101 and 102 will introduce students to the world of market forces (supply and demand). They will also supply perspective. Maybe a course in stock and commodities would be helpful. Even if they do not pursue a career in business, students will be investors one day.

That's about it. An undergraduate student, especially one whose major is not business, should not go off on a business tangent. A sampling of courses just named will equip her for a significant part of her life even if she never pursues a business career.[9]

Undoubtedly, some advisors and mentors will pooh-pooh the advice about education and its heightened importance for women. Any person, man or woman, who becomes CEO of a major business organization, has ample access to persons who can supply the accounting, finance or other background the CEO lacks. I would answer back that no substitute exists for having a good grounding (not necessarily encyclopedic knowledge or technical virtuosity). For proof, I would point to the experience of capable women CEOs Jill Barad and Carly Fiorina, who had first-rate marketing and sales expertise but whose lack of financial literacy more than other deficiency proved their undoing, despite access to the best and the brightest who could support them and provide what they lacked.[10]

Line Experience

Sitting on committees to recommend judicial candidates or law school dean finalists is similar to sitting on a corporate CEO search committee. One central question voiced in every search is similar to searches for CEO candidates: "Has she ever had to meet a payroll?" "I want someone who has had profit and loss responsibility."

The advice books for women in business, such as Sheila Wellington's, make the point:

> There's a big secret out there that a lot of women in the workforce aren't told: certain jobs, no matter how good they are, won't take you to the very top of most organizations. If you set your sights on the pinnacle . . . you must have some experience with the bottom line. That means a line job—one with profit and loss responsibility.[11]

The basic assertion is on balance correct but not completely so. It might be better stated as "*should* have line experience" rather than "*must*." Additionally, male chauvinists, who exist on many corporate search committees, will use an assertion so strongly stated to exclude meritorious candidates, many of them women.

Ann Mulcahy, arguably the most successful woman CEO portrayed in this book, who resurrected Xerox from near death, did not rise through the organization by means of a series of line jobs. She rose to vice-president-human resources before the Xerox board picked her as CEO. Jill Barad (Mattel) and Carleton Fiorina (Hewlett-Packard) spent their entire pre-CEO careers in marketing and sales. They never headed up a plant, work center, division, or subsidiary which actually produced and shipped the items or services which produced revenue. Brenda Barnes's career consisted, first, of marketing corn chips and, second, carbonated soft drinks at Frito Lay and then at its parent, PepsiCo. Susan Ivey marketed cigarettes. Angela Braly rose through a series of staff appointments. She went from general counsel to the corner suite.

Several points are in order. First, in many businesses, the marketing function may be as important as any line position, because sales and marketing are as important as production. That may be particularly true of endeavors in consumer products, such as snack foods, soft drinks, baked goods, other food products, toys, and tobacco products, or in service industries. Second, line experience is important in many corporations but it need not take the form of line experience leading right up to CEO candidacy, or a string of ever more weighty line positions (as, for example, in the case of Pat Woertz). An important line experience or two, somewhere in a career progression, should be sufficient, if other attributes are present. Third, the emphasis on making career choices should be not to abjure staff positions, concentrating solely on line jobs. The emphasis should be on avoidance of being trapped behind a "glass wall," especially in those staff positions thought most amenable to women executives (head of human resources, foundation chief of staff, legal counsel).[12] Overall, though, being a mid-ranking staff person in legal or finance at corporate headquarters may advance a career better than a COO position at a peripheral or distant subsidiary. The goal should not be line experience to the exclusion of all else.

Belief in Core Values

Fourth, there is one characteristic that all of these women CEOs share, save perhaps one. It is not line experience in their career progression but an abiding, steadfast belief in the company, its products, its services, and in its culture. Anne Mulcahy came from staff jobs and human resources but she was a Xerox person from the soles of her feet and she let people know it. In contrast, Carleton Fiorina, a very capable person, was openly dismissive of "the HP way," the company culture, and even its mix of products and services. Her lack of belief and confidence prevented her from ever getting traction in the CEO position, contributing to her downfall. All the other of these women who have made it to the CEO suite, while they might work to change this or that aspect of a company's culture, or shift its mix of products, overall came there (to the CEO suite) having demonstrated an abiding faith in the company, its culture, and its people. On their rises through the ranks, these women all proved themselves not only capable of but also proud and willing to represent the company anywhere, to anyone, in London, New York, Peoria, Salina, or Timbuktu.

In *Good to Great*, author Jim Collins finds:

> [T]here are no specific "right" core values for becoming an enduring great company [or the leader of one]. . . . A company need not have a passion for its customers (Sony didn't), or respect for the individual (Disney didn't), or quality (Wal-Mart didn't) . . . in order to become enduring and great. This was one of the most paradoxical findings from *Built to Last* [about Hewlett-Packard] . . . The point is not *what* core values you have, but that you have core values at all, that you know what they are, that you build them explicitly into your organization, and that you preserve them over time.

> The notion of preserving your core ideology is a central feature of great companies [and the persons who lead them].[13]

It is the capability of being able to build and preserve core values, while not necessarily being a cheerleader or a rah-rah person, rather than line experience, which seems to differentiate women who have become CEOs from other aspiring executives.

Children

> Of the Elite Eight [Women CEOs in Office in 2004], only three—Andrea Jung, Anne Mulcahy, and Meg Whitman—have children (each of them has two children).[14]

Nineteen of 21 women CEOs this book profiles, or 90.5 percent, have children. Several, such as Susan Ivey or Carleton Fiorina, are adoptive parents for children from spouses' earlier marriages, but they have served as parents nonetheless, at the same time serving as CEOs of major companies. Professor Barnard did not include them as parents in the study she conducted. The total number of children is 42, for 21 women, an average of two children per CEO.

Brenda Barnes (Sara Lee), Angel Braly (Wellpoint), Pat Woertz (Archer Daniels Midland), Ellen Kullman (DuPont) and Carol Bartz (Yahoo!), all of whom became CEOs after the Barnard study was complete, have three children each. These findings (90 percent plus, three children women CEOs) contradict all the studies of women in business generally, which purport to find that successful women do not have children, or have fewer children, or should limit themselves to one child.

Brenda Barnes, CEO of Sara Lee Corp., contradicted widespread thinking when she told an interviewer that rather than her children needing her, the shoe was on the other foot. In the hectic, swirling world of a modern-day CEO, she needs her children more than her children need her.[15] Having other persons who give you unconditional love, are dependent on you the way in which staff and other employees are not, and complete your person in a variety of social, school, and home settings, affords balance to a person whose life otherwise would be tilted completely toward business. It becomes apparent that having children and a home life may be more important again as one reaches the top.

The last thought on the subject is that women in business who want to have children might give thought to having them sooner rather than later. Frau Anne-Kathrin Deutrich, ex-CEO of SICK, a German public company, made the point to an audience in Frankfurt-Am-Main, Germany, discussing career choices for aspiring women.[16] The birth of children before a career begins in earnest allows for a smoother, relatively uninterrupted career progression afterwards. The evidence from women CEO profiles bears this out. Jill Barad (2 boys), Ann Mulcahy (2 boys), Marion Sandler (1 boy, 1 girl),

Angel Braly (2 boys, 1 girl), Pat Woertz (3 children), Brenda Barnes (2 boys, 1 girl), and Meg Whitman (2 boys), among others, had their children before they began their careers in earnest, or soon thereafter.

The profiles of women CEOs establishes for the first time that the received wisdom about children and business careers is wrong when it comes to women who have made it to the very top.

Mentoring

Prevalent in every career progression formula is finding and utilizing mentors. "Everyone Who Makes It Has a Mentor" was a title prominent in the 1978 *Harvard Business Review*.[17] Sheila Wellington, president of Catalyst, titled her 2002 book *Be Your Own Mentor*.[18]

Mentors can provide many things. They may advise on how to close a deal, handle a personnel problem, or put out a brush fire. They also can provide strategic advice: suggesting possible steps for a woman to reach her career goals, examining the political landscape within the company, and offering advice on how to deal with it.

Mentors are very much like stocks. A woman should have more than one, and preferably a diversified portfolio. She should have several peers who are confidantes as well as several seniors, both remote and near, with whom she can confer, as mentors. She should have mentors outside the company as well as within it, in the same or similar business and elsewhere. She might have mentors who are not in business at all but who have expertise to which she can turn with financial questions, personnel issues, engineering problems, or for sage advice overall, or for moral support.

Many times the capable mentor may be close at hand. "Good bosses make great mentors. Where it works, that's the best mentorship you can have," says Anne Mulcahy. Sheila Wellington distills her 30 years' experience at the beginning of her book:

> [T]he single most important reason why . . . equally talented men tend to rise higher than women is that most men have mentors and women do not. . . . Mentors are more important to career success than hard work . . . talent . . . [or] intelligence. Why? Because you need to learn how to operate in the work world and mentors teach you how. [T]hat translates into a person who can hook you up with the experiences and people you need to move ahead . . . Mentors can show you the ropes. And pull strings.[19]

Although the advice books are replete with lists of the uses mentors can have for women in business, none lists the drawbacks, save for perhaps the difficulty of finding other women to act as role models, especially because as one moves up in an organization women become scarce, much like trees as you approach the tree line on a mountain.

Three of mentoring's drawbacks are the encounter, by women especially, of the over protective mentor ("the office uncle" and "plastic bubble" phenomena), succumbing to the temptation to misuse mentor relationships to bypass hierarchy or the chain of command, and the meld of a pernicious star system with mentoring.

Mentors disappear. They transfer to another location or move to a competitor. They may be the victims of downsizing. Mentors can also be counterproductive when they become the father or uncle figure whose faults sociologist Rosabeth Kanter identifies:

> Many women object to the protectiveness that they perceived in their [mentors] that "encased" them "in a plastic bubble" . . . and rendered them ineffectual. Anyone who is protected loses power, for successes are attributed to the helpful actions of others, rather than the person's own actions. Women complained about the "people who want to move walls for me" instead of saying, "Here's a wall. Let's strategize working through it."[20]

Some mentors engage in "negative mentoring," advising women especially to move into human resources or staff positions which will shelter the occupants from sudden storms or political intrigues that may arise in line or other staff positions. They attempt to protect female colleagues much like fathers protect daughters. Women end up in staff positions that may not help their careers advance. They may become trapped by "glass walls" which constitute insurmountable barriers to getting back to where they might resume an upward career path.

Mentors, or sponsors, often provide "the occasion for lower level organization members to *bypass the hierarchy*: to get inside information, to short-circuit cumbersome procedures, or to cut red tape . . . [Mentor's presence] also provides an important signal to other people, a form of *'reflected power.'* " Proper use of a mentor may be an elusive thing, capable of abuse by certain mentees, "who must be careful about the way they use the reflected power of the sponsor." For example, Kanter warns, "You can't use it [reflected power] with your own manager or you get into trouble."[21] A "fast tracker," a "rising star," or a "42 long" should never use reflected or derived power to run roughshod over the chain of command. To use relationship with a mentor in that way may be fatal.

Mentoring or Star System?

What is to one person mentoring or sponsorship may be to another person a "star system." Or what began as productive mentoring system may evolve to be a pernicious star system. An aspiring woman manager should know the difference, remaining alert for changes such an evolution brings with it.

On a star system, stars of the first magnitude, those upper level managers in an organization within one or two reporting levels of the CEO, have two or three stars of a lesser magnitude whom they may mentor but whom they also champion. Merit may become less relevant. The young or lesser stars rise because they have become the favorites of the stars of greater magnitude.

What determines who become stars?

> Sponsorship is sometimes generated by good performance, but it can also come . . . "because you have the right social background or know some of the officers from outside the corporation or look good in a suit" [the 42 long]. . . . Boy wonders rise under certain power structures. They are recognized by a powerful person because they are very much like him. When women acquired sponsors, the reasons were often different . . . [O]fficers were looking for a high performing woman they could make into a showpiece to demonstrate the organization's openness to women.[22]

But, in such a system, and unlike in a true mentoring arrangement, the leading star may fall from the firmament, in which case the lesser star will fall further. The whims of the CEO, and those around him, determine who is in favor that week. The system resembles royal courts in eighteenth-century England or France.

From career standpoint, a star system in a corporation is a snake pit. Backstabbing and rumor mongering are the order of the day. A well-credentialed, capable and diligent manager, steadily on an upward career trajectory, may find herself out in the streets in a matter of weeks.

So any rising woman manager should ask herself whether what she sees in a particular corporation is a good faith mentoring system, a corrupt star system, or something in between. She can then act accordingly, aware of the potential detriments, and benefits as well, and the ins and outs of mentoring. The larger lesson is that, although on balance a beneficial and necessary ingredient in career success, mentoring has negative attributes (office uncles, plastic bubbles, negative mentoring, and star system, to name a few) which the how-to books ignore.

Informal Networks

"Mentoring" conjures up visions of advisers who are senior, some of whom may be remote. By contrast, "network" conjures visions of co-workers, peers, approachable bosses, knowledgeable subordinates, and others, both in the workplace or outside, most of whom are proximate. Advice books for women place primacy on the formation of informal networks.[23]

" 'Exclusion from informal networks stands as one of the top barriers to success reported by women" to Catalyst. "We women watch men leave together for lunch as we bolt down a cup of yoghurt at our desks. [W]e see men heading out together for drinks and more talk, while we go pick up the kids, pick up dinner, pick up the dry cleaning, pick up the house."[24] The standard advice is that "[y]ou should be building your network while you're looking for your first job, your next job, your tenth job, and you should network starting at entry level."[25]

In the extreme, "how to" books tell women to take up golf. Others push Monday Night and NFL football: "Men do business on the golf course and in the sky box at sporting events, because that's where the networks are."[26] A woman who can knowledgeably criticize last night's game will gain entrance to an informal network.

There is only a kernel of truth to any of this. Women might take up golf because they find that they enjoy it. They may make additional friends from participation in the Tuesday or Wednesday Twilight Golf League. But such advice is wide of the mark because it misapprehends the reasons why women should seek out an informal network as well as how to do it.

Being open, approachable and caring for fellow workers and subordinates, in the workplace and in normal working hours, is sufficient to develop a network. Have members of your network to lunch; clip articles and hand deliver them to network associates who might find them interesting; work to get an associate or two on a committee on which you serve; stop by for a short chat. None of the contortions and manipulations the books for women advocate are needed.

And why do you need an informal network? A few, a very few, of those who dispense advice for women do not advocate a network, at least in the traditional way. "For years, books and magazines [have] focused on those bulging Rolodexes and the need for female managers to glad-hand their way to the top." Psychologist Carol Gallagher advises women to be more selective. "[N]uture more substantive relationships or *alliances* with fewer people." To her:

> [N]etworking connotes pressing the flesh, handing out business cards, and developing relatively superficial relationships at social functions and "networking" gatherings. . . . In fact, of the initial seventy women I interviewed . . . *nearly all scorned this approach*. Most admitted they were not at all good at it. Besides, they didn't have time for it, and they didn't enjoy it![27]

However described, women managers need a network because a network functions as a support group. In this day and age of 360 degree reviews, peers and even subordinates will play an important role in evaluations, annually and preliminary to a promotion. Often a good word from a co-worker may do the most in sparking a promotion to a higher position.

A network also will aid in preventing too far a fall from grace should a woman manager stumble. Men who fall from grace often rebound off the glass floor into a nearly equivalent or another executive position, while many women who fall from grace are never seen again. They fall so far because no informal network exists to retard their decline.[28]

Last of all, the existence of a properly functioning network may prevent a stumble in the first place. The presence of associates will prevent the dominants in a group from "ganging up" in a committee meeting or during a presentation by a minority woman manager. A member of the network may advise you to give consideration to something you overlooked.

A supervisor advocated swapping time off for Martin Luther King Day in January, for Presidents' Day in February, on the grounds that time off for Martin Luther King Day came too soon after the Christmas holiday. Being very much a go-it-alone woman, she didn't have an informal network, a member or two of which might have suggested to her how offensive the suggestion might be to African American co-workers. She published a memo suggesting the change. It set off a barrage of criticism rising to a chorus, chanting racism. A properly functioning network would have averted the public error in judgment and the fallout which followed.

In the same way, when a woman has plugged into an informal network she runs a much reduced risk of being sandbagged at presentations, of having her ideas plagiarized, and of behind-the-back criticisms and other forms of backstabbing.

Lessons Learned

The time has come to shift from the descriptive to the prescriptive. Examination of the careers of 21 women CEOs produces many teachings, many of them counterintuitive, and directly contrary to what the advice books say:

- Education matters, much more so for women than men. There seems to be great value in obtaining an MBA, which a woman can do through an executive MBA program as well as full-time attendance.
- Financial literacy is necessary. Even if one majors in liberal arts, which may be a beneficent thing to do, give thought to beginning some grounding in financial subjects early.
- Emphasis on line experience at some point in a career is advice to listen to and probably, but not necessarily, heed. Key staff, marketing, or sales jobs may be as important in many organizations.
- Beware of overemphasis on line experience. It often seems to be the Trojan horse the chauvinists use to gain entry into promotion and search processes.
- Belief in an organization, in its culture, and that it has core values (not necessarily a given set of values), without necessarily being a cheerleader or wearing it on your sleeve, are central to career advancement. With such a tool kit, you can represent the organization anywhere, on any occasion—instill it, and lead it.
- Parenting children is not as inimical to a woman's career as tradition holds.

- Children may in fact become more important as an executive reaches for the higher rungs of the corporate ladder, because children offer a counterpoint to what you do all day, and give you solace, love and balance in your life.
- Mentoring is important but may not be all that advice books crank it up to be. The plastic bubble phenomenon, over protective and negative mentoring, and star systems masquerading as mentoring are pitfalls.
- Take advice about networking with a grain of salt. Concentrate on quality more than quantity. Understand why a network is important.

20 Lessons Learned

I play on masculine pride and natural instincts to protect the weaker sex. "I can't figure this out, and I'm exhausted," I will say . . . "[I]f it's not done tomorrow, I'm dead."

"I'll do it," he'll invariably say.

But his rescue mission won't be truly satisfying to him unless I show appreciation for the sacrifice he is making. . . .

"No, no, you're swamped, too," I'll say.

"I'll make time for it."

"Thank you. I love you."

"I know. You're welcome."

It's like great sex. Everyone walks away fulfilled.[1]

Nina DiSesa, *Seducing the Boys' Club* (2008)

[G]ames little boys play such as basketball, baseball, football . . . are hierarchical. Sports are structured as pyramids with coaches at the top; team captains, star players, and average players in the middle . . . Someone always wins and someone always loses. Girls live in a "flat" social structure. They play games in which power is shared equally. There is never a captain . . .

Boys' games are focused. A boy will never say. "Let's get the game started and figure out where the goal is later." The main purpose of playing is to win—score the most points. By contrast, the main thrust of girls' play . . . lies in relating to others. There is no winning or losing . . .

The impact of these differences on the business world is profound.[2]

Pat Heim & Susan Golant, *Smashing the Glass Ceiling:
Tactics for Women Who Want to Win in Business* (1995)

The first lesson that becomes clear after immersion in the processes of choosing women CEOs and managers is that the myriad advice and "how to" books contain at most a kernel of truth. Among the worst are those with a tinge of sexual innuendo, such as *Skirt Rules* or *Seducing the Boys' Club*.[3] Use of feminine wiles to clinch a promotion, get help with a key report, or win over a new client, especially for this day and age, is plain bad advice.

Nonetheless, those titles are among the most recent, supplanting an earlier generation of advice books for women that used sports metaphors ("Hit a home run," "Score a touchdown," "Throw the knockout punch"). Many of these 1990s books, such as *Smashing the Glass Ceiling*, are "one note Joanie's," spinning an entire theme around a sports analogy: *Hardball for Women*[4] and *Play Like a Man, Win Like a Woman.*[5]

The difficulty with such books is their tilt toward aggressive, assertive behavior is outmoded. The advice places primary reliance on what Ellen Goodman terms "shoulder pad feminism"—entry-level women bedecked in Prada and Armani suits. Assertiveness may get a capable women her first, and perhaps second, promotion but ultimately will sidetrack, or altogether derail, an otherwise promising career. Working in the Silicon Valley and with high-tech companies, social psychologist Jan Hollands coined a name for it, the "bully broad" phenomenon. In her book, *Same Game, Different Rules*, Hollands cautions against aggressive, overly assertive behavior, counseling women with careers in business to avoid the bully broad pitfall.[6]

The take that business closely resembles sports—boys play sports and girls don't, or that, if girls involve themselves in games, the rules and nature of the competition are radically different for boys than they are for girls—are 1950s relics. Girls have been playing competitive sports—soccer, basketball, softball, and even ice hockey—for a generation now, many times in a more bruising environment than the boys. Except for a few outliers, boys and girls play sports by the same rules. Saying that boys' and girls' sports and games are different is outdated. Too much emphasis on sports themes and metaphors leads to the wrong advice (too much aggression).

The Advice Books

Betty Friedan published *The Feminine Mystique* in 1963.[7] She found that "[t]he problem that has no name—which is simply [that] American women are kept from growing to their full human capacities—is taking a far greater toll on the physical and mental health in our country than is any known disease."

It took nearly two decades before other authors took up the cudgels from Friedman. Since that time, however, publication of management and advice books for women has been a land office business. Titles include:

- Susan Adams, *The New Success Rules for Women* (2000)
- Donna Brooks & Lynn Brooks, *Seven Secrets of Successful Women* (1997)
- Esther Wachs Book, *Why the Best Man for the Job Is a Woman* (2000)
- Catalyst, Inc., *Advancing Women in Business* (1998)
- Nina DiSesa, *Seducing the Boys' Club* (2008)
- Gail Evans, *Play Like a Man, Win Like a Woman* (2000)
- Carol Gallagher, *Going to the Top* (2000)
- Pamela B. Gilberd, *The Eleven Commandments of Wildly Successful Women* (1996)
- Harvard Business Review Books, *Reach for the Top* (1994)
- Sylvia A. Hewlett, *Off Ramps and On Ramps* (2007)

- Pat Heim & Susan Golant, *Hardball for Women* (1992, rev. edn. 2005)
- Pat Heim & Susan Golant, *Smashing the Glass Ceiling* (1993)
- Linda Hirshman, *Get to Work* (2006)
- Kelly L. Johnson, *Skirt! Rules: For the Workplace* (2008)
- Ann Morrison et al., *Breaking the Glass Ceiling* (1987; rev. edn 1992)
- Anthony Stith, *Breaking the Glass Ceiling* (1998)
- Sheila Wellington, *Be Your Own Mentor* (2002).

The advice tends to be anecdotal: "this happened to me," or "happened to a friend." When books purport to be scientific, they sample women at random, sampling from middle level management positions (undefined) or senior executive positions (also undefined).

The idea of analyzing the careers of 21 women who actually have become CEOs of *Fortune 500* companies is more scientific than anything that has been done previously. What does it teach us?

Ten Tentative Teachings Made Final

Develop a "Can Do" Reputation

Advice applicable to all who aspire to high positions is to "develop a reputation as one who can solve problems"[8] but this seems especially true for women in business. Several women in this book exemplify this trait, either once they made it to the CEO suite or en route to it, although a strong element of it is present in every case:

- Andrea Jung: in her early days as CEO of Avon, she confronted a predicament, namely, the seeming obsolescence of Avon's selling methods, coupled with the need to retain hundreds of thousands of loyal sales reps, the resolution of which had befuddled three previous CEOs. She invented new sales methods, expanded the product mix and the geographical reach, and kept the reps as well.
- Marion Sandler: she built a tiny two office savings and loan into the second largest in the United States, surviving several crises along the way, crises which played a significant role in the demise of 3,500 of 4,500 thrift institutions which used to exist in the United States.
- Anne Mulcahy: she turned around a fallen angel, which suffered from a severe case of the bloat, whose market share had fallen from 90 percent to 13 percent and whose share price from $64 to $4.93.
- Susan Ivey: she turned around a corporation which, due to settlement of a massive lawsuit by states' attorneys general and increased competition from less expensive generic cigarettes, had seen its market share fall drastically. She did so by resurrecting old brands, venturing into smokeless tobacco, and converting premium to everyday brands.

- Pat Woertz: she superintended construction of the Alberta to California pipeline and got it done and oversaw the gigantic Chevron distribution network.
- Meg Whitman: she imposed business methods on a tech startup without compromising its culture, shepherding it through its teenage years and resulting in one of the most successful tech startups of all time.
- Angela Braley: she almost single handedly created room for Blue Cross of Missouri to convert to for-profit status and to enter the twenty-first century.

Don't Too Much a "Tall Poppy" Be

One manifestation of the egalitarian spirit is the tendency to cut down anyone who has become a "tall poppy." Americans do much the same to those who "have become too big for their britches." An ancient proverb states that "Greatness is always built on this foundation: the ability to appear, speak, and act, as the most common man [or woman]."[9] It behooves a woman who seeks to rise to the higher heights of an organization to avoid accumulating a reputation as a prima donna, tall poppy, or "too big for her britches."

Prepare Yourself for the Accounting and Financial Sides of Business

As CEOs, women will have CFOs and comptrollers who deal with such matters on a day-to-day basis. Every CEO, though, must have a working knowledge of managerial accounting, corporate finance, stocks, commodities, the share markets, basic economics, and marketing. It is acceptable to be overweighted in one area, such as marketing or sales, as were Jill Barad, Andrea Jung, Carleton Fiorina, Susan Ivey, Brenda Barnes, and Indra Nooyi, to name several, but not to the exclusion of a facility in all necessary areas, which Barad lacked at Mattel and Fiorina did at Hewlett-Packard.

But Avoid Being Lopsided

Learn about revenues, profits, forecasts, and share prices, as well as sales. Jill Barad's tenure at Mattel highlights her fixation with marketing Barbie dolls. At Lucent and at HP, Fiorina's experience and interests, while primarily in sales, were broader. She was interested in making herself the image of Hewlett-Packard, interested in being the architect of business organization and strategy. But both women failed to give the necessary attention to revenues, profits, forecasts, and share prices, and those deficiencies led to their downfalls.

Directors are willing to appear patient but revenue and sales growth, meeting forecasts, and share price levels are never far from board members' consciousness. Any woman who aspires to be a CEO has to develop a feel for that.

Education Matters

A counterintuitive finding of this book is that all 21 women were graduated from college or university and more than two-thirds (14 of 20) have graduate degrees (12 MBAs). Most have demonstrated that they possess the financial acumen which is necessary for anyone who holds the top spot. The MBA degree started them in that direction.

The Glass Cliff Theory Appears to Have Robust Support

Anne Mulcahy at Xerox and Patricia Russo at Lucent are paradigmatic "Glass Cliff" cases. This theory holds that, while boards today are more likely to choose a woman as CEO, boards are more likely to take a chance on a woman when the company is in the midst of tough times, or in an extremis situation. Xerox with Anne Mulcahy and Lucent with Pat Russo bear witness to the theory, as does Avon with Andrea Jung, and as do Reynolds America with Susan Ivey, Sara Lee Corp. with Brenda Barnes, Rite Aid with Mary Sammons, and Yahoo! with Carol Bartz. When a woman reaches the top, she should be aware that she may have a shorter time in which to prove herself because of the circumstances in which she may come into office, and that a "can do" reputation may be disproportionately more significant for women than men CEO candidates. This is because women more often come into situations which place a premium on getting the job (the turnaround) done and done quickly.

Changing Careers Often Aids Career Advancement

Changing employers (company to company) or sectors (for example, profit to not-for-profit, or profit to government) may have a beneficial strategic effect, as Pat Russo's departure to Kodak or Irene Rosenfeld's to Frito Lay show. By contrast, too much "side stepping" may give off the appearance of a lack of stability or "careerism," a characterization Meg Whitman narrowly avoided on her way to eBay. Anne Mulcahy proves the exception to the rule. She has spent virtually her entire career at the same corporation, Xerox.

Overall, though, side stepping within the corporate sector seems to benefit a woman's career. The following women changed employers at least three times in their careers: Andrea Jung, Jill Barad, Paula Reynolds, Pat Woertz, Brenda Barnes, Christine Gold, Angela Braley, Indra Nooyi, Pat Russo, Meg Whitman, and Ellen Kullman. By contrast, in addition to Anne Mulcahy, the following women had all, or nearly all, their professional lives with one or two companies (entry level "transition jobs" excluded): Marion Sandler, Susan Ivey, Carleton Fiorina (2), Mary Sammons (2), and Carol Meyrowitz.

You Can't Let the Snowball Roll Over You

Pat Russo has made this one of her mantras. When senior executives give an aspiring executive a test to turn around a product, a plant, division, or subsidiary, as well as when a woman becomes the CEO of a company in a turnaround situation as Russo did, she has to take the challenges of the job one by one and set about as the problem solver, the one who can fix it if anyone can. They can't let themselves be overwhelmed, either by tough job assignments or sandbagging, pack attacks, or backstabbing by dominant males or queen bees in their midst.

Go Where They Aren't

The choice is not for everyone but every woman in business should give it thought, either initially or after her first or second promotion. Certain industries remain male dominated but the instances of outright or even subtle discrimination are vastly reduced. Susan Ivey in tobacco, Paula Reynolds in utilities and then insurance, and Pat Woertz in petroleum and agribusiness are the generation following the pioneers. Lynn Elsenhans, also in petroleum, Ellen Kullman, in paint and chemicals, and Carol Bartz, in information technology, did much the same as Ivey, Reynolds and Woertz. Their successes, which include ultimately promotion to CEOs of major corporations, herald the elimination of hurdles and obstacles that existed only 15–20 years ago, which will continue to fall.

Prioritize Careers with Your Partner?

Many two-career married couples pursue both careers for a time. Then, it seems, the very successful ones have a discussion and, based upon that discussion, consciously relegate one career to the other. Christina Gold, Indra Nooyi, Lynn Elsenhans, Carleton Fiorina, Anne Mulcahy, and Susan Ivey and their husbands are examples. Marion and Herb Sandler choose to partner instead, but they could do so because they owned the business. Only Brenda Barnes and her spouse attempted to pursue executive management careers simultaneously, both with PepsiCo. The subject is a very personal one, but couples which include a woman who is succeeding in her business career should have a discussion of the option.

Teachings For Everyone

Keep Your Ego in Check and Learn to Partner

Carleton Fiorina was a celebrity CEO wannabe who always had to be center stage, loved to travel, make speeches, and be pictured on magazine covers. She was bold and inventive as an architect of corporate strategy and organization but woefully short on follow-through.

"[A] narcissist personality ... needs to partner with an obsessive," Dr. Michael Maccoby concludes.[10] "[T]hink of Steve Ballmer [second at Microsoft to Bill Gates], Roy Lane [second to Larry Ellison at Oracle], and Colleen Barrett [second to Herb Kelleher at Southwest Airlines]—in building the company, watching the bottom line, and managing people."[11] Ship captains have executive officers, deans have associate deans, university chancellors have provosts, pastors have curates, and so on. A second-in-command is ubiquitous in most walks of life, including business.

Fiorina's refusal to consider a second-in-command, despite repeated requests to hire one, put her squarely in opposition to the HP directors. It also contributed to the failure of HP to perform as it should have earlier on and its run away financial success under command of a "low key problem solver" successor CEO. The broader lesson is that every manager should consider partnering so that attention to detail and follow through are assured.

Know When to Duck, Know When to Admit Error, Know When to Apologize

Jill Barad and Carleton Fiorina were never able to do these things. They thus had short tenures. By contrast, Anne Mulcahy and Pat Russo lasted longer than Barad and Fiorina did. Neither made quantified projections or, for the most part, generic ones either. Through periods of red ink, massive layoffs, downsizing, and poor stock market performance, they keep a low profile.

Make Dissenters into Leaders; Get Opposites Communicating

Encourage out-of-the-box thinking. Do not be a micro-manager or otherwise over-controlling. Leave room for juniors and subordinates to create and to contribute.

Get the engineers to communicate with the sales and marketing people, and vice versa. Get the downstream sales organization talking with the upstream production people, or the design team communicating with the retail parts of the organization. To get subordinates talking, insist on the no penalty culture in order to foster communication. If you hire capable and diligent people, make it as easy as possible, not more difficult, for them to communicate with each other. Google has a flag protocol: anyone in a company cafe or restaurant who wants to meet someone new puts a flag on their table. Many conversations and friendships between people with disparate jobs or backgrounds begin that way. Google also provides complementary restaurant and recreational facilities where employees can mingle and cross-communicate in all sorts of ways.

These are some of the management precepts first-rate CEOs have taped to their bathroom mirrors.

Don't Be Greedy

Accept only properly approved (board approved) salary and perquisites. Do not accept IPO allocations in other companies, backdated stock options, or excessive housing, travel or other perks. Meg Whitman's acceptance of IPO allocations to her account (spinning) may yet put a cloud over her head that will hinder her campaign for governor despite her achievements. Steven Jobs and all he has achieved at Apple are diminished by his receipt of stock options backdated to when the market, and therefore his exercise price, were lower. These instances of what appears to be unbridled greed can leave a stain that is indelible.

Bring a Global Attitude, if not Expertise, to the Table

Andrea Jung, Susan Ivey and Indra Nooyi exemplify this new requirement for any CEO, man or woman. Large corporations such as Avon Products, Reynolds America or PepsiCo must be ready to market products around the globe, to 6.2 billion persons. These companies are not only ready but doing so because of the women who lead them.

On the production side, Anne Mulcahy at Xerox saw the need and successfully outsourced the production of products to Singapore. Pat Russo did something of the same, arranging for the production of Lucent telecommunications equipment in East Asia.

In recent years, at most companies, specifications call for CEO candidates with international experience and a global outlook. What are those specifications? Not "how to," strictly speaking, for the CEO and those who work for her will assemble the foreign legal, real estate, manufacturing, and marketing experts needed. The "need to" and the "will to" are attributes companies seek. The candidate needs to be able to lead a management team through the process of devising objectives and scale (or lack thereof) for the foreign outreach. She needs to help participate in understanding the tolerable levels of risk. Do we go it alone? Do we joint venture with an established foreign firm? She needs to understand how the rapid progress toward implementation of international accounting standards may affect her business, even if she does not have to master the technical intricacies of the accounting principles themselves.[12]

Global thinking and leadership require diplomatic and leadership skills very similar to those the CEO position has required all long, but on a grander, more visionary scale. Any man or woman who aspires to a high management position in any larger business organization must make evident her ability to implement the global thinking that the twenty-first century requires, as several of these women's biographies (Jung, Ivey, Nooyi, Mulcahy, Russo) demonstrate.

21 Conclusion: Evolving a New Paradigm for a New Century

Back to Hillary Clinton, where we began. In her endorsement speech at the 2008 Democratic Convention, Senator Clinton rallied her supporters, noting that if it were not shattered, the glass ceiling "has 18 million cracks in it." Clinton obtained 18 million votes in the 2008 presidential primaries, the same as the male nominee, Barack Obama.

If the glass ceiling has 18 million cracks in it, shards of glass falling from what now may be a more porous barrier still retard women's progress. What else can explain that, while women constitute 50 percent of the middle managers in businesses, they still constitute only 8 percent of the senior managers and 3 percent of the CEOs?

The metaphor, though, is a good one. There are cracks—many more opportunities for women to advance, not just in politics, professions and not-for-profits, but in business organizations as well. It is the twenty-first century. In this new century, what must women do to advance through falling shards of glass, moving toward and through those cracks in the glass ceiling?

Most emphatically, abandon the role models and the advice books in the spirit of the last century. Consign almost all of them to the trash heap. Emphasize education and financial literacy. Show that you can think and act globally. Develop a reputation in an area or field. Develop a reputation for being able to fix problems and to represent the organization in whatever quarter it may become necessary to do so. It is no longer necessary to wear power suits from Prada, to watch professional football, or to take up golf, if that ever was the case. The emphasis on obtaining mentors, building informal networks, and moving through line positions, needs to be toned down and added to, in significant measure.

Most of all, become aware that not one paradigm stands for all time, or for a considerable time, any more. Instead, the route a woman may have to take will twist and turn as she moves upward. The paradigm shifts, seemingly much more for a woman than a man. A male can advance in a business career by being assertive, by developing a reputation as Mr. Fix It, or by being a "42 long" (suit size). A woman has to triumph over several paradigm shifts over the same period of time.

Paradigm One—The Tightrope

At lower level management track positions, say, in sales or production, an assertive approach will position the woman manager for the next promotion. The line women must walk, however, is a tightrope. Too much aggressiveness and "[i]t's all the classical stuff: of a man they say 'He's hard-charging; he takes command,' but when a woman acts the same way, she's pushy."[1] "When a man applies the word *aggressive* to another man, he means that he's bold and forceful, that he has the strength and capabilities to achieve his goal. But when guys use the word to describe women . . . [t]he woman becomes pushy, argumentative, domineering," Gail Evans warns.[2]

"[T]he most common terms describing male executives [are] 'quarterback,' 'absolute winner,' 'aggressive,' 'boastful,' 'desire to win,' 'holding power,' [and] 'tough skinned.' "[3] Women managers might do well to mimic some of the traits those male paradigms suggest but not to overdo it.

Gail Evans frequently contrasts men's with women's mannerisms. In meetings, "[w]omen often take those peripheral chairs, because they think the table is for the boss and the key people."[4] "Men will tell you that women are too timid when they talk at the office, or too evasive, or too circuitous, or too unsure of themselves. [S]peaking forcefully isn't about speaking loudly . . . It's about learning how to use your voice effectively."[5]

Do not get a chip on your shoulder. Take slights in your stride. Remember that it may be more difficult for women. Ginger Rodgers danced all the same steps as Fred Astaire—but she did it backwards and in high heels.[6]

Paradigm Two

At some point, say after the second or third promotion, the paradigm for a woman shifts. As long ago as 1977, Margaret Henning noted the change:

> The skills you may need to get close to the executive level (and I'd be the first to admit that you may have to be relatively aggressive) may not serve you well once you get there. After you become a member of the "team," you need to learn to be a team player, and that requires a different set of behaviors. Indeed, managers especially women, unfortunately—often antagonize others [by being] perceived as overly ambitious or a threat.[7]

"Women have to shift their focus from how well they do their job to what job they have." They must become, and appear to have become, more diplomatic, more strategic: "[U]nderstand the big picture. Have a clear sense of what will work and what won't, given competing trends, demands and situations," social psychologist Carol Gallagher urges.[8] Sheila Wellington hints at the transformation:

> If your only strategy is working like a dog, you're likely to find the path to upper management blocked. So what's the missing ingredient?

Something called style. The women who've reached executive levels today say their success depended on developing a style with which men felt comfortable working.[9]

A host of different axioms crowds out early rules to live by ("be aggressive") or co-exist with others ("Deliver results on time or ahead of time. Deliver more than people expect.").

Some of those axioms which form the mid-career composite:

- Develop areas in which you are an expert. Prove yourself continually by invoking your expertise. "Expertise impresses."[10]
- "Style matters. Style is the sum total of yourself presentation. It consists of how you look and how you act. [It] includes not only the sartorial . . . but also your carriage, your attitude, the way you do things. It is the way you speak, the subliminal messages you send, the way you manage your workload."[11]
- At this middle stage, "you have to be approachable and generous with praise, gratitude, and your time in order to succeed . . . Business is a very human interaction. [T]he higher people rise in the corporate pyramid, the more their future promotions are based upon relationships with superiors, colleagues, and subordinates."[12]
- "No one is surprised to hear a man raise his voice, see him show his anger . . . [In contrast] [w]hen a woman does display anger, people are often uneasy, frightened; they perceive her as difficult, unladylike . . . [M]en perceive a show of anger as something out of character for a woman, they judge it as a loss of control."[13]
- Learn the art of the humorous comeback. Radiate confidence. Carry things off with aplomb. Take slights with a grain of salt. Let negative comments slide. Keep things in perspective.
- Be seen as a team player. "Most women really are team players. The difference is that [women] seldom draw attention to the work they have done. Women join a team, participate in the planning, get their assigned tasks, go off and do a bang-up job on them, and move on. Men on a team tend to talk about what they have to do, talk about what they're doing, and talk about what they've done."[14]

Paradigm Three

As an executive approaches upper middle management, she will see the paradigm shift again. Some aggressive behavior creeps back in. As a team member, a shift is made from being a team player to being a team leader: "Develop a reputation as someone who can provide sound advice but also solve problems; move the ball forward, work effectively with other people, manage projects, manage people, bring people together, facilitate the reconciliation of conflicting viewpoints."[15] She must not only be diplomatic but be seen as being a diplomat and a leader: "If you're a vice president, act like a vice president, talk like a vice president, do the work of a vice president. . . . You are sitting at a certain level of the pyramid. Act accordingly."[16]

The Final Paradigm

At the fourth stage, the mix of aggressive behavior with strategic and diplomatic behaviors has added to it progressively larger doses of self-promotion and the appearance of "executive presence."

- Your organization wants to know that it can send you anywhere in the world on any assignment or to solve any problem, that you will project the right image anywhere, that you will never embarrass it.
- Take calculated risks. "Women have to be aggressive with everything, taking risks with tough jobs, big moves, and putting themselves out in front in [certain] situations."[17]
- Judicious use of press coverage may be part of a success strategy. Good internal publicity within the company and visibility in the community become more important at this stage. Seek out public speaking opportunities. Spearhead discussion at staff workshops. Attend conferences. While there, be visible, and ask questions.

There is not *one* paradigm for women who wish to succeed in business, contrary to the advice books.[18] It is not one size fits all. Even the how-to tomes that seem to recognize the evolution of behaviors thought necessary do not seem to recognize that toward the top the paradigm comes nearly full circle. Bully Broads, or Iron Maidens, come across too strong, too tough, and too pushy, in mid-career. The reality or the perception then stalls their careers. If, however, they become suitably strategic, diplomatic, and a team player, as managers, women continue to progress.

But then at some further point, when on the cusp of senior management's ranks, women have to come on strong again, with behaviors that at an earlier stage would have been deemed overly pushy and possibly have doomed their hoped-for career progression. There is reversion.

But not quite. After this twisting and tortuous path they must follow, women should see that the circle does not close at the top. If they fail to discern that, and revert to behavior that might have won them their initial promotion, they may fall completely from grace. The principal lessons to be learned from those careers, along with lessons that may be discerned from a close reading of other careers documented in this book, are two in number: one, is that the paradigm which will get women to the top shifts and changes, coming almost full circle; and two is that, despite those paradigm shifts, the circle does not quite close at the top.

No one paradigm exists or stands for very long anymore. A woman who seeks to advance in a business organization may do well to examine the careers of women who have preceded her and have succeeded, not in the sense of doing what they say they did or what they would advise but in the sense of examining the actual pathways their career took as they moved to the top. There are still a small number of women who have reached the pinnacle, the CEO suite, but the number is large enough that women will benefit from examining successful women's careers. Providing the data and the narratives with which women and governance watchers can do that may be the highest aspiration this book can have.

Forty years ago Bella Abzug, Gloria Steinam, Betty Fridman and others planted the seeds for the modern-day women's movement. The business women featured in this book are not the seeds but the first crop of flowers to bloom. They will be succeeded by further flowerings, each hopefully more plentiful and splendid than the last.

Notes

Preface

1. Congressional Directory, 111th Congress, at 2 *passim* (2009); Leadership Directories, Inc., Congressional Yellow Book, at 31–218 (2009). As of January 30, 2009, 17 of the 100 U.S. senators were women. Idem.
2. OECD, *OECD in Figures 2007* (OECD Publishing) at 84 (graph).
3. See note 1, *supra*. They are Lisa Murkowski (Alaska); Blanche Lincoln (Arkansas); Dianne Feinstein and Barbara Boxer (California); Mary Landrieu (Louisiana); Olympia Snowe and Susan Collins (Maine); Barbara Milkulski (Maryland); Debbie Stabenow (Michigan); Amy Klobuchar (Minnesota); Claire McCaskill (Missouri); Jeanne Shaheen (New Hampshire); Kirsten Gillibrand (New York); Kay Hagan (North Carolina); Kay Hutchinson (Texas); Patty Murray and Maria Cantwell (Washington).
4. Catalyst, Inc., "Number of Women Chief Executives Doubles in 2001" (April 18, 2001).
5. Del Jones, "Female CEOs Make More Gains in 2007," *USA Today*, Jan. 3, 2008, at 2B (listing 12 women CEOs, leaving out Patricia Russo of Alcatel-Lucent). *Cf.* Douglas M. Branson, *No Seat at the Table—How Corporate Governance and Law Keep Women Out of the Boardroom* at 146–47 (New York, NYU Press, 2007) (listing eight female CEOs as of late 2005).
6. According to the most recent census, in 2000, 57.5 percent of all women worked outside the home and women constituted 46.7 percent of those gainfully employed. U.S. Census Bureau, American Fact Finder, at QT-P27 (2005) ("Occupation by Sex").
7. See, for example, *No Seat* at 150–52. Women received 19.7 percent of the MBAs universities awarded in 1979 while 28.1 percent of the 1979 law graduates were women.
8. There is little or no magic in the titles corporate officers may hold: it is a matter of what the principal internal operating document, the bylaws, may provide and what currently is in vogue. The corporate president of bygone days today is the Chief Executive Officer, or CEO. Yesterday's Executive Vice-president is today's Chief Operating Officer (COO). The Treasurer may be the Chief Financial Officer (CFO) in one company but may co-exist, and generally be subservient to, the CFO in the next. House counsel (the lawyer) may be titled the Chief Legal Officer (CLO) and Vice-president Marketing has become the Chief Marketing Officer, or CMO. Only the corporate Secretary seems frozen in time as to title: she is still termed "the Secretary."

   Older corporate statutes exist in several states which require corporations to have at least a president and a secretary. In those states, the head person may have the title President and Chief Executive Officer, or President alone. But most modern statues provide that a corporation need have only those officers for which the bylaws provide. See Model Business Corporation Act § 8.40 (1984).

9. An early pioneer is Linda Wachner, CEO at Warnaco Group (lingerie, Calvin Klein, Speedo), whom the Warnaco board of directors removed from office in November 2001. See "Warnaco Outs CEO Amid Restructuring," *Los Angeles Times*, Nov. 17, 2001, at C-1. Warnaco Group is not a Fortune 500 public company.

10. See note 7 *supra*.

11. *No Seat* at 108.

12. Idem at 96 (lack of "marketing reciprocity" among many retail and consumer product companies).

13. *No Seat* at 106–08 (airlines, grocery chains and financial services companies also have deficient records).

14. See, for example, Joan Lublin, "Behind the Rush to Add Women to Norway's Boards," *Wall St. Journal*, Dec. 10, 2007, at B-1 (uncritical acceptance of 14.8 percent as relative proposition of U.S. directors who are women).

15. Kimberly Weisul, "Make Way for Madame Director," *Business Week*, Dec. 22, 2003, at 57; Catalyst, Inc., Press Release, Dec. 10, 2008, "Catalyst Census of Fortune 500 Reveals Women Gained Little Ground Advancing to Business Leadership Positions" (15.2 percent of directors in 2008; 14.8 percent in 2007).

16. *No Seat* at 97.

17. Idem Avita Raghhavan, "Many CEOs Say 'No Thanks' to Board Seats," *Wall Street Journal*, Jan. 28, 2005, at B-1.

18. Douglas M. Branson, "Where Are the Women?," The Conference Board Review, Sept.–Oct., 2007, 51, at 52; *No Seat* at 99 (listing nine super trophy directors in 2006: Susan Bayh, Brenda Barnes, Barbara Bowles, Shirley Jackson, Penelope Hughes, Bonnie Hill, Ann McLaughlin Korogolos, Lynn Martin, and Jackie Ward). Other super trophy directors include former University of California (Berkeley) M.B.A. school dean Laura Tyson; economics professor Wendy Gramm, wife of ex-U.S. Senator Phil Gramm; University of Michigan School of Business professor Marina Whitman; Gwendolyn King, ex Commissioner of Social Security; director of presidential personnel Constance Horner; and former State Department negotiator and ambassador Rozanne Ridgeway. *No Seat* at 94, 100.

19. Dan Ackerman, "Black Directors: Diversity Without Diversity," *Forbes*, Aug. 8, 2002.

20. Another factor that could affect the female CEO pool is the lackluster progress in numbers of women matriculating at MBA schools. The number dropped precipitously, to less than 25 percent, in the 1990s. Staff, "For Women, Fewer MBAs As the Degree's Value and Cost Are Questioned," *Wall Street Journal*, Sept. 27, 1992; "Female Enrollment Falls In Many Top MBA Programs," idem, Sept. 25, 1992; Terry R. Johnson and Steven D. McLaughlin, *Declining Number of Female MBAs: An Analysis from the GMAT Registrant Survey*, available from Graduate Management Admissions Council, 1750 Tyson's Blvd., McClean, Va. 221012. It has since rebounded but has often been one step forward, two steps back. "We'd see a half percentage or full percentage point increase, but then it often would fall back in the following year," reported Ellissa Ellis-Sangster of the Forte Foundation, Austin, Texas, which exists to promote female matriculation at the graduate schools of business. Career Journal, "How To Raise Female M.B.A. Enrollment," *Wall Street Journal*, July 17, 2007, at B-6.

21. Sources include the 2007 SEC Proxy Statements ("definitive 14A's"), available SEC.GOV, EDGAR (Electronic Data Gathering and Retrieval) (last visited, Jan. 31, 2008), and the various corporations' websites.

22. William M. Bulkeley, "Xerox Names Burns Chief As Mulcahy Retires Early," *Wall Street Journal*, May 22, 2009, at B-1.

23. Nina DiSesa, *Seducing the Boys Club—Uncensored Tactics From a Woman at the Top* at 211 (New York, Ballantine, 2008).
24. Jessica Seid, "10 Best Paid Executives: They're All Men," CNNMoney.com. Oct. 13, 2006.
25. Scott Decarlo, "Top CEO Compensation in 2007," *Forbes*, April 30, 2008, available www.forbes.com/ceos/ (last visited Sept. 6, 2008). The figures for 2006 were higher: Steve Jobs, Apple Computer, $647 million; Ray Irani, Occidental Petroleum, $322 million; Barry Diller, IAC, $259 million; William Foley, Fidelity National, $180 million; and Terry Semel, Yahoo!, $174 million. Scott DeCarlo, "Big Paychecks," *Forbes*, May 21, 2007, at 112.
26. Male CEO, and especially female CEO, compensation levels seem insignificant when compared to hedge fund managers' compensation: James Simons, Renaissance Technologies, $1.5 billion; Steven Cohen, SAC Capital, $1.2 billion; Kenneth Griffin, Citadel Investment Group, $1.2 billion; T. Boone Pickens, BP Capital, $1.1 billion; and George Soros, Soros Fund Management, $950 million. Michael K. Ozanian and Peter J. Schwartz, "Wall Street's Highest Earners," *Forbes*, May 21, 2007, at 104.
27. Staff, "Who Made the Biggest Bucks," *Wall Street Journal*, April 11, 2002, at B-7; Staff, "Oracle's Ellison Has Windfall on Options," idem, Sept. 4, 2001, at B-6.
28. See Lucien Bebchuk and Jesse Fried, *Pay Without Performance: The Unfulfilled Promise of Executive Compensation* (Cambridge, MA, Harvard University Press, 2004); Jesse Eisinger, "Lavish Pay Puts a Bite on Profits," *Wall Street Journal*, Jan. 11, 2006, at C-1.

1 The Fall of Jill Barad at Mattel Toy

1. Unidentified Mattel board member, "Jury's Out," *Delaney Report*, April 5, 1999, at 1.
2. Abigail Goldman, "Beleaguered Mattel CEO Resigns as Profit Sinks," *Los Angeles Times*, Feb. 4, 2000, at A-1.
3. See "Fortune's 50 Most Powerful Women," *Fortune*, Oct. 12, 1998, at 76; G. Wayne Miller, "Manager's Journal: The Rise and Fall Of Toyland's Princess," *Wall Street Journal*, Feb. 7, 2000, at A-38 (in *People* Barad appeared "in a full page spread in which she sprawled on satin bedding with 35 Barbies dressed in bikinis and evening gowns").
4. Between the time she became CEO and September 1999, Jill Barad was featured in 717 stories by the national media. See "Princess on a Steeple," *The Economist*, Oct. 9, 1999, at 84.
5. *Compare* Patricia Sellers, "Women, Sex & Power," *Fortune*, Aug. 15, 1996, at 46 (nurturing) *with* Kathleen Morris, "The Rise of Jill Barad," *Business Week*, May 25, 1998, at 112 (vicious and "not a team player").
6. Miller, *supra*, at A-38.
7. See Morris, *supra*, at 21.
8. Idem. See also Sheila Wellington, *Be Your Own Mentor* at 239–40 (New York, Random House, 2001), quoting Barad explaining her "basic success strategies": " 'doing things that make you uncomfortable,' such as when her career side stepped out of marketing into product development, rewarding her with vital new experience."
9. A "Pioneer Profile" of Barad is contained in *Be Your Own Mentor* at 240.
10. Idem.
11. Sellers, *supra*, at 44.
12. See Kelley Holland & Eric Schine, "Toys 'R' Her," *Business Week*, Sept. 2, 1996, at 47.

13. See generally Lisa Bannon, "Mattel Names Jill Barad Chief Executive," *Wall Street Journal*, Aug. 23, 1996, at B-2.
14. See Morris, *supra*, at 114.
15. Philip D. Broughton, "The Rise and Fall of Bossy Barbie," *Daily Telegraph* (London), Feb. 12, 2000, at 21.
16. "The Woman Who Saved Barbie Gets a $30 Million Payoff," *Daily Express*, March 14, 2000, at 97.
17. See generally Bannon, *supra*, at B-2; Morris, *supra*.
18. Denise Gellene, "Fits of Pink: Barbie Collectors Go Toe-To-Toe with Mattel," *Washington Post*, May 16, 1997, at B-2.
19. Holland & Schine, *supra*, at 47.
20. See generally Morris, *supra*; "Top Businesswomen [who] Exceed $1 Million in Pay," *Wall Street Journal*, Dec. 17, 1996, at C-20.
21. Nancy Rivera Brooks & Martha Groves, "Woman to Run the House That Barbie Built," *Los Angeles Times*, Aug. 23, 1996, at A-23.
22. See generally Jennifer Lanthier, "Hits and Misses: Mattel Lost Its Bid for Hasbro," *National Post*, May 15, 1996, at 11. See generally G. Wayne Miller, *Toy Wars: The Epic Battle Between G.I. Joe, Barbie, and the Companies That Make Them* (New York, Times Books, 1998).
23. See Linda Sandler & Robert McGough, "Mattel's Marriage to Disney Falters as Toys Based on 'Hunchback' Get Little Play Time," *Wall Street Journal*, Aug. 6, 1996, at C-2.
24. Holland & Schine, *supra*, at 47.
25. Lisa Bannon & Andy Pasztor, "Mattel CEO Moves to Shred Some Units as Fourth Quarter Earnings Come in Flat," *Wall Street Journal*, Feb. 6, 1997, at B-8.
26. On the Tyco acquisition, see generally Lisa Bannon & Joseph Pereira, "No. 1 Toy Maker Mattel Agrees to Buy No. 3 Tyco in $755 Million Stock Deal," *Wall Street Journal*, Nov. 19, 1996, at A-13; George White, "Mattel Agrees To Buy Tyco for $755 Million," *Wall Street Journal*, Nov. 19, 1996, at D-1.
27. See Jan Howells, "There's Life In the Old Doll Yet," *Daily Telegraph* (London), April 22, 1997, at 6.
28. See generally Tara Parker-Pope & Lisa Bannon, "Avon's New Calling: Selling Barbie in China," *Wall Street Journal*, May 1, 1997, at B-1.
29. "Mattel's CEO Got $1.5 Million [base cash compensation] in 97 for Salary, Bonus," *Wall Street Journal*, Mar. 16, 1998, at B-8.
30. See Lisa Bannon, "Mattel Had Profit 1st Quarter, Despite Setbacks," *Wall Street Journal*, April 17, 1998, at A-4; Bannon, "Mattel Plans to Double Sales Abroad," idem, Feb. 11, 1998, at A-3.
31. Lisa Bannon, "Mattel Reports Profit Fell 20 percent in Second Period," *Wall Street Journal*, July 17, 1998, at A-6.
32. Lisa Bannon, "Mattel Cuts Forecast for Yearly Profit in Wake of Toys 'R' Us Restructuring," *Wall Street Journal*, Sept. 25, 1998, at B-7.
33. Stacy Kravetz & Jon G. Auerbach, "Mattel Reveals Profit Shortfall," *Wall Street Journal*, Dec. 15, 1998, at B-1.
34. Idem.
35. Stacy Kravetz, "Mattel Forecasts Sluggish Sales, Posts 70 percent Drop in 4th Quarter Net," *Wall Street Journal*, Feb. 3, 1999, at B-14.
36. Lisa Bannon, "Mattel, As Expected, Posts Loss but Says It Is on Track to Meet 1999 Forecast," *Wall Street Journal*, July 23, 1999, at B-6.
37. See Lisa Bannon, "Mattel's New Profit Shortfall Punishes Stock and Raises Questions about CEO," *Wall Street Journal*, Oct. 5, 1999, at A-3; Bannon, "Mattel Still Doesn't Grasp Sanfu at Learning Company," idem, Oct. 8, 1999, at A-3. Cf. Bannon, "Learning Co. Is On Track, Says Mattel," idem, Oct. 22, 1999, at A-3.

38. Lisa Bannon & Joann S. Lublin, "Jill Barad Abruptly Quits the Top Job at Mattel," *Wall Street Journal*, Feb. 4, 2000, at B-1.
39. Reported in Constance Hays, "Mattel Chief Quits After Losses," *International Herald Tribune*, Feb. 5, 2000, at 12, and in Abigail Goodman, "Beleaguered Mattel CEO Resigns After Profit Sinks," *Los Angeles Times*, Feb. 4, 2000, at A-1.
40. See Andrew Cave, "Mattel Boss Pays $1 for Limo in Severance Deal," *Daily Telegraph* (London), Feb. 9, 2000, at 8; Lisa Bannon, "Mattel Filing Says Former Executives To Get $50 Million," *Wall Street Journal*, March 13, 2000, at B-6. Upon learning that Mrs. Barad was to receive all or most of $50 million, Mattel shareholders raised a ruckus at the June 2000 annual meeting. Bannon, "Mattel's Shareholders Make It Clear That They Aren't To Be Toyed With," *Wall Street Journal*, June 8, 2000, at B-16.
41. See Jim Collins, *Good to Great—Why Some Companies Make the Leap and Others Don't* at 10 (New York, Harper Collins, 2001): "Larger-than-life celebrity leaders . . . are *negatively* correlated with taking a company from good to great."
42. Analyst Sean McGowan of Gerard, Klauer & Mattison, quoted in Lisa Bannon, "Co-Founders of Mattel Learning Co. Unit Depart in the Wake of Shortfall Surprise," *Wall Street Journal*, Nov. 11, 1999, at B-10.
43. Recounted in Edward Helmore, *The Toy Queen Is Toppled, The Observer*, Feb. 6, 2000, at 3.
44. *Be Your Own Mentor* at 223.
45. See also Symposium, "The Essays of Warren Buffett," *Cardozo Law Review*, 19, 5, 740 (1997) ("More big dumb acquisitions are made in the name of strategic plans than any other").
46. See Susan Adams, "Look Before You Buy," *Forbes*, March 6, 2000, at 32, reviewing a Nov. 1, 1999 *Forbes* article predicting that the Mattel acquisition of TLC would turn out to have been a "mistake."
47. Abigail Goldman, "Mattel Will Shut Last U.S. Manufacturing Site," *Los Angeles Times*, April 4, 2000, at C-2; "Mattel, Inc: Last Manufacturing Plant in the U.S. Will Be Closed," *Wall Street Journal*, April 4, 2000, at B-8.
48. See Lisa Bannon, "Mattel to Sell Learning Co; Price Seen Low," *Wall Street Journal*, April 3, 2000, at B-3.
49. Lisa Bannon, "Mattel, After Learning Co., Faces Big Job," *Wall Street Journal*, Oct. 2, 2000, at B-8.
50. Nicholas Casey, "Mattel Profits Despite Barbie," Wall Street Journal, Feb. 1, 2008, at A-11. Although Barbie remains the "no. 1 in girls toys," falling domestic sales cancel out rising international sales, resulting in "flat world wide sales for the Barbie brand." Nicholas Casey, "As Barbie Sales Fall, Mattel Looks to Simplify Its Iconic Line," idem, April 22, 2008, at B-3.
51. L.A. Johnson, "Golden Girl: As Barbie Turns 50, Women Share Memories and Meaning of the Doll Who Has It All," *Pittsburgh Posy-Gazette*, March 8, 2009, at E-1.
52. Nancy Holt, "Workspaces," *Wall Street Journal*, Feb. 5, 2003, at B-8.

2 Carleton Fiorina at Hewlett-Packard

1. Reported in Peter Burrows, *Backfire—Carly Fiorina's High Stakes Battle For the Soul of Hewlett Packard* at 87 (Hoboken, NJ, Wiley & Sons, 2003).
2. Eric Nee, "Open Season on Carly Fiorina," *Fortune*, July 23, 2001, at 114.
3. *Backfire* at 97.
4. See Karl T. Greenfield, "What Glass Ceiling? Carly Fiorina Takes Over Hewlett-Packard, Becoming the First Woman CEO of a Dow 30 Firm," *Time*, Aug. 2, 1999, at 72.
5. Carly Fiorina, *Tough Choices* (New York, Penguin, 2007).

6. Idem at xii.
7. Idem at 320.
8. *Backfire* at 27 ("Others find her impulsive, calculating, deeply focused on goals that . . . are misguided").
9. See Gary Rivlin, "Hewlett-Packard to Lay Off 14,500 in Turnaround Effort," *New York Times*, July 20, 2005, at C-1 ("Mr. Hurd was taking steps to decentralize Hewlett, in contrast to Ms. Fiorina's efforts to centralize . . . [D]ecentralization, he said, will mean greater innovation within individual units").
10. With the fall of HP's share value, in part due to the market's reaction to September 11, 2001, and in part due to the near universal condemnation of the Compaq acquisition, HP's share price dived and, with it, the transaction's value dipped, to $19.5 billion.
11. Reported in *Backfire* at 175.
12. See Symposium, "The Essays of Warren Buffett," *Cardozo Law Rev.* 19, 5, 740 (1997) ("More big dumb acquisitions are made in the name of strategic plans than any other").
13. Gary Rivlin, "Hewlett Profits Come In Lower Than Expected," *New York Times*, Aug. 13, 2004, at C-1.
14. Matt Richtel, "With Earnings Up 38 percent, HP Raises Its Forecast," idem, Feb. 20, 2008, at C-3; Damon Darlin, "Hewlett Says Earnings Jumped 51 percent," idem, May 17, 2006, at C-1; Darlin, "Profit Jumps 30 percent at Hewlett A Year Into Chief's Tenure," idem, Feb. 16, 2006, at C-11.
15. Staff, "A Buyback at HP," idem, March 17, 2007, at C-2.
16. Darlin, "Hewlett-Packard Nears Goal of Overtaking I.B.M.," idem, Aug. 17, 2006, at C-3.
17. See Michael Meyer, "In a League of Her Own: There's No Glass Ceiling For Carleton Fiorina, Now the Nation's Highest-Ranking Female Executive," *Newsweek*, Aug. 2, 1999.
18. Patricia Sellers, "The Fifty Most Powerful Women in American Business," *Fortune*, Oct. 12, 1998, at 76.
19. Idem.
20. *Backfire* at 104.
21. Shipping increased quantities of a product and billing therefore in the days immediately before an accounting period closes, thus recognizing revenue in the instant quarter even though cash may not be received until some future time, or not received at all, if customers return the merchandise.
22. Idem at 117.
23. Quentin Hardy, "The Cult of Carly," *Forbes*, Dec. 13, 1999.
24. Michael A. Hiltzik, "William R. Hewlett, High-tech Entrepreneur Co-founded Hewlett-Packard," *Pittsburgh Post Gazette*, Jan. 13, 2001, at C-5.
25. See generally David Packard, *The HP Way: How Bill Hewlett and I Built Our Company* (Boston, Harper Business, 1995) (with Karen Lewis).
26. David Packard, Idem; Jim Collins & Jerry Porras, *Built To Last* (New York, Harper Business, 1994).
27. Richard S. Tedlow, *Giants of Enterprise* at 371 (New York, Harper Business, 2001).
28. *Compare* David Hamilton, "Inside Hewlett-Packard, Carly Fiorina Combines Discipline, New-Age Talk," *Wall Street Journal*, Aug. 22, 2000, at A-1 ("83 autonomous businesses") *with* "Rebuilding the Garage," *The Economist*, July 15, 2000, at 59 (130 product groups).
29. Hardy, *supra*.
30. *Backfire* at 83.
31. *Today Show*, Nov. 15, 1999, "One-on-One with HP CEO Carly Fiorina," interview with Jamie Gangrell.

32. Sellers, *supra*, at 94.
33. Carly Fiorina, quoted in Sheila Wellington, *Be Your Own Mentor* at 116 (New York, Random House, 2001).
34. Idem at 103.
35. Don Clark, "H-P Awards Chairman Title to Fiorina, Expects to Meet Profit, Revenue Targets," Sept. 25, 2000, at B-13, col. 1–2.
36. "Rebuilding the Garage," *supra* at 60.
37. Hamilton, *supra*, at A-18.
38. Recounted in Eric Nee, "Open Season on Carly Fiorina," *Fortune*, July 23, 2001, at 114.
39. Hamilton, *supra*, at A-18.
40. See Hardy, *supra*.
41. *Backfire* at 157–8.
42. Carly Fiorina, quoted in "Rebuilding the Garage," *supra*.
43. Financial results and quotations from Nee, *supra*.
44. Clark, *supra* note.
45. See Molly Williams & Bridget O'Brian, "H-P's Task Is to Sell Its Deal to Skeptics," *Wall Street Journal*, Sept. 6, 2001, at A-3 ("The acquisition will add 20 percent to the earnings per share in the first fiscal year, according to Ms. Fiorina.").
46. David Packard had announced his intention to leave the HP board before Fiorina came aboard. He was unhappy that HP was to spin off the original test and instrument business into Agilent Corp., a split up that Fiorina termed a "mistake," *Tough Choices* at 190. His term ended on Fiorina's watch during which she made no attempt to convince him to stay, even though he was Dave Packard's oldest son and the principal Packard family representative.
47. James Surowiecki, "The Financial Page—The Urge to Merge," *The New Yorker*, Sept. 17, 2001, at 72.
48. Idem (quoting a 1981 letter from Warren Buffet to Berkshire Hathaway shareholders).
49. Molly Williams, "H-P's Net Falls 89 percent, but Share Price Climbs 9.1 percent," Nov. 15, 2001, at A-3.
50. See Molly Williams & Gary McWilliams, "H-P Deal's Fate Rest With Skeptical Heirs Of Company Founders," Nov. 9, 2001, at A-.1.
51. Molly Williams, "Hewletts Reject Deal to Join H-P, Compaq," *Wall Street Journal*, Nov. 7, 2001, at A-3. See also Andrew R. Sorkin, "Hewletts Vow to Oppose Hewlett-Packard Merger with Compaq," *New York Times*, Nov. 7, 2001, at C-1.
52. See Molly Williams & Gary McWilliams, "Packard Group Opposes Compaq Deal," *Wall Street Journal*, Dec. 10, 2001, at A-3, col. 1–3.
53. Steve Lohr, "A Growing Group of Disgruntled Relatives May Seal the Fate of Hewlett-Packard and Compaq," *New York Times*, Nov. 8, 2001, at C-6.
54. Williams & McWilliams, *supra*, at A-9.
55. "Son of H-P Founder To File Proxy in Fight Against Compaq Deal," *Wall Street Journal*, Nov. 19, 2001, at B-5.
56. *Tough Choices* at 237.
57. Idem at 293.
58. Idem at 67.
59. Rivlin, *supra*.
60. Damon Darlin, "Hewlett Says Earnings Jumped 51 percent," idem, May 17, 2006, at C-1 ("The key was laptop sales, which increased 27 percent").
61. Damon Darlin, "Hewlett-Packard Nears Goal of Overtaking IBM," *New York Times*, Aug. 17, 2007, at C-3.
62. Damon Darlin, "Hewlett-Packard Says Quarterly Results Will Top Forecast," idem, May 9, 2007, at C-3.

63. Justin Scheck, "PC Demand Boosts HP Profit," *Wall Street Journal*, Feb. 20, 2008, A-3; Matt Richtel, "With Earnings Up 38 percent, H.P. Raises Its Forecast," *New York Times*, Feb. 20, 2008, C-3.
64. See, for example, *Tough Choices* at 136.
65. See, for example, *Tough Choices* at 96, 97, 101, 104, 146, 147.
66. Idem at 32.
67. Idem at 172.
68. *Backfire* at 132 ("There are very, very few companies that have that").
69. "Over the years I turned down requests from *Glamour, People, Vogue,* Diane Sawyer, Oprah Winfrey, and more." *Tough Choices* at 172.
70. *Be Your Own Mentor* at 100–02.
71. Idem at 224.
72. Idem at 276.
73. Idem at 286.
74. Idem at 224.
75. *Tough Choices* at 250.
76. Michael Maccoby, *The Productive Narcissist—The Promise and Peril of Visionary Leadership* at 24849 (New York, Broadway Books, 2003).
77. Idem at 191.
78. Idem at 88.
79. Gary Rivlin, *supra*, at C-1.
80. *Tough Choices* at 185.
81. *Backfire* at 171.
82. See, for example, Justin Scheck & Ben Worthen, "Hewlett-Packard Takes Aim at IBM," *Wall Street Journal*, May 14, 2008, at B-1 (under Mark Hurd, HP completed negotiations for $13.5 billion acquisition of Electronic Data Processing (EDS)).
83. *Tough Choices* at 237.
84. Idem at 249, 266.
85. *Tough Choices* at 250 (agreeing with Jay Keyworth).
86. Idem at 250.
87. Idem at 255 (agreeing with Jay Keyworth).
88. Idem at 246.
89. Idem at 248, 256.
90. Idem at 250.

3 A CEO Success—Andrea Jung at Avon Products

1. Sales by Mary Kay Cosmetics, Avon Products, and other direct sellers had come to represent only 6.8 percent of cosmetic sales by 2000. See Nanette Byrnes, "Avon—The New Calling," *Business Week*, Sept. 18, 2000, 136, at 138.
2. See, for example, Lisa Marsh, "Sears Dumps Avon Partnership Deal," *New York Post*, July 11, 2001, at 38. Avon then entered a similar agreement with J.C. Penny, who pulled the cosmetics after several months. Jung believed that Penny had not done enough to build up the cosmetics' presence in the stores. "We didn't bet the ranch on it and it was a great learning experience." Claudia Deutsch, "In a Dull Economy Avon Finds a Hidden Gloss," *New York Times*, June 1, 2003, §3, at 4.
3. Jung's strategy is highlighted in Jennifer Pellet, "Ding Dong Avon Stalling?," *Chief Executive*, June 1, 2000, 26, at 30.
4. CBS *Early Show* host Bryant Gumbel to Andrea Jung, July 26, 2001, CBS News transcripts, 2001 Burrelle's Information Services.
5. Katrina Brooker, "It Took a Lady to Save Avon; Elegant and Poised, with a Will of Iron, Andrea Jung Knows How to Win," *Fortune*, Oct. 15, 2001, at 202.

6. Staff, "Andrea Jung Elected Chairman of Avon's Board of Directors," *PR Newswire*, Sept. 6, 2001.
7. Ellen Byron, "Is Avon's Latest Scent the Sweet Smell of Success?," *Wall Street Journal*, Oct. 15, 2007, at B-1.
8. Robin Finn, "Spearheading a Marketing Makeover at Avon," *New York Times*, May 10, 2001, at B-2.
9. Patricia Sellers, "Behind Every Successful Woman There Is . . . A Woman," *Fortune*, Oct. 25, 1999, at 129.
10. Avon's early history is re-counted by Pellet, *supra*, at 26.
11. See, for example, Randall E. Stross, *eBoys*, at 252–60 (New York, Crown, 2000).
12. Byrnes, *supra*, at 140.
13. Micro lending programs by entities such as the Heinz Foundation enable women in poor regions to purchase needles and thread to become seamstresses, or chickens to become poultry farmers, thus alleviating chronic poverty. See, for example, James Surowieki, "The Financial Page: What Microloans Miss," *New Yorker*, March 17, 2008, at 35. Avon does much the same: "[W]e front our sales representatives their first order and that 'mini loan' is paid back after the first order." Byron, *supra*, at B-1 (quoting Andrea Jung).
14. Andrea Jung, quoted in Byron, *supra*, at B-3 ("Things have changed in many ways . . . high-touch meets high tech," but emphasis remains on Avon reps and direct selling).
15. Idem at 142.
16. Sheila Wellington, *Be Your Own Mentor* at 98 (New York, Random House, 2001).
17. Del Jones, "Avon Takes Breast Cancer Fight Personally: CEO Andrea Jung Leads Company's Fundraising Efforts," *U.S.A. Today*, March 7, 2000, at 3B.
18. J. Cramer & C. Mason, *Jim Cramer's Stay Mad* (New York, Simon & Schuster. 2007).
19. See, for example, Staff, "But Jim, What Do You Really Think," *Business Week*, at 46 ("I have said that as long as Andrea Jung is running the company, it will not go up. She is one of my top 5 CEOs who must leave.").
20. Staff, "Avon's Makeover Isn't Cosmetic," *Wall Street Journal*, Oct. 22, 2007, at C-1.
21. Jim Cramer, "Mad Money ReCap," *Yahoo! Finance*, Nov. 2, 2007 (visited February 8, 2008).
22. See Patricia Sellers, "America's Most Powerful Business Women: Patient But Not Passive," *Fortune*, Oct. 15, 2001, at 188.
23. See, for example, *Be Your Own Mentor, supra*, at 24 (develop five-year plans and in doing so entertain the idea of four or five careers, with different specialties and different corporations).
24. *No Seat at the Table* at 94–95, 105–06.
25. Idem at 87, 100.
26. *Be Your Own Mentor, supra*, at 86.
27. Staff, "Avon's Makeover Isn't Cosmetic," *Wall Street Journal*, Oct. 22, 2007, at C-1.
28. Recently, Ms. Jung became the first female director at Apple, Inc. Peter Carey, "Apple Appoints Woman to All-Male Board," *San Jose Mercury News*, Jan. 8, 2008.

4 Plowhorse—Marion Sandler at Golden West Financial

1. Staff, "The Cult of Carly," *Forbes*, Dec., 1999 (cover story).
2. James Collins, *Good To Great: Why Some Companies Make the Leap . . . And Others Don't* (New York, Harper Collins Business, 2001).
3. "Best Selling Business Books," *Wall Street Journal*, Feb. 15, 2008, at W-4 (ranked no. 3).

4. Jim Collins, "Beware the Self-Promoting CEO," *Wall Street Journal*, Nov. 26, 2001, at A-18.

5. Idem.

6. Dennis K, Berman, Carrick Mollenkamp & Valerie Bauerlein, "Wachovia Strikes $26 Billion Deal For Golden West," *Wall Street Journal*, May 8, 2006, at A-1.

7. Kathy M. Kristof, "Women at the Top—Almost," *Los Angeles Times*, May 28, 1990, at D-1.

8. At least one other public company, smaller than Golden West but publicly held, has a husband and wife co-CEO team. It is Tootsie Roll, Inc., the Chicago-based maker of Tootsie Rolls, Dots, Junior Mints, Charms and other popular candies. Melvin and Ellen Gordon function as co-CEOs based upon a controlling shareholding that Ms. Gordon's family has held for over 65 years. See Esther Wachs' Book, *Why the Best Man For the Job Is a Woman*, at 167–75 (New York, HarperCollins Business, 2000).

9. Matthew Schifrin, "What's the Payback?," *Forbes*, Jan. 6, 1992, at 144.

10. Due diligence is different in the initial sale and purchase of securities (the public offering, including the initial public offering, or IPO). There, the buyers are widespread and, before the offer, largely unknown. The law, therefore, places the due diligence responsibility upon the seller of the securities and its principal delegate, the managing underwriter, the investment banking firm that will bring the securities to market. See Securities Act of 1933 §11; *Escott v. BarChris Construction Co.*, 283 F. Supp. 643 (S.D.N.Y. 1969) (leading due diligence court case).

11. Staff, "An S&L With the Midas Touch," *Business Week*, May 19, 1980, at 130.

12. In fact, each year for three days in Beverly Hills Milkin and Drexel Burnham Lambert bought together potential buyers and sellers of junk bonds at the "predators' ball," where allegedly more than good investment prospects were available. Ensconced at the Beverly Hills Hotel, S&L managers from Tulsa, Toledo, or Fresno got to mingle with Wall Street investment banker types. The S&L managers could also regale friends back home with stories about the cocaine and prostitutes that were available. See generally Connie Bruck, *The Predator's Ball* (New York, Viking Penguin, 1989).

13. Seth Lubove, "Stick to Your Knitting—Golden West Is the Nation's Best-Managed Financial Company," *Forbes*, March 1, 2004, at 66.

14. And which Wachovia discontinued after it had acquired Golden West. Homeowners adopting options under Pick A Payment mortgages were allowing loan balances to increase too much. Valerie Bauerlein & Ruth Simon, "Wachovia to Discontinue Option-ARMs," *Wall Street Journal*, July 1, 2008, at C-3.

15. Michael Hilzik, "Golden State—Duo's Success Built on Old-School Approach," *Los Angeles Times*, March 3, 2003, at 3–1 (91 percent of Golden West mortgages are ARMs).

16. Reported in Don L. Burroughs, "Golden West: Eating Humble Pie, Making Lots of Bread," *U.S. News & World Rep.*, April 6, 1992, at 50.

17. Cable News Network Financial, "Street Sweep: Golden West Financial's CEO," April 26, 2000, CCN transcript 00042605FN-106; Staff, "Golden West Financial Corp.—On the Record: Marion and Herb Sandler," *San Francisco Chronicle*, July 18, 2004, at 11 (industry went from 4,500 S&Ls in 1970s to approximately 1,000 today).

18. "The 50 Most Powerful Women in Business 2000," *Fortune*, Oct. 15, 2001.

19. Esther Wachs Book, *supra*, at 199.

20. Kristof, *supra*.

21. E. Scott Rechard, "Putting Their Money into the Right to Know—A Pair of Ex-bankers Are Launching ProPacifica, a Nonprofit Investigative News

Organization," *Los Angeles Times*, Nov. 19, 2007, at C-1; Staff, "The Top Givers," *Business Week*, Nov. 27, 2007, at 72.
22. See David Erhich, "Street Jeers Wachovia," *Wall Street Journal*, April 15, 2008, at C-1.

5 Anne Mulcahy at Xerox and Patricia Russo at Alcatel-Lucent—Fix It CEOs

1. Geraldine Fabrikant, "Executive Is First to Back Women at Augusta," *New York Times*, Oct. 5, 2002, at D-1. They rejected his proposal; Augusta National's membership remains all male.
2. Pamela Moore, "She's Here to Fix the Xerox," *Business Week*, Aug. 6, 2001, at 47.
3. Edward Moltzen, "Her 'Partner or Perish' Rally Cry Brings Xerox Back from the Brink," *Computer Reseller News*, June 25, 2007, at 20.
4. Associated Press, "A Dividend at Xerox," *New York Times*, Nov. 20, 2007, at C-5 (first dividend in six years).
5. Claudia H. Deutsch, "Openers; Suits; Miles to Go," idem, March 27, 2005, at 32.
6. Bloomberg News, "Citicorp. Adds 2 to Board," idem, Sept. 21, 2004, at C-2.
7. Betsy Morris, "The Accidental CEO: She Was Never Groomed to Be the Boss," *Fortune*, June 23, 2006, at 58.
8. See Claudia H. Deutsch, "At Xerox, the Chief Earns (Grudging) Respect," *Sunday New York Times*, Money and Business, June 2, 2002, at 1.
9. See Moore, *supra*, at 47 (Xerox "killing its entire line of desktop inkjet printers—a one year old business that employed 1,500 people worldwide and had been championed by Mulcahy herself").
10. See James Bandler & John Hechinger, "SEC Says Xerox Misled Investors," *Wall Street Journal*, April 12, 2002, at A-3.
11. James Bandler & Mark Maremont, "Xerox to Pay $10 Million in SEC Case," idem, April 2, 2002, at A-3 (highest previous was $3.5 million paid by America Online).
12. See James Bandler & Mark Maremont, "Deeper Accounting Woes at Xerox," idem, June 28, 2002, at A-3.
13. Deutsch, *supra*, at 1.
14. Claudia Deutsch, "Prices Are Lower But Profits Are Up at Xerox," *New York Times*, April 21, 2007, at C-4.
15. Reported in Deutsch, *supra*.
16. Xerox hired a high-profile law firm (Akin, Gump, Strauss) to investigate but then Xerox's house lawyers, including General Counsel Christina Clayton, limited the law firm to Mexico, even after Akin Gump had indications that the lease accounting manipulations were widespread. Xerox lawyers would "second guess everything," one source reported. James Bandler & Mark Maremont, "SEC's Xerox Case May Broaden To Ex-Executives and to KPMG," *Wall Street Journal*, April 10, 2002, at A-1.
17. See Rachel McTague, "Pitt Met With Xerox CEO at Time SEC Was Investigating Firm," 34 BNA Fed. Sec. Reg. & L. Rep. 831 (May 27, 2002).
18. See, for example, "Can SEC's Pitt Judge Former Clients?" *Wall Street Journal*, June 12, 2022, at C-1 (report of private meeting with Anne Mulcahy).
19. See Michael Schroeder, "Help Wanted: SEC Chief Pitt Is Gone," *Wall Street Journal*, Nov. 7, 2002, at C-1.
20. Biographical details from Xerox Executive Biographies, available, http://www.2.xerox.com.about_xerox (visited March 3, 2008).
21. Moore, *supra*.

22. See Anthony Bianco & Pamela L. Moore, "Downfall—The Inside Story of the Management Fiasco at Xerox," *Business Week*, March 5, 2001, 82, at 85.
23. See generally Michael Hiltzik, *Dealers of Lightening: Xerox PARC and the Dawn of the Computer Age* (New York, Harper Business, 1999).
24. Idem.
25. Reuters, "Chief Executive of Xerox to be Chairwoman Too," *New York Times*, Dec. 4, 2001, at C-4.
26. Patricia Sellers, "Patient But Not Passive—The Top Fifty Female Executives of 2001," *Fortune*, Oct. 15, 2001, at 188.
27. Deutsch, *supra*, at 12.
28. Idem.
29. Moore, *supra*, at 48.
30. Deutsch, *supra*, at 12.
31. Bloomberg News, "Xerox Receives $557 Million in Financing," *New York Times*, March 28, 202, at C-3.
32. Bloomberg News, "Xerox Profit Doubles; Forecast Is Raised," idem, July 24, 2004, at C-4.
33. Feder, *supra*, at C-5.
34. Barnaby J. Feder, "Xerox Alters Tack to Win Business Back," idem, May 1, 2003, at C-5.
35. Sellers, *supra*, at 190.
36. Julie Cresswell, "How Suite It Isn't: A Dearth of Female Bosses," *New York Times*, Dec. 17, 2006, Sunday Money and Business, at 31.
37. Idem.
38. Ellen Galinsky, "Work Life Award Interview with Anne Mulcahy," April 11, 2006
39. Claudia Deutsch, "The Boss: Shaped by Family Debates," *New York Times*, Oct. 10, 2001, at C-6.
40. Idem.
41. See Dennis K. Berman, "Lucent Veteran Russo to Return as CEO," *Wall Street Journal*, Jan. 7, 2002, at A-3.
42. Linda A. Johnson, "New Lucent CEO Russo Seen As Strong Manager, Morale Builder," *Pittsburgh Post Gazette*, June 6, 2002, at E-8.
43. See Berman, *supra*, at A-3.
44. "Get Big Fast" is the title of Jeff Bezos's biography, Robert Spector, *Amazon.Com: Get Big Fast* (New York, Harper Collins, 2000).
45. Peter Borrows, *Backfire* at 111 (Hoboken, NJ, John Wiley & Sons, 2003).
46. Dennis K. Berman & Joann S. Lublin, "Russo's Goal as Lucent's New Chief: Restore Luster," *Wall Street Journal*, Jan. 8, 2002, at B-1.
47. Jonathan Weil, "Lucent's Sales Outlook Is Central to Suit Filed By Former Official," *Wall Street Journal*, Dec. 20, 2000.
48. Claudia Deutsch, "Departure Expected to Have Little Impact on Kodak," New York Times, Jan. 8, 2002, at C-8.
49. Patrick McGeehan, "Executive Pay: A Special Report—Money Follows the Pin-stripes," idem, April 6, 2003, at 31.
50. Berman & Lublin, *supra*, at B-1.
51. See Stephanie N. Mehta, "First/Hot," *Fortune*, Feb. 4, 2002, at 23.
52. See generally Stephanie N. Mehta, "Pat Russo's Lucent Vision," *Fortune*, April 15, 2002, at 126.
53. Staff, "Technology Journal: Traveling Light," *Wall Street Journal*, Jan. 24, 2002.
54. Comment of Edward Whitacre, CEO of SBC Communications, quoted in Berman & Lublin, *supra*, at B-1.
55. Mehta, *supra*, at 127.

56. Matt Richtel, "Lucent Reports Profit in Quarter for the First Time in 3 Years," *New York Times*, Oct. 23, 2003, at C-4.
57. Richtel, "Lucent's Chief Offers Bad News, and Optimism," idem, July 4, 2003, at C-1.
58. See Ken Belson, "Lucent Profit Declines 49 percent; Revenue is Short of Forecasts," idem, Jan. 20, 2005, at C-8; Belson, "Its Sales Down 15 percent, Lucent Cuts Revenue Forecast for the Year," idem, Jan. 14, 2005, at C-4.
59. Andrew R. Sorkin & Ken Belson, "Talks for Lucent May Signal End for 90s Symbol," idem, March 24, 2006, at A-1.
60. Staff, "The Splice That Binds Two Giants," idem, March 25, 2006, at C-1.
61. Vikas Bajaj, "Merger Deal Is Reached by Lucent and Alcatel," idem, April 3, 2006, at C-1.
62. Andrew R. Sorkin, "A Transatlantic Merger of Equals? Not Exactly," idem, April 9, 2006, at 33.
63. Staff, "Revenue Falls 16 percent at Alcatel Lucent," idem, Jan. 24, 2007.
64. James Kanter, "Alcatel-Lucent Warns of Further Losses," idem, April 25, 2007, at C-18.
65. Vixtoria Shannon, "Alcatel-Lucent Posts Loss But Revenue Climbs 18 percent," idem, Feb. 9, 2008, at C-3.
66. Reported in James Kanter, "Shareholders in Paris Approve Merger of Alcatel and Lucent," idem, Sept. 8, 2006, at C-3.
67. Sorkin, *supra*, at 33.
68. Wilson Rothman, "Pat Russo," *Time*, April 30, 2006.
69. Jethro Mullen & Leila Abboud, "Alcatel Talks Up Its Prospects to Holders," *Wall Street Journal*, May 31, 2008, at B-6.
70. Leila Abboud, Sara Silver & Joann S. Lublin, "Alcatel Seeks New Leaders As Chairman, CEO to Leave," idem, July 30, 2008, at B-1; David Gauthier-Villars, Joann Lublin & Leila Abboud, "Alcatel Goes on the Hunt for New Leaders," idem, Aug. 5, 2008, at B-1; David Gauthier-Williams, "Alcatel CEO Covets New Technology," idem, Sept. 3, 2008, at B-3 (Ben Verwaayen appointed CEO of Alcatel-Lucent).
71. Idem, July 30, 2008 (internal quotation marks omitted).
72. Idem.

6 Go Where They Aren't

1. Brent Adams, "Reynolds America CEO: A Fiery Competitor," *The Business Journal*, Oct. 31, 2003.
2. See Edward Martin, "A Woman's Work: It's Almost Never Done as CEO of a Major Company," *Business North Carolina*, April 2005, at 32.
3. Shelly Branch, "Ivey to Take Helm at Tobacco Giant B&W, a BAT Unit," *Wall Street Journal*, Nov. 10, 2000, at B-8.
4. "B&W's Ivey Eyes Greater Relevance, Local Flavor, for Lucky Strike & Kool," *Brandweek*, Feb. 7, 2000, at 9.
5. See, for example, Bill Dedman, "Executive Says He's Uncertain About Tobacco's Harm," *New York Times*, March 3, 1998, at A-16 (40 states); Richard Perez-Dena, "New York Politics Hold Up Most of Nation's Tobacco Cash," idem, April 11, 1999, at 11 (remaining $206 billion to be distributed among 46 states).
6. Vanessa O'Connell & Deborah Ball, "Tobacco Merger to Give Top Job to Susan Ivey," *Wall Street Journal*, Oct. 29, 2003, at B-1.
7. *New York Times*, Oct. 29, 2003, at C-8.
8. "2007 Outperformers," *USA Today*, Jan. 3, 2008, at B-2.
9. "Pay and Performance," *Fortune*, Oct. 15, 2007, at 149.

10. See Chapter 12 in this volume.
11. Martin, *supra*.
12. Richard Carver, "Ivey Lists Tips for Women on the Way Up," *Winston Salem Journal*, Oct. 3, 2006, at B-1.
13. Linda Bell, "Women Led Firms and the Gender Gap in Top Executive Jobs," http://ssrn.com/abstract=773964, July 2007, at 16–17.
14. Spencer Stuart, *No Longer Your Father's Utility: Women in Power in Today's Energy Industry* (2002).
15. Idem at 2.
16. Susan Hitchcock, "Energy's Her Game—Inclusive Her Style," (2001), http://www.turknett.com/sectionR/Rosput1.html.
17. Catalyst, Inc., *The Double-Bind Dilemma for Women in Leadership: Damned If You Do, Doomed If You Don't* at 32 (2007).
18. See Douglas M. Branson, *No Seat at the Table—How Corporate Governance and Law Keep Women Out of the Boardroom* (New York, NYU Press, 2007) (side stepping as a route for women in obtaining seats on boards of directors).
19. Staff, *Index to the Fortune 500 and the Fortune 1,000*, April 30, 2007, at F-75.
20. Spencer Stuart Study, *supra*, at 5.
21. See Hitchcock, *supra*.
22. Marci Alborghetti, "Energized for Action," http://www.entrepreneur.com/tradejournals/article/58252788.
23. Eric Minton, "Catherine Land Waters," http://entrepreneur.com/tradejournals/article/63267770.
24. Kate Colburn, "Suzanne Sitherwood of AGL: A Passion for Diversity," http://diversitycareers.com/articles/pro/05_octnov/ann_suzanne.
25. Hitchcock, *supra*.
26. Idem.
27. Spencer Stuart, *supra*, at 4.
28. Melissa Allison, "Utility Exec New Safeco CEO," *Seattle Times*, Dec. 8, 2005, at E-1.
29. Katherine Long, "Safeco Sold: HQ Goes, Name Stays," *Seattle Times*, April 27, 2008, at A-3; Staff, "Liberty Mutual Buys Safeco Insurance Company for $6.2 Billion," idem, April 24, 2008.
30. Jon Birger, "ADMs New Boss—The Outsider," *Fortune*, Oct. 16, 2006, 166, at 168.
31. Idem.
32. T. Boone Pickens, *Boone* at 149–235 (Boston, Houghton Mifflin, 1987).
33. Greg Burns, "Bringing New Energy to ADM," *Chicago Tribune*, Dec. 2006, at 29.
34. See Richard Lieber, *Rats in the Grain: Dirty Tricks and Trials at Archer Daniels Midland* (New York, Four Walls Four Windows, 2000).
35. Scott Kilman & Joann Lublin, "ADM Chooses an Energy-Savvy Outsider as Its New CEO," *Wall Street Journal*, April 28, 2006, at B-1.
36. Birger, *supra* (quoting a food industry executive search consultant).
37. "From One Male Bastion to the Other," *Business Week*, May 15, 2006.
38. Birger, *supra*.
39. Doug Cameron & Jennifer Hoyt, "ADM Profit Plunges 61 percent But Sales Soar as Prices Rise," *Wall Street Journal*, Aug. 6, 2008, at B-3.
40. Chapter 14, in this volume, describes stereotypes, including "Queen Bee."
41. Kathleen Kingsbury & Julie Norwell, "People to Watch in Business," *Time*, July 24, 2006, at 16.
42. Lloyd Watson, "Chevron Exec Is Industry's Top Female Operating Chief," *San Francisco Chronicle*, Aug. 11, 1993, at B-3.

7 Two Additional CEO Portraits

1. See, for example, Patricia Sellers, "Can Meg Whitman Save California," *Fortune*, March 30, 2009, at 64 (cover story). See also Ellen Byron & Stu Woo, "Ebay Ex-Chief Spurs Political Speculation," *Wall Street Journal*, Jan. 6, 2009, at B-3 (Whitman to announce candidacy); Julliet Williams, "Run For Governor Could Be Revealing," *San Diego Union Tribune*, Jan. 7, 2009, at A-4 (same).
2. See Douglas M. Branson, *No Seat at the Table—How Corporate Governance and Law Keep Women Out of the Boardroom* at 99 (2007) (Barnes at Sears Roebuck, Sara Lee, Pepsico, Staples, Avon Products, Lucas Film Corp. and *New York Times*).
3. Reported in Greg Burns, "Nobody's Business But Her Own: Brenda Barnes Was Accused of Betraying Working Women When She Quit to Be With Her Family; Now She's a CEO Again and Unapologetic About Her Personal and Career Choices," *Chicago Tribune* Sunday Magazine, Oct. 14, 2007, 12.
4. John Schmeltzer, "Brenda Barnes—Focus on Education Started Journey to Top Spot at Sara Lee," *Chicago Tribune*, Oct. 28, 2005, C-1 (quoting John Gogonas).
5. Idem.
6. See Chapter 7 in this volume.
7. Idem.
8. See, for example, Sally Weale, "Career vs. Children—Superwoman is Coming Home—To Family," *The Guardian* (London), Sept. 26, 1997, at 5.
9. Joan Blakewell, "One Pepsi Short of the Real Thing," *Sunday Times* (London), Sept. 28, 1997.
10. Lisa Belkin, "The Opt-Out Revolution," *New York Times* Sunday Magazine, Oct. 23, 2003, at 42.
11. Burns, *supra*.
12. Burns, *supra*.
13. See Staff, "The Top Business Schools," *Wall Street Journal*, April 5, 2001, at R-3 (5th); idem, Sept. 9, 2002, at R-5 (4th); idem, Sept. 17, 2003, R-5 (4th); idem, Sept. 25, 2005, at R-4 (4th). In 2006, Northwestern fell out of the top 5, ranking 6th, and fell further the following year, ranking 12th. Idem, Sept. 20, 2006, at R-4 and Sept. 17, 2007, at R-2.
14. Schmeltzer, *supra* (service on boards at *The New York Times*, Staples, Inv., and Lucas Film, Ltd.).
15. Lissa L. Broome, "The Corporate Boardroom: Still a Male Club," *Journal of Corporation Law*, 33, 665, 669–70.
16. See, for example, Institutional Investor Services, ISS 2007 U.S. Proxy Voting Guidelines; Concise Summary at 2 (2008).
17. T. Shawn Taylor, "Executives Reflect on Fiorina's Ouster," *Chicago Tribune*, Feb. 16, 2005, at C-1.
18. See Schmeltzer, *supra*; John Schmeltzer, "Sara Lee's Barnes Set to Add Chairman's Title," *Chicago Tribune*, Oct. 25, 2005, at C-3.
19. Julie Jargon, "High Costs Put Sara Lee CEO in a Bind," *Wall Street Journal*, July 23, 2008, at B-1.
20. Staff, "Chock Full O' Brands: Sara Lee," *The Economist*, Nov. 12, 2005, at 65; Julie Jargon, "Sara Lee to Maintain Spending Pace," *Wall Street Journal*, Nov. 8, 2007, at C-6.
21. Jargon, *supra*.
22. http://finance.yahoo.com/q?s=SLE (last visited February 25, 2008).
23. Jargon, *supra*.
24. Burns, *supra*.
25. Becky Yerak, "Women Missing From Top Wage Earners at 35 Big Firms," *Chicago Tribune*, Jan. 22, 2006 (statistics from Chicago Network).
26. Judith Dobrzynski, "Female CEOs Still Rare Sight," *Chicago Tribune*, March 28,

2007, at C-23 (statistics by Chicago Network). See also John Schmeltzer, "CEO Pushes Women to Succeed," idem, April 12, 2007, at C-3.

27. Dobbrzynski, *supra*.
28. Mylene Mangalindan, "Next on the Block: A Bid to Succeed eBay CEO," *Wall Street Journal*, Jan. 28, 2008, at B-1.
29. See Maria Farkas, *Meg Whitman at eBay* at 3 et seq. (Boston, Harvard Business School Press, 2000).
30. Ken Howe et al., "Interview with Meg Whitman: CEO and President, eBay," *San Francisco Chronicle*, Nov. 19, 2006, at C-1.
31. eBay's early history is recounted in Randall Stross, *eBoys* at 49–55 (New York, Crown Publishers, 2000).
32. Mark Gimein, "CEOs Who Manage Too Much," *Fortune*, Sept. 4, 2000, at 234, in an appendix list ten "CEOs Who've Gone Dot-Com," including Whitman.
33. Farkas, *supra*, at 7.
34. Idem at 12–14.
35. Summarized in Michael Maccoby, *The Productive Narcissist*, at 243–44 (New York, Broadway Books, 2003).
36. See, for example, Valerie Bauerlein & David Enrich, "Wachovia Board Ousts CEO As Bank's Missteps Mount," *Wall Street Journal*, June 3, 2008, at A-1.
37. Indeed, that is the title of the leading book about the success of Jeff Bezos and Amazon, Inc., Robert Spector, *Get Big Fast* (New York, HarperCollins, 2000).
38. Heidi E. Moore, "Deal Journal: US Executives Decry Insularity," *Wall Street Journal*, June 12, 2008, at C-3.
39. See Therese Poletti, "Market Watch First Take: Whitman Leaves Behind Mixed Legacy at EBay," *Dow Jones Bus. News*, Jan. 24, 2008.
40. Two expositions on spinning are: Sean Griffith, "Spinning and Underpricing: A Legal and Economic Analysis of the Preferential Allocation of Shares in Public Offerings," *Brooklyn Law Review*, 69, 583 (2004); Therese H. Maynard, "Spinning in a Hot IPO—Breach of Fiduciary Duty or Business as Usual?, *Wm. & Mary Law Review*, 43, 2023 (2002).
41. Staff, "eBay Inc.: Executives to Pay $3.4 million in Shareholder Suit Settlement," *Wall Street Journal*, April 29, 2005, at A-11.
42. See, for example, Andrew Parry, "The Most Respected CEOs: From Around the World, 30 Who Make a Real Difference," *Barron's*, March 28, 2005, at 23.
43. Mylene Mangalindan, "EBay Chief Whitman, Web Pioneer, Plans to Retire," *Wall Street Journal*, Jan. 22, 2008, at A-3.
44. Erika Brown, "Much Ado About Meg," *Forbes*, Jan. 24, 2008.
45. http://finance.yahoo.com/eBay (last visited May 23, 2008).
46. See Mylene Mangalindan & Joann Lublin, "After Disney Try, EBay's Whitman Sees Star Rise," *Wall Street Journal*, March 14, 2005, at B-1. The article makes no mention of Whitman's part in the spinning episode.
47. Post-Whitman, eBay has been a company in transition, from the middleman of an online auction site, a virtual flea market, to representation of various mass market secondary sellers, bargain basements of out-of-season or over-stocked goods. The latter sell at a fixed but discounted price, enticing consumers with quick service and free shipping, rather than conducting auctions. See Geoffrey A. Fowler, "Auctions Fade in eBay's Bid for Growth," *Wall Street Journal*, May 26, 2009, at A-9.

8 Five Who Leave Few Footprints

1. Staff, "People in Business," *St. Louis Post-Dispatch*, May 9, 1995, at 13-C.
2. Judith Vandewater, "Judge Questions Blue Cross Deal, Takes Over Assets," idem, Oct. 31, 1998 at 32.

3. Vandewater, "Blue Cross Challenges Judge's Order," idem, Nov. 3, 1998, at C-6; Terry Ganey, "Public Hearings in St. Louis Will Study Operations of State's Blue Cross," Idem Nov. 20, 1998, at C-8.
4. Staff, "Wellpoint CEO Glasscock to Retire, Braly Tapped," St. Louis Business Journal, Feb. 26, 2007.
5. Daniel Lee, "A Historic Handoff at Wellpoint," *Indianapolis Star*, Feb. 27, 2007 (quoting former colleague John Riffle).
6. John Ketzenberger, "John Ketzenberger's Column," *Indianapolis Star*, Feb. 27, 2007, Business, at 1 (quoting outgoing CEO Larry Glasscock).
7. Staff, "Braly Named Woman to Watch by WSJ," *St. Louis Business Journal*, Nov. 19, 2007.
8. See Vanessa Fuhrmans & Carol Hymowitz, "Wellpoint's CEO Takes the Reins, Facing Challenges," *Wall Street Journal*, June 6, 2007, at B-1.
9. Daniel Lee, "Wall Street Pummels Wellpoint Shares," *Indianapolis Star*, March 11, 2008, Business, at 1.
10. Yahoo! Finance, http://finance.yahoo/wellpoint/basic chart/5yr max (last visited February 27, 2008).
11. Lee, "Wellpoint Execs Handle Stock Tumble Together," *Indianapolis Star*, March 15, 2008, News, at 1.
12. Dinah Wisenberg Brin, "Wellpoint Profit Falls 25 percent," *Wall Street Journal*, April 24, 2008, at B-6.
13. Vanessa Fuhrmans, "Wellpoint Net Falls, Yet Pricing, Cost Moves Please Investors," *Wall Street Journal*, July 24, 2008, at B-3. See also Vanessa Fuhrmans, "Wellpoint Clients Leave as Prices Rise," idem, Sept. 3, 2008, at B-1.
14. Shirleen Dorman, "Wellpoint to Cut About 1,500 Jobs," *Wall Street Journal*, Jan. 20, 2009, at B-5.
15. Vanessa Fuhrmans, "Wellpoint Profit Slides 61 percent as Plan Numbers Fall," *Wall Street Journal*, Jan. 29, 2009, at B-6.
16. "Wellpoint Named as One of Diversity Inc.'s Top 50 Companies," *PR Newswire*, April 8, 2008.
17. See generally Claudia Deutsch, "Profile: Relighting Fires at Avon," *New York Times*, April 3, 1994, at F-6.
18. Carleton University, Great Grads File, http://alumni.carleton.ca/alumni/gratgrads_profile.cfm? (last visited April 2008).
19. Almost all, if not all, major corporations maintain a website on which, among other things, they describe their goods and services. Information about Western Union's services come from its website. See http://corporate.westernunion.com/services.html (last visited April 24, 2008).
20. Staff, "Western Union's Christina Gold Named One of Fortune's 50 Most Powerful Women," Fortune, Oct. 20, 2006.
21. "[W]e do not make the personal details of our CEO publicly available. Thank you for your interest in our CEO and in our company." Email from Annmarie Farretta, manager of corporate communications, investor & public relations, the TJX Companies, to the author, May 21, 2008.
22. TJX Companies, http://www.tjx.com/about.asp (last visited April 1, 2008). TJX also operates 170 Winner's and 50 HomeSense stores in Canada and 190 T.J. Maxx stores on Europe. Idem.
23. Jessica Pallay, "Meyrowitz Moving On, Herrman Moving Up at TJX," *Daily News Record*, Nov., 15, 2004, at 28.
24. "Carol Meyrowitz at the Helm of Home Fashions Retailer TJX," (Oct. 7, 2005), available at www.fibrefashions.com (last visited April 1, 2008).
25. "TJX Companies, Inc. Victimized by Computer Systems Intrusion," *Business Wire*, Jan. 17, 2007.

26. See *In re TJX Companies Retail Security Breach Litigation*, No. 07–10162, MDL No. 1838 (D. Mass. 2007).
27. "The TJX Companies, Inc., Agrees to Settlement of Customer Class Actions, Subject to Court Approval," *Business Wire*, Sept. 21, 2007.
28. Joseph Pereira et al., "U.S. Indicts 11 in Credit-Card Scheme," *Wall Street Journal*, Aug. 6, 2008, at B-1.
29. TJX Companies, Inc., http://www.tjx.com (last visited April 2008).
30. Yale School of Management, "Alumni Leader Profile: Indra Nooyi," available at http://mba.yale.edu/alumni/alumni_leaders/nooyii.shtml (last visited April 17, 2008).
31. Jyoti Thottam, "The Iron Woman Is Ready to Rock: Indra Nooyi at Pepsico," *Time*, Dec. 1, 2003, at 73.
32. See Betty Morris, "The Pepsi Challenge," Fortune, March 3, 2008, at 54.
33. Staff, "Women in Business: The Pepsi Challenge," *The Economist*, Aug. 19, 2006, at 51.
34. Damayanti Datta, "Mate Today," *India Today*, Dec. 25, 2006, at 94.
35. Vinnee Tong, "Pepsi Taps Indian Woman as Nest CEO," *Globe and Mail* (Toronto), Aug. 15, 2006, at B-9.
36. Chard Terhune & Joann Lublin, "Pepsi's New CEO Doesn't Keep Her Options Bottled Up," *Wall Street Journal*, Aug. 15, 2006, at B-1.
37. Bill Saporito, "Indra Nooyi," *Time*, May 14, 2007, at 156.
38. Terhune & Lublin, *supra* (quoting Ramesh Vangal).
39. Staff, "The Ceiling Breakers: Up and Away," *India Today*, Jan. 13, 2003, at 14.
40. Terhune & Lublin, *supra* (quoting Roger Enrico).
41. Idem; Yahoo! Finance, available at http://financeyahoo.com/pep (last visited February 27, 2008).
42. Betsy McKay, "PepsiCo CEO Adapts to Tough Climate," *Wall Street Journal*, Sept. 11, 2008, at B-1.
43. Anajali Cordeiro & Valerie Bauerlein, "PepsiCo Battles Soda Slowdown at Home," *Wall Street Journal*, Feb. 14, 2009, at B-5.
44. Christina Rogers, "Pepsi Exec Likens America to the Middle Finger," *New York Sun*, May 19, 2005, at 13.
45. Terhune & Lublin, *supra*.
46. Morris, *supra*, at 54.
47. Bloomberg News, "Former Rite Aid Chief Gets 8 Years in Prison," *New York Times*, May 28, 2004, at C-ll. See also Kenneth Gilpin, "Ex-Rite Aid Officials Face U.C. Charges of Financial Fraud, idem, June 22, 2002, at A-1; Richard Opel, Jr., "Chief Is Ousted at Rite Aid and Earnings Are Restated," idem, Oct. 19, 1999, at C-6.
48. Floyd Norris, "Rite Aid to Pay $200 Million to Settle Shareholder Suits," idem, Nov. 10, 2000, at C-4.
49. Tracie Rozhon, "Shock Therapy to Resuscitate Rite-Aid Chain," idem, May 19, 2007, at C-3.
50. Floyd Norris, "Rite Aid Names a New Management Team," idem, Dec. 6, 1999, at C-2.
51. David Pinto, "CDR Names Mary Sammons Retailer of the Year," *Chain Drug Review*, 24, Jan. 7, 2002, at 3.
52. Staff, "Rite Aid Launches a National Television Ad Campaign," *Business Wire*, Aug. 27, 2001.
53. See Mike Vogel, "Sammons Challenges Rite Aid to Be Even Better," *Chain Drug Review*, 26, Aug. 30, 2004, at 3.
54. Staff, "Rite Aid Receives Stockholder OK," 29 *Chain Drug Review*, Feb. 2, 2007, at 2. See also Jessica Blair, "Analysts, Executives Weigh In on Rite Aid's Integration Process," *Central Pennsylvania Bus. J.*, 23, Oct. 19, 2007, 9.

55. Staff, "We Have to Differentiate Ourselves," *Chain Drug Review*, 29, Nov. 19, 2007, at 3 (comments of Mary Sammons).
56. http://finance.yahoo.com.RAD (visited May 20, 2008).
57. Norris, *supra*.
58. Amy Merrick & Jennifer Hoyt, "Acquired Stores Weigh on Rite Aid," *Wall Street Journal*, June 27, 2008, at B-3.
59. Amy Merrick, "Rite Aid See Wider Loss, Makes Management Changes," *Wall Street Journal*, Sept. 26, 2008, at B-3.
60. Shirleen Dorman, "Rite Aid Board Approves Reverse Stock Split," *Wall Street Journal*, Oct. 20, 2008, at B-2.
61. David Pinto, "What Comes After the Assimilation Is Over: Rite Aid's Option is to Recast the Chain as the Consumers' Top Choice for Wellness," *Chain Drug Review*, 29, Nov. 19, 2007, at 1.
62. See the discussion in Chapter 11 this volume.

9 CEO Additions of 2008–09

1. Catalyst, Inc., Press Release. "Women CEOs of the Fortune 1000," Feb., 2009 (listing 15 in the *Fortune 500* but omitting Irene Rosenfeld). See also Del Jones, "Women Slowly Gain on Corporate America," *USA Today*, Jan. 2, 2009, Money, at 6B (listing 13 as of Jan. 1).
2. SUN, XOM, RDS-B and BP—Profiles & Key Statistics, Yahoo! Finance (visited March 31, 2009).
3. Staff, "Refiner Sunoco Names Elsenhans First Female CEO," *USA Today*, July 16, 2008.
4. Francesca Donner, "At Sunoco, Lynn Laverty Elsenhans Vaults to the Top," *Wall Street Journal*, July 16, 2008.
5. Christopher Dow, "Lynn Elsenhans," *Rice Magazine*, issue no, 1, 2008.
6. Kate Galbraith, "Strategic Shift Is Expected From New Chief at Sunoco, *New York Times*, July 17, 2008.
7. Dow, *supra*.
8. Idem.
9. Vicki McKinney, Darryl Wilson, Nita Brooks, Anne O'Leary & Bill Hardgrave, "Women and Men in the IT Profession," *51 Communications of the ACM*, issue no. 2, at 81 (2008).
10. Douglas M. Branson, *No Seat at the Table—How Corporate Governance and Law Keep Women Out of the Boardroom* at 106 (New York, NYU Press, 2007).
11. Kathleen Melymuka, "Why Women Quit Technology," *Computer World*, 39, 16, at 35 (2008).
12. Jessica E. Vascellare & Joann S. Lublin, "Yahoo Names Bartz as CEO, Decker Resigns," *Wall Street Journal*, Jan. 14, 2009, at B-1.
13. Carol Bartz, "Carol Bartz: No Time to Change for Others," *Forbes ASAP*, Dec., 1997, at 140.
14. Reported in Melymuka, *supra*, at 35.
15. Meg Whitman & Pat Russo, "The Steps to Tackle the Female Brain Drain," *Computer Weekly*, Oct. 19, 2004, at 46.
16. John Ballard, Karen Scales & Mary Ann Edwards, "Perceptions of Information Technology Careers Among Women in Career Development," *Information Technology Learning and Performance J.*, 24,2, at 2 (2006).
17. Cathy Gulli, "Do Women Avoid IT Jobs on Purpose?," *Macleans*, 121, 23, 32 (2008).
18. McKinney et al., *supra*, at 82.
19. Ballard et al., *supra*, at 8 (quoting George Friedman).

20. See Edward Cone, "Behind the Decline in Women in IT," *CIO Insight*, June 27, 2007, at 82.
21. See the biography in Miguel Helft, "Yahoo's New Chief Makes a Decisive First Appearance," *New York Times*, Jan. 16, 2009, at B-1. Bartz is also featured in Julie Creswell, "How Suite It Isn't: A Dearth of Female Bosses," *Money & Business*, Dec. 17, 2006, at 1; Staff, "Biography of Carol Bartz," *Business Week*, March 6, 2006, at 87.
22. Marta Mendoza, "The World According to Carol Bartz," *More Magazine*, June 2006.
23. Recounted in Creswell, *supra*, at 1.
24. Staff, "One Tough Yahoo," *The Economist*, Jan. 17, 2009, at 66.
25. Creswell, *supra*, at 1 (remarks of Kim Polese).
26. Idem.
27. Lawrence Fisher, "Profile" Carol Bartz—Imposing a Hierarchy On a Gaggle of Techies," *New York Times*, Nov. 29, 1992, section 3, at 4.
28. Idem.
29. Creswell, *supra*.
30. Carol Hymowitz, "Yahoo's New Chief With Deep Roots in the Valley, *Forbes.com*, Jan. 13, 2009.
31. Fisher, *supra*.
32. Rebecca Buckman, "The Exacting Standards of Carol Bartz," *Forbes.com*, Jan. 15, 2009.
33. Creswell, *supra*.
34. G. Paschal Zachary, "The Survivor," *Business*, 2.0, Dec. 1, 2004.
35. Buckman, *supra*. Autodesk's 2008 revenues were $2.2 million. Vascellaro & Lublin, *supra*.
36. Zachary, *supra*.
37. Fisher, *supra*.
38. See, for example, Jessica Vascellaro, "Bartz Helps Boost Chance of Yahoo-Microsoft Deal," *Wall Street Journal*, Jan. 15, 2009, at B-3.
39. Yahoo! announced Ms. Bratz's appointment on Jan. 13, 2009. Vascellaro & Liblin, *supra*.
40. Martin Peers, "No Yahoo for Tech Company's New Chief," *Wall Street Journal*, Jan. 14, 2009, at C-14.
41. Jessica Vascellaro, "Yahoo Posts Loss as New Chief Plots Strategy," *Wall Street Journal*, Jan. 28, 2009, at B-1.
42. See Miguel Helft, "Yahoo Chief Rearranges Managers Once Again," *New York Times*, Feb. 27, 2009, at B-5; Jessica Vascellaro, "Yahoo CEO Set to Install Top-Down Management," *Wall Street Journal*, Feb. 23, 2009, at B-1.
43. Jessica Vascellaro & Nick Wingfield, "Microsoft, Yahoo Hold Talks About Partnership," *Wall Street Journal*, April 11, 2009, at B-1.
44. Mendoza, *supra*.
45. Idem.
46. Staff, "One Tough Yahoo," *The Economist*, Jan. 17, 2009, at 66.
47. Creswell, *supra*.
48. Bartz, *supra*.
49. Idem.
50. Creswell, *supra*.
51. Bartz, *supra*.
52. Shirleen Dorman & Doug Cameron, "DuPont Posts Loss, but Sees Steady Prices Despite Market," *Wall Street Journal*, Jan. 28, 2009, at B-6.
53. DuPont News, Press Release, "Ellen Kullman to Become President, Director, and CEO," Sept. 24, 2008.
54. Ana Campoy, "New DuPont CEO Led Diversification Drive," *Wall Street Journal*,

Sept. 24, 2008, at B-1; Jessica Shambora, "DuPont's CEO Reinvests Herself," *CNN Money*, Sept. 23, 2008. The six are Indra Nooyi at PepsiCo, Irene Rosenfeld at Kraft Foods, Pat Woertz at Archer Daniels Midland, Angela Braly at Wellpoint, Lynn Elsenhans at Sunoco, and Ellen Kullman at DuPont.

55. Staff, "Rising Stars," *Chemical Weekly*, Aug. 2, 1995, at 40.

56. Geoffrey Colvin, "Star Power: They're Already Major Players," *Fortune*, Feb. 6, 2006, at 54.

57. Staff, "A Special Report: Women to Watch—50 Women to Watch," *Wall Street Journal*, Nov. 19, 2007, at R-3.

58. Campoy, *supra*.

59. Carol Hymowitz, "Women Swell Ranks As Middle Managers, But Are Scarce at the Top," *Wall Street Journal*, July 24, 2006, at B-1.

60. Dorman & Cameron, *supra*.

61. Andrew Eder & Eric Ruth, "A New Era Dawns at the DuPont Co.," *Wilmington (DE) News Journal*, Sept. 24, 2008, at 1A.

62. Irene B. Rosenfeld, "Lewis H. Durland Memorial Lecture," Johnson Graduate School of Business, Cornell University, Oct. 18, 2007.

63. "Irene Rosenfeld: Interview Transcript," *Marketplace*, Feb. 10, 2009.

64. David Lieberman, "CEO Forum: Rosenfeld Keeps Kraft From Being Too Cheesy," *USA Today*, Dec. 10, 2008.

65. Idem.

66. Lieberman, *supra*.

67. Linda Meyers, "Queen of Brands: Kraft CEO Breathes New Life Into Old Favorites," *Cornell Enterprise*, fall, 2007.

68. Lieberman, *supra*.

69. Idem.

70. BJ's Wholesale Club, Press Release, "BJ's Wholesale Club Announces the Election of Laura Sen as CEO," Dec. 11, 2008.

71. John Jannarone, "Put BJ's Shares in Your Shopping Cart Along Discount Isle," *Wall Street Journal*, April 11, 2009, at B-8.

72. Email from Cathy Maloney, vice-president, investor relations, BJ's Wholesale Club, to Douglas M. Branson, dated March 30, 2009.

10 Why Women?

1. Catalyst, Inc., "Catalyst Study Reveals Financial Performance Is Higher for Companies with Women at the Top," Jan. 26, 2004 (study of 353 *Fortune 500* companies over years 1996–2000).

2. Sanjai Bhagat & Bernard Black, "The Uncertain Relationship Between Board Composition and Firm Performance," *Business Lawyer*, 54, 917, at 922–23, 942 (1999).

3. Catalyst, Inc., Press Release, "Companies With More Women Directors Experience Higher Financial Performance," Oct. 1. 2007 (53 percent higher return on equity; 43 percent higher return on sales; and 66 percent higher return on invested capital than firms with the fewest number of women directors).

4. Sanjai Bhagat & Bernard Black, *supra*.

5. See, for example, Caspar Rose, "Does Female Representation on Corporate Boards Influence Firm Performance: The Danish Experience," *Corporate Governance: An International Review*, 15, 404, at 412 (2007) (finding no effect of board gender diversity); Kathleen Farrell & Philip L. Hersch, "Additions to Corporate Boards: The Effect of Gender," *Journal of Corporate Finance*, 85, 103 (2005) (no effect on ROA (Return on Assets) or market returns); Charles B. Shrade et al., "Women in Management and Firm Performance," *Managerial Issues*, 9, 355, at 365 (2007) (no relationship between number of women directors and ROA,

ROE or profit margin); Shaler A. Zahra & Wilbur Stratton, "The Implications of Board of Directors' Composition for Corporate Strategy and Performance," *International Journal of Management*, 5, 229, at 232–33 (1988) (no effect of women on the board). Cf. David A. Carter et al., "Corporate Governance, Board Diversity, and Firm Value," *Financial Review*, 38, 33, at 38, 51 (2003) (finding that Tobin's Q is positively related to the number of female directors); Niclas L. Erhardt et al., "Board of Director Diversity and Firm Financial Performance," *Corporate Governance: An International Review*, 11, 102, at 107 (2003) (increases in female directors is positively related to greater ROE and ROA).

6. George Packer, "The Political Scene: The Choice," *New Yorker*, Jan. 28, 2008, 28, at 29.

7. See, for example, Lisa Fairfax, "The Bottom Line On Board: A Cost-Benefit Analysis of Business Rationales for Diversity on Corporate Boards," *Wisconsin Law Review*, 795, at 810–20 (2005).

8. Vicki M. Kramer, Alison M. Conrad, Sunru Erkeu & Michelle J. Hooper, "Critical Mass on Corporate Boards: Why Three or More Women Enhance Corporate Governance," *NACD Directors Monthly*, Feb. 2007, at 18.

9. The subject is elaborated upon further in Chapter 15, "The Legacies of Tokenism," in this volume.

10. See Linda Bell, "Women-Led Firms and the Gender Gap in Top Executive Jobs," http://papers.ssrn.com (2007) (visited February 17, 2008).

11. Staff, "The 50 Most Powerful Women in Business," *Fortune*, Oct. 16, 2006, at C-1.

12. See Jean Hollands, *Same Games, Different Rules: How To Get Ahead Without Being a Bully Broad, An Ice Queen, or "Ms. Misunderstood,"* at 108 (New York, McGraw Hill, 2002).

13. In contrast to women, Professors Devon Carbado and Mitu Gulati conclude that "[T]here is reason to believe that racial minorities at the top of the corporate hierarchy neither racially reform the corporation nor engage in any door-opening activities, for minorities at the bottom." Carbado & Gulati, "Race to the Top of the Corporate Ladder: What Minorities Do When They Get There," *Washington and Lee Law Review*, 61, 1645, at 1692 (2004).

14. See *No Seat at the Table*, at 151–52 (citing authorities).

15. See Carolyn Kay Brancato & D. Jeanne Paterson, *Diversity in U.S. Corporations: Best Practices for Broadening the Profile of Corporate Boards*, at 8 (The Conference Board, New York, 1999).

16. See, for example, Fairfax, *supra* note, at 820–25 ("the market rationale").

17. Thomas J. Peters, Tom Peters & Robert Waterman, *In Search of Excellence: Lessons From America's Best Run Companies* (New York, Harper & Row, 1988); Tom Peters, *Re-Imagine* (London, Dorling Kindersley, 2003).

18. "Author: More Women Should Be in Charge," *USA Today*, Dec. 8, 2003, at 13B.

19. Carol Hymowitz, "Corporate Boards Lack Gender, Racial Equality," *Wall Street Journal*, July 9, 2003, at B-1; Fairfax, *supra* note, at 823, n. 119.

20. Irving Janis, *Victims of Groupthink: A Psychological Study of Foreign Policy Decisions and Fiascos* (New York, Houghton Mifflin, 1978).

21. Marleen A. O'Connor, "The Enron Board: The Perils of Groupthink," *University of Cincinnati Law Review*, 71, 1233, at 1257 et seq. (2003).

22. Groupthink may lead to:

1. A sense of invincibility;
2. Belief in [the] inherent morality of goals;
3. Collective rationalization;
4. Stereotyping of out-groups;
5. Appearance of unanimity;

6. Self-censorship;
7. Pressures on dissenters; and
8. Self-appointment as mind guards.

Idem. at 1259–60.

23. Carly Fiorina, *Tough Choices*, at 321 (New York, Penguin, 2007).
24. Idem at 322.
25. Pew Foundation, Jeffrey Passel & D'Vera Cohn, Pew Research Center, "U.S. Population Projections, 2005–2050 (February 11, 2005) (whites will have become a 47 percent minority by 2050).
26. A.G. Lafley, chairperson and CEO, Proctor & Gamble, Inc., in E. Bud Simpson, "Doing Business with Alaska Native Corporations," *Business Law Today*, July–Aug., 2007, 37, at 41.

11 How We Choose CEOs

1. Richard S. Tedlow, *Giants of Enterprise* at 433 (New York, Harper Business, 2001).
2. Rakesh Khurana, *Searching For the Corporate Savior—The Irrational Quest for Corporate CEOs* at 303 (Princeton, NJ, Princeton University Press, 2002), quoting Peter Tenin, *The Stability of the American Business Elite* at 34 (1998).
3. Michael Bezilla, "Samuel Rhea," *Railroads in the Age of Regulation, 1900–1980*, at 361 (Keith Bryant, Jr., ed.) (New York, Facts on File, 1988).
4. Joann Lublin & Don Clark, "Star Search: Hewlett-Packard Seeks Successor to Fiorina," *Wall Street Journal*, Feb. 10, 2005, at B-1.
5. *Corporate Savior* at 94.
6. See generally *Corporate Savior* at 94–96.
7. This chapter deals with external executive searches for CEOs. When the search for a successor CEO is internal to the company, women fare even more poorly. Professors Dan Dalton and Catherine Price have found that in internal searches, the successor CEO was first an inside director 85 percent of the time. Of 1,250 inside directors in the *Fortune 500*, only eight were women. Michelle Conlin, "The CEO Still Wears Wingtips," *Business Week*, Nov. 22, 1999, at 82. The number of women inside directors has not increased at all. See Douglas M. Branson, *No Seat at the Table—How Corporate Governance and Law Keep Women Out of the Boardroom* at 87 *passim* (2007) (only nine inside women directors in *Fortune 500*).
8. See Roger Crockett, "The New Kingmakers," *Business Week*, Jan. 30, 2006, at 68.
9. DHR International is a Chicago-based executive search firm with offices in several cities. See, for example, David Hoffman & Alexandra Henderson, "Driving Diversity in the Boardroom," *Chief Executive*, Dec. 2006, at 1.
10. See John Byrne, *The Headhunters* (New York, Macmillan, 1988).
11. *Corporate Savior* at 104.
12. Crockett, *supra* note.
13. *The Headhunters* at 207.
14. Crockett, *supra* (quoting Joseph McCool, former editor, *Executive Recruiter News*).
15. Idem at 108.
16. Idem at 173.
17. Carol Hymowitz, "The Perils of Picking a CEO," *Wall Street Journal*, March 15, 2005, at B-1.
18. *Corporate Savior* at 111.
19. Idem at 113.
20. Idem at 29 ("Search Firm Statistics Contrasting CEO Search with VP Marketing Search").

21. *Corporate Savior* at 118.
22. Max Weber explained that the root meaning, "gift of grace," religion aside, first appeared in political settings. He described charisma as the ability to evoke in others feeling of devotion, confidence, illumination, and heroism. Max Weber, *Economy and Society* (1947).
23. Crockett, *supra* (quoting James Citrin and Gerald R. Roche at Spencer Stuart).

12 Glass Ceilings, Floors, Walls, and Cliffs

1. Gail Evans, *Play Like a Man, Win Like a Woman* at 7 (New York, Broadway Books, 2000).
2. Martha Chamallas, *Introduction to Feminist Legal Theory* at 184 (New York, Aspen Law and Business, 2000). See also Anthony Stith, *Breaking the Glass Ceiling: Sexism and Racism in Corporate America: The Myths, the Realities, and the Solutions* (Toronto, Warwick Publishers, 1998); Pat Heim & Susan K. Golant, *Smashing the Glass Ceiling* (New York, Simon & Schuster, 1995); Ann Morrison, Ellen Van Velsor & Randall P. White, *Breaking the Glass Ceiling* (Cambridge, Perseus Publishing, 1992). See also Naomi Cahn & Michael Selmi, "The Glass Ceiling," *Maryland Law Review*, 65, 435 (2006) (the glass ceiling as viewed looking upward by women and minorities on the lowest rungs of the economic latter).
3. Maureen Dowd, "Victimized by Gender," *Pittsburgh Post-Gazette*, Oct. 12, 2006, at B-7; Carleton Fiorina, *Tough Choices* at 171 (New York, Penguin, 2006) ("When I said the 'glass ceiling does not exist,' it made headlines").
4. Email from Karen Ruger, senior vice-president, Corporate Communications, Rite Aid Corporation, to Douglas Branson, dated March 20, 2008 (Mary Sammons "declines interviews relating to being a 'female' CEO, believing that gender shouldn't matter").
5. Federal Glass Ceiling Commission, "Good for Business: Making Full Use of the Nation's Human Capital," *BNA Daily Labor Report*, March 17, 1995, at 634–37.
6. Leading works espousing these views include Richard Epstein, *Forbidden Grounds: The Case Against Employment Discrimination* (Cambridge, Harvard University Press, 1992), at 41–42, 102, and Richard Posner, "An Economic Analysis of Sex Discrimination Laws," *University of Chicago Law Review*, 56, 1311 (1989).
7. Alice H. Early & Lindi L. Carli, *Through the Labyrinth: How Women Become Leaders* (Cambridge, Massachusetts, Harvard Business School Press, 2007) (based upon advancement of women in not-for-profit and educational fields rather than in business).
8. Douglas M. Branson, *No Seat at the Table: How Corporate Governance and Law Keep Women Out of the Boardroom* at 87 (New York, NYU Press, 2007).
9. The expression seems to have originated with Judith H. Dobrzynski, "When Directors Play Musical Chairs," Money and Business, *New York Times*, Nov. 17, 1996, at 1.
10. See Chapters 7 (Woertz) and 8 (Barnes and Whitman) in this volume.
11. *No Seat at the Table* at 87, 97–98.
12. See Anna Raghhavan, "Many CEOs Say 'No Thanks' to Board Seats," *Wall Street Journal*, Jan. 25, 2005, at B-1.
13. *Tough Choices* at 39, 43, 68, 69, 89, 106, 109, 146.
14. See also idem at 52: "[G]ender alone could deny me the presumption of competence. [Many] people wouldn't give me the benefit of a doubt [because I was a woman]"; at 53 ("I could see [sex] bias in [co-workers'] faces and body language"); at 145 (There is "no Fifty Most Powerful Men in Business" but business periodicals feel compelled to issue one for women).
15. Alice H. Eagly & Linda L. Carli, "Women and the Labyrinth of Leadership,"

Harvard Business Review, Sept. 2007, 61, at 64, previewing Alice Eagly & Linda Carli, *Through the Labyrinth: The Truth About How Women Become Leaders, supra.*

16. Rudiger Fahlenbrack, Bernadette Morrison & Carrie H. Pan, "Former CEO Directors: Lingering CEOs or Valuable Resources as Comeback CEOs?" (2008) (on file with the author).

17. See Janet Adamy, "Schultz Takes Over to Try to Perk Up Starbucks," *Wall Street Journal*, Jan. 8, 2008, at B-1 ("Mr. Schultz's return to the CEO post at Starbucks is similar to the recent returns of company founders, such as Jerry Yang at Yahoo!, Inc., Michael Dell at Dell Computer, Inc., Steve Jobs at Apple, Inc., Charles Schwab at Charles Schwab Corp., Ted Waitt at Gateway Inc., and Thomas Frist. Jr., at HCA Inc.").

18. Joann Lublin, "The Serial CEO," *Wall Street Journal*, Sept. 19, 2005, at B-1 (sitting or former CEOs are often the safe choice but "highlight a shortage of in-house talent and weak succession planning at many companies").

19. Catalyst, Inc., "Women in Corporate Leadership: Progress and Prospects," at 136 (1996).

20. Sheila Wellington, *Be Your Own Mentor* at 185 (New York, Random House, 2002).

21. See, for example, Mark Henderson, "Women Who Break Through the Glass Ceiling Face a Cliffhanger," *The Times* (London), Sept. 7, 2004, at 3.

22. Michelle K. Ryan & Alexander Haslam, "The Glass Cliff: Evidence That Women Are Over-Represented in Precarious Leadership Positions," *British Journal of Management*, 16, 81 (2005). See also Jayne W. Barnard, "At the Top of the Pyramid: Lessons from the Alpha Woman and the Elite Eight," *Maryland Law Review*, 65, 315 (2006).

23. Those who came to power in precarious corporate settings (10) include: Jill Barad at Mattel; Andrea Jung at Avon; Ann Mulcahy at Xerox; Patricia Russo at Lucent; Susan Ivery at Reynolds; Patricia Woertz at AMD; Brenda Barnes at Sara Lee; Mary Sammons at Rite Aid America; Christina Gold at Western Union; and Carol Bartz at Yahoo!. Those female CEOs of whom the same thing cannot be said (11) include Carleton Fiorina at Hewlett-Packard; Marion Sandler at Golden West Financial; Paula Rosport Reynolds at Safeco; Angela Braly at Wellpoint; Indra Nooyi at Pepsico; Carol Meyrowitz at TJX; Meg Whitman at Ebay; Lynn Elsenahns at Sunoco; Ellen Kullman at DuPont; Irene Rosenfeld at Kraft; and Laura Sen at BJ's Wholesale Club.

13 Work–Life Issues and the Price of Motherhood

1. Ann Crittenden, *The Price of Motherhood—Why the Most Important Job in the World Is Still the Least Valued* at 16 (New York, Metropolitan Books, 2001).

2. Lisa Belkin, "Will Dad Ever Do His Share? When Mom and Dad Share It All," *New York Times* Sunday Magazine, June 15, 2008, 44, at 46.

3. Department of Labor, "Bureau of Labor Statistics Chart Book" (1993). By the 2000 census, the number of women in the workplace had peaked and then fallen, to 57.5 percent of women, holding 46.7 percent of the jobs available. United States Census 2000, at Chart QT-P24. Ten years earlier, 53 percent of women worked, holding 45.7 percent of the jobs. United States Census 1990, at Table 233.

4. Catherine Ross, "The Division of Labor at Home," *Social Forces*, 65, 816 (March 1997).

5. Sue Shellenbarger, "Pregnant Pause: Deciding When to Tell a New Boss You are Expecting a Baby," *Wall Street Journal*, Oct. 14, 2004, at D-1.

6. Lisa Belkin, "The Opt-Out Revolution," *New York Times* Sunday Magazine, Oct. 23, 2003, at 42.

7. See David Brooks, "Empty Nests, and Hearts," *New York Times*, Jan. 15, 2005, at A-15.

8. The phrase "mummy track" was coined by Felice N. Schwartz, the founder and first president of Catalyst, Inc. See Ann Crittenden, *The Price of Motherhood* at 44 (New York, Metropolitan Books, 2001).

9. *The Price of Motherhood* at 35.

10. Georgia Post, "Study Shows More Mothers Prefer to Work Part Time," *Pittsburgh Post Gazette*, July 23, 2007, at A-13 (Pew Research survey of 2,020 working women).

11. As a result of the study's findings, Deloitte devoted specific resources to the hiring and advancement of women with its Initiative for the Advancement of Women/Flexibility & Choice, described in Williams et al., *infra*, at 450–452.

12. Piper Fogg, "Female Professors Assail Remarks by Harvard's President, Who Says It's All a Misunderstanding," *Chronicle of Higher Education*, Jan. 19, 2005, at 3. Summers soon thereafter resigned his position at Harvard after the controversy continued unabated.

13. *The Price of Motherhood* at 2.

14. Idem at 5.

15. See, for example, Joan Williams, Cynthia Thomas Calvert & Holly Green Cooper, "Better on Balance? The Corporate Counsel Retention Project—Final Report," *William and Mary Journal of Women and the Law*, 10 367, at 377 (2004).

16. Idem at 417–18.

17. 127 Supreme Court 2162 (2007).

18. H.R. 11, 106th Congress, 1st Session (2009).

19. Joan Williams, *Unbending Gender* (New York, Oxford University Press) at 17, quoting Deborah Fallows, *A Mother's Work* (New York, Houghton Mifflin, 1985) at 11.

20. Ellen Goodman, "Involuntarily Opted Out," *Pittsburgh Post-Gazette*, Aug. 1, 2008, at B-7 (study shepherded by Rep. Carolyn Maloney).

21. Beverly Sills & Lawrence Linderman, *Beverly: An Autobiography* at 117 (New York, Bantam Books, 1987).

22. Belkin, *supra*, at 44 (citing U.S. census data).

23. Idem at 45.

24. Reported in Belkin, *supra*, at 44.

25. *The Price of Motherhood* at 13.

26. Council of Economic Advisers, "Families and the Labor Market 1969–1999: Analyzing the 'Time Crunch,' " at 4 (1999).

27. Candy Saigon, "Dinner Time," *Washington Post*, Mar. 3, 1999.

28. *The Price of Motherhood* at 26–7.

29. Belkin, *supra*, at 47.

30. Idem.

31. *The Price of Motherhood* at 29.

32. Claudia Goldin, "Career and Family: College Women Look to the Past," National Bureau of Economic Research Working Paper No. 5188 (1995).

33. Judith P. Walker & Deborah J. Swiss, *Women and the Work/Family Dilemma* (New York, Wiley & Sons, 1993).

34. Reported in Catherine MacKinnon & Reva P. Siegel, *Directions In Sexual Harassment Law* at 1092 (New Haven, CT, Yale University Press, 2003).

35. See Gary S. Becker, *Human Capital* (Chicago, IL, University of Chicago Press, 3rd edn, 1994); Gary S. Becker & Nigel Tomes, "Human Capital and the Rises and Fall of Families," *Journal of Labor Economics*, 43 (July 1986).

36. Belkin, *supra*, at 58.

37. Williams et al., *supra*, at 414.

38. Rosabeth Moss Kanter, *Men and Women of the Corporation* at 305 (New York, Basic Books, 1977, rev. edn 1993).
39. Reported in *Price of Motherhood* at 95.
40. U.S. Bureau of the Census, "Current Population Reports: Money Income in the U.S.," at 46–49 (2000).
41. Robert G. Wood, Mary E. Corcoran & Paul N. Courant, "Pay Differences Among the Highly Paid: The Male-Female Earnings Gap in Lawyer's Salaries," *Journal of Labor Economics*, 11, 417 (1993).
42. *Price of Motherhood* at 96.
43. Catalyst, Inc., "Women and the MBA: Gateway to Opportunity" (2000).
44. Idem at 107.
45. The author appeared on a panel in Frankfurt, Germany, in July 2007, with Frau Deutrich, at the law firm of Hengler Mueller.
46. The phrase comes from a landmark U.S. Supreme Court discrimination case, *Griggs v. Duke Power Co.*, 401 U.S. 424, 432 (1971).
47. *The Price of Motherhood* at 256–74 ("How to Bring Children Up Without Putting Women Down").
48. Williams et al., *supra*, at 422–32.
49. Williams, *supra*, at 432. See also Edward S. Adams, "Using Evaluations To Break Down the Male Corporate Hierarchy: A Full Circle Approach," *University of Colorado Law Review*, 73, 117 (2002).
50. In the order in which this book presents them, the women CEOs followed by the number of children are: Jill Barad (2); Andrea Jung (2); Marion Sandler (2); Ann Mulcahy (2); Patricia Russo (2); Carleton Fiorina (2); Susan Ivey (2); Paula Rosport Reynolds (1); Pat Woertz (3); Angela Braly (3); Christina Gold (0); Carol Meyrowoitz (2); Indra Nooyi (2); Mary Sammons (1); Brenda Barnes (3); and Meg Whitman (2).
51. Betsy Morris, Kate Bonamici, Susan Kaufman & Patricia Neering, "How Corporate America Is Betraying Women," *Fortune*, Jan. 10, 2005, at 64.

14 In a Different Register

1. Deborah Tannen, *Talking from 9 to 5—Women and Men in the Workplace: Language, Sex and Power* at 14, 23 (New York, Avon, 1994).
2. Idem at 315.
3. John M. Conley, William M. O'Barr & E. Allen Lind, "The Power of Language: Presentation Style in the Courtroom," *Duke Law Journal*, at 1375 (1978).
4. Deborah Tannen, *Gender and Discourse* at 31 (New York, Oxford University Press, 1994).
5. See, for example, Sheila Wellington, *Be Your Own Mentor* at 92 (New York, Random House, 2001); Gail Evans, *Play Like A Man, Win Like A Woman* at 31 (New York, Broadway Books, 2000) ("Women must learn that we are playing in a world where our opponents have been taught to hide their emotions.").
6. Mary Ann Mason, "Some Thoughts on Female Leadership in Male-Dominated Fields," *San Francisco Chronicle*, Feb. 20, 2009, at A-17.
7. See generally Erving Goffman, *Gender Advertisements* (New York, Harper & Row, 1979).
8. *Gender and Discourse* at 217.
9. Robin T. Lakoff, *Language and Woman's Place* (New York, Harper Trade, 1975).
10. In a number of tribal languages, the linguistic usages of male and female speakers differ dramatically. Men and women actually speak distinct variants of the language. See, for example, Edward Sapir, *Selected Writings of Edward Sapir in Language, Culture and Personality* (Berkley, CA, University of California Press, 1949); *Language, Gender, and Sex in Comparative Perspective* (Susan Phillips et al.,

eds.) (New York, Cambridge University Press, 1987). With English and the languages of other industrialized nations, certain syntactic and other character-istics may be disproportionately distributed according to gender but the sexes do not use their own language variants.

11. Deborah Tannen, *You Just Don't Understand* (New York, William Morrow, 1990).
12. *Gender and Discourse* at 31–37, 65–70, 195 et seq.
13. See, for example, David Graddol & Joan Swann, *Gender Voices* (Malden, MA, Blackwell Publishing, 1989).
14. See, for example, *The Sociology of The Languages of American Women* (Betty L. DuBois & Isabel Crouch, eds.) (New York and Berlin, Walter De Gruyter, Inc., 2nd edn, 1979). See also Bent Preisler, *Linguistic Sex Roles in Conversation: Social Variation in the Expression of Tentativeness in English* (New York and Berlin, Walter De Gruyter, Inc., 1986); *Women in Their Speech Communities* (Jennifer Coates & Deborah Cameron, eds.) (White Plains, NY, Longman Publishing, 1989); Jennifer Coates, *Language and Gender: A Reader* (Malden, MA, Blackwell Publishing, 1997).
15. See William O'Barr, *Linguistic Evidence: Language, Power, and Strategy in the Courtroom* (London, Elsevier Science & Technology, 1982).
16. Janet E. Ainsworth, "In a Different Register: The Pragmatics of Powerlessness in Police Interrogation," *Yale Law Journal*, 103, 259 (1993).
17. Idem at 274.
18. See, for example, Tannen, *supra*, at 53–83 ("Chapter Two: Interpreting Interruption in Conversation").
19. *Language and Woman's Place* at 18.
20. *Gender and Discourse* at 34.
21. Mary R. Key, *Male/Female Language* at 75–76 (Lanham, MD, Scarecrow Press, 1975).
22. Ainsworth, *supra*, at 280.
23. Idem at 276.
24. *Play Like A Man, Win Like A Woman* at 147.
25. *Language and Woman's Place* at 53–54.
26. Ainsworth, *supra*, at 282–83.
27. *Language and Woman's Place* at 17.
28. See, for example, Ruth M. Bend, "Male-Female Intonation Patterns in American English," in *Language and Sex: Difference and Dominance* (Barrie Thorns & Nancy Henley eds.) (London, The Stationery Office, 1975).
29. *Gender and Discourse* at 30.
30. *Be Your Own Mentor* at 85. See also idem at 92: "Lower the pitch of your voice. A lower voice commands more attention and respect."
31. Ainsworth, *supra*, at 283.
32. *Language and Woman's Place* at 205.
33. Stephanie Coontz, *The Social Origins of Private Life* (New York, Norton & Co., 1988) at 85, quoted in Joan Williams, *Unbending Gender* at 23 (New York, Oxford University Press, 2000).
34. Jean Holland, *Same Game, Different Rules—How to Get Ahead Without Being a Bully Broad, Ice Queen, or "Ms. Misunderstood"* (New York, McGraw-Hill, 2002).
35. See Debra E. Meyeson & Joyce K. Fletcher, "A Modest Manifesto for Shattering the Glass Ceiling," *Harvard Business Review*, Jan.–Feb., 2000, 127, 133.
36. Williams, *supra*, at 1.

15 Legacies of Tokenism: Retreats into Stereotypes

1. Rosabeth Moss Kanter, *Men and Women of the Corporation* at 210 (New York, Basic Books, 1977, rev. edn, 1993).

2. Idem at 216.
3. See, for example, Carol Gallagher, *Going to the Top* at 109 (New York, Viking Penguin, 2000).
4. *Men and Women of the Corporation* at 221.
5. Idem at 223.
6. These were the facts in *Hemmings v. Tidymans, Inc.*, 285 F.3rd 1174 (9th Cir. 2002) (en banc), in which two women sought promotions into an exclusively male management group.
7. *Men and Women of the Corporation* at 226.
8. Idem at 236.
9. Jean Hollands, *Same Game, Different Rules: How To Get Ahead Without Being a Bully Broad, an Ice Queen, or "Ms. Misunderstood,"* at 163 (New York, McGraw Hill, 2002).
10. Idem at 164.
11. *Going to the Top* at 109.
12. Idem at 108.
13. *Same Game, Different Rules: How To Get Ahead Without Being a Bully Broad* at 5, 19.
14. Idem at 202.
15. See, for example, idem at 226–27 ("the Sounding Off Tyrant," "the Selectively Silent Type," "Sarcastic-Aggressive," and "the Silent Judge"); *Going to the Top* at 108–09 ("Bride of Dracula").
16. *Men and Women of the Corporation* at 316.
17. See, for example, David Cope, *The Fundamentals of Statistical Analysis* at 15–16 (New York Foundation, 2005).
18. Wellesley Center for Women, *The Critical Mass Project* (2006); Vicki Kramer, Allison M. Konrad, Samru Erkut & Michele J. Hooper, "Critical Mass on Corporate Boards: Why Three or More Women Enhance Governance," *National Association of Corporate Directors (NACD) Directors Monthly*, Feb., 2007, at 19.

16 Narcissists, Malignant Narcissists, and Productive Narcissists

1. Richard Y. Hathorn, *Greek Mythology* at 105 (Beirut, Lebanon, American University of Beirut Press, 1977).
2. *Interpretations of Greek Mythology* (Jan Bremmer, ed.) (London, Croom Helm, 1987).
3. Sigmund Freud, *On Narcissism: An Introduction* (London, Hogarth Press, 1914).
4. Raymond J. Corsini, *The Dictionary of Psychology* at 626 (Philadelphia, Taylor & Francis, 1999). See also James Drever, *The Dictionary of Psychology* at 177 ("excessive preoccupation with oneself and one's own concerns") (Baltimore, Penguin Books, 1963).
5. Michael Maccoby, "Narcissistic Leaders: The Incredible Pro's, and the Inevitable Con's," *Harvard Business Review*, Jan.–Feb., 2000, at 68.
6. Michael Maccoby, *The Productive Narcissist—the Promise and Peril of Visionary Leadership* (New York, Broadway Books, 2003). Earlier works by Maccoby include *The Leader: A New Face for American Management* (New York, Simon & Schuster, 1981), and *The Gamesmen: The New Corporate Leaders* (New York, Simon & Schuster, 1977).
7. Michael Maccoby, *Narcissistic Leaders: Who Succeeds and Who Fails* (Cambridge, Harvard Business School Press, 2007).
8. Maccoby, *supra Harvard Business Review*, at 69.
9. Idem at 75 (Paglia), 136 (Stewart). Camilla Paglia is the author of *Sex, Art and American Culture* (New York, Vintage Books, 1992).
10. See Mike Wilson, *The Difference Between God and Larry Ellison: Inside Oracle Corporation* (New York, Morrow, 1997).

11. *Narcissistic Leaders* at 9.
12. J. Brooks Bouson, *The Emphatic Reader—A Study of the Narcissistic Character and the Drama of the Self* at 16–17 (Amherst, MA, University of Massachusetts Press, 1989).
13. Idem at 20.
14. *Narcissistic Leaders* at 44–45. "The downside of the erotic personality is dependency, in all its forms: neediness, emotional clinging, an inability to leave a bad relationship, and dependency." Idem at 47.
15. See Walter Issacson, *Benjamin Franklin—An American Life* (New York, Simon & Schuster, 2003).
16. *Narcissistic Leaders* at 51. Buffet would agree, as his metaphor for life indicates: "[T]he important thing is to find wet snow and a really long hill." See Alice Schroder, *The Snowball: Warren Buffett and the Business of Life* (New York, Random House, 2008) (rear dust cover).
17. Idem at 52.
18. Idem at 55.
19. See Kenneth Blanchard, *Who Moved My Cheese: An Amazing Way to Deal With Change in Your Work and Life* (New York, Putnam, 1998); Steven R. Covey, *The Seven Habits of Highly Effective People* (New York, Fireside Books, 1990), and Kenneth Blanchard, *The One Minute Manager* (New York, Berkeley Press, 1983).
20. Patrick Lencioni, *The Five Dysfunctions of a Team: An Illustrated Leadership Fable* (New York, Wiley & Sons, 2008); Gary Harpst, *The Six Disciplines Execution Revolution: Solving the One Business Problems That Makes Solving All Other Problems Easier* (Finlay, Ohio, Six Disciplines Publishing, 2008).
21. *Narcissistic Leaders* at 66.
22. Idem at 67.
23. Sigmund Freud, *On Narcissism: An Introduction* (London, Hogarth Press, 1914); Freud, *Leonardo Da Vinci and a Memory of His Childhood* (London, Hogarth, 1910).
24. *Narcissistic Leaders* at 69.
25. Maccoby uses Will Durant, who founded General Motors, and Richard Branson, who began Virgin Records and Virgin Airlines, as example of narcissists in business. He also alludes to Alexander the Great and Frank Lloyd Wright as having had narcissistic personalities. Idem at 73–75.
26. See Michael Lewis, *The New, New Thing—A Silicon Valley Story* at 68 *et seq.* (New York, W.W. Norton, 2000).
27. Idem at 120.
28. Idem at 133.
29. See, for example, Jennifer Edstrom & Marlin Eller, *Barbarians Led By Bill Gates—Microsoft from the Inside* at 51–62 (New York, Henry Holt & Son, 1998).
30. Idem at 141.
31. Idem at 142.
32. Daniel Goleman, *Emotional Intelligence* (New York, Bantam Books, 1995).
33. *Narcissistic Leaders* at 149, 154.
34. Idem at 162.
35. Jack Welch, *Jack—Straight From the Gut* at 186–90 (New York, Warner Books, 2001).
36. *Narcissistic Leaders* at 175.
37. Idem at 185. See also David Enrich & David Reilly, "Citigroup Head of Risk Panel to Step Down—Armstrong Relinquishes Post Amid Investor Push for His Ouster from Board," *Wall Street Journal*, April 8, 2008, at C-1.
38. Idem at 187.

17 Good-to-Great Companies and Plowhorse CEOs

1. Jim Collins, *Good to Great—Why Some Companies Make the Leap and Others Don't* at 165, 13 (New York, Harper Collins Business, 2001).
2. Keith R. McFarland, *The Breakthrough Company: How Every Day Companies Become Extraordinary* (New York, Crown Business, 2008).
3. *Good to Great* at 7.
4. Idem at 211 (in the study, "[m]any companies show a sharp rise for 5 or 10 years" but very few for 15).
5. Idem at 101–03.
6. Idem at 70.
7. Subsequent to Collins's book at least two of the good-to-great companies have fallen on hard times. Circuit City, because it stumbled badly, tried to sell itself (with no takers), and liquidated rather than attempting reorganization in Chapter 11 bankruptcy. See Miguel Bustillo, "Retailer Circuit City to Liquidate," *Wall Street Journal*, Jan. 17, 2009, at B-1. Fannie Mae, first because of accounting scandals and earnings restatements (it understated rather than overstated profits, to keep regulators off its back, and to store accounting profits for a rainy day— a so-called "cookie jar" case)—and, second, because of the subprime mortgage crisis of 2008–09. Another (Gillette) has been acquired (by Proctor & Gamble) while a fourth (Phillip Morris) changed its named (to Altaria).
8. Idem at 10.
9. See Chapter 10 in this volume. See generally Rakesh Khurana, *Searching For the Corporate Savior—The Irrational Quest for Corporate CEOs* at 303 (Princeton, NJ, Princeton University Press, 2002).
10. *Good to Great* at 11.
11. See Chapter 15 in this volume. See generally Michael Maccoby, *The Productive Narcissist—the Promise and Peril of Visionary Leadership* (New York, Broadway Books, 2003).
12. *Good to Great* at 11.
13. Two of the women CEOs, Ann Mulcahy at Xerox and Brenda Barnes at Sara Lee Corp., have made their marks through aggressive downsizing and divestitures, the opposite of acquisitions.
14. *Good to Great* at 11.
15. Idem at 20–23.
16. Idem at 22.
17. Idem at 27–28.
18. Idem at 25, 21.
19. Idem at 28.
20. There were two autobiographies: Lee A. Iacocca, *Talking Straight* (New York, Bantam, 1988) (with Sony Kleinfeld), and Iacocca, *Iacocca: An Autobiography* (New York, Bantam, 1984) (with William Novak).
21. "President Iacocca," *Wall Street Journal*, July 28, 1982, at A-1.
22. See John Byrne, *Chainsaw Al: The Notorious Career of Al Dunlap in the Era of Profit-at-Any-Price* at 26 (New York, Harper Business, 1999); Elizabeth Kiesche, "Scott Merger Just a Piece of Dunlap Story," *Chicago Sunday Times*, July 23, 1995, at 23.
23. Two books about Chainsaw Al are his autobiography: Alfred Dunlap, *Mean Business—How I Save Bad Companies and Make Good Companies Great* (New York, Simon & Schuster Fireside, 1996) (with Bob Andelman), and *Chainsaw Al, supra*. Journalists also gave Dunlap the names "The Shredder," "Ming the Merciless," and "Dunlap the Terrible." *Mean Business* at 132–35.
24. *Good to Great* at 27.
25. Idem at 39–40 (chapter summary).
26. Idem at 91.

27. Warren Buffett & Larry Cunningham, "The Essays of Warren Buffett," *Cardozo Law Review*, 19, 5 at 88 (1997).
28. "Warren Buffett's Favorite Banker," *Forbes*, Oct. 13, 1993, at 46.
29. James Kelly & Scott Nadler, "Leading From Below," *Wall Street Journal*, March 3, 2007, at R-4 (survey by ERM Consulting of environmental health and safety directors).
30. *Good to Great* at 121.
31. Idem.
32. HP director and venture capitalist Tom Perkins compared the compliance board represented by Ms. Dunn with the historic best practices board, which he termed the "Guidance board." "The Guidance board is typically very involved: strategy, tactics, background, hiring, firing, technology, and engineering reviews." He finds "[t]here is a huge difference between the Guidance board, with its focus on technical strategy, marketing so on, and the Compliance board with its focus on legal issues." "A Compliance board is a very, very busy board. It works hard . . . There are so many matters to comply with . . . [The] compliance board listens to consultants and attorneys before deciding matters . . . [f]ocused on regulatory aspects . . . Like it or hate it, what I have described is the evolving standard model in corporate America today." Perkins, "The 'Compliance' Board," *Wall Street Journal*, March 2, 2007, at A-11. So, too, a manager should aspire to be a guidance manager or guidance executive, resisting the pull so prevalent in today's milieu to become a compliance manager, a scold and a paper shuffler rather than a leader.
33. See, for example, John Strohmeyer, *Crisis in Bethlehem* at 30–35 (Pittsburgh, University of Pittsburgh Press, 1986). Ironically, Leigh University acquired Bethlehem's new hilltop headquarters facility, renaming it after one of its most distinguished alumni, Lee Iacocca.
34. See Ken Iverson, *Plain Talk* (New York, John Wiley & Sons, 1986).
35. *Good to Great* at 134.
36. Idem at 167.

18 The Plowhorse Versus the Showhorse

1. Ellen J. Pollack (quoting Ira Millstein), "Twilight of the Gods: CEO as American Icon Slips Into Down Cycle," *Wall Street Journal*, Jan. 5, 1999, at A-1. Idem (an unidentified mutual fund manager).
2. Nelson D. Schwartz, "CEO Evolution: Phase 3," *New York Times*, Nov. 10, 2007, at C-1.
3. Their appointments as CEO form material for espousal of the "glass cliff" phenomenon but the theory relates more to the motivation for their appointments as opposed to their performances once they occupied the corner office. See Chapter 11 in this volume.
4. Editorial, "The Un-imperial CEO," *Wall Street Journal*, Sept. 16, 2006, at A-8 ("CEOs used to serve for an average of about a decade; today the average CEO lasts only about four years.").
5. Schwartz, *supra*.
6. Richard Gibson, "Pitchman in the Corner Office," *Wall Street Journal*, Oct. 24, 2007, at D-10.
7. David Novak, *The Education of an Accidental CEO* (New York, Crown Business, 2007) (with John Boswell). Mr. Novak is CEO of Yum Brands, Inc. (KFC, Pizza Hut, Taco Bell, Long John Silver and A&W).
8. Michael Maccoby, "*The Productive Narcissist—The Promise and Peril of Visionary Leadership* at 248 (New York, Broadway Books, 2003).
9. Idem at 249.

10. Idem at 147.
11. Idem at 151.
12. Idem at 154.
13. Idem at 152.
14. *Good to Great* at 46–47.
15. Idem at 54.
16. Idem at 56.
17. Idem at 59.
18. Idem at 72.
19. Idem at 73.
20. Idem at 83.
21. George Anders, "Tough CEOs Often the Most Successful, Study Finds," *Wall Street Journal*, Nov. 19, 2007, at B-3.
22. Maureen Dowd, "Dueling Victims: Should the Democrats Overcome Misogyny or Racism First?," *Pittsburgh Post-Gazette*, March 6, 2008, at B-5.

19 Education, Mentoring, and Networking

1. Jayne Barnard, "At the Top of the Pyramid: Lessons from the Alpha Woman and the Elite Eight," *Maryland Law Review*, 65, 315, at 336 (2006).
2. Ron Suskind, *The Price of Loyalty: George Bush, the White House, and the Education of Paul O'Neill* (New York, Simon & Schuster, 2006).
3. Michael Maccoby, *The Productive Narcissist—The Promise and Peril of Visionary Leadership* at 15 (New York, Broadway Books, 2003).
4. Idem.
5. Staff at the TJX Companies refused to release any information about CEO Carol Meyrowitz, including about education beyond that Ms. Meyrowitz had obtained a bachelor's degree. See Chapter 7 in this volume.
6. Suze Orman has published 12 books. Her latest books include *Women and Money: Owing the Power to Control Your Destiny* (New York, Spiegel & Grau, 2007); *9 Steps to Financial Freedom* (New York, Three Rivers Press, 2006); *Money Book for the Young, the Fabulous and Broke* (New York, Riverhead Books, 2005); *Road to Wealth: a Comprehensive Guide to Your Money—Everything You Need to Know in Good Times and Bad* (Riverhead Books, 2001); and *You Earned It; Don't Lose It: Mistakes You Can't Afford When You Retire* (New York, New Market Press, 1998). She also wrote a series of *Ask Suze* monographs which relate to specific topics, such as insurance, social security, love and money, and the like.
7. Association To Advance Collegiate Schools of Business, Women Business School Deans at Member Schools, http://www.aacsb.edu/members/communities/interestgrps/womendeans.asp (visited July 30, 2008).
8. There are other costs as well: according to one study, women who have MBAs are more than twice as likely (12 percent versus 5 percent) as comparable males to be divorced. Anita Raghavan, "For Women, Graduate Degrees Greater Marriage Test," *Wall Street Journal*, April 11, 2008, at D-9. But the statistic compares better (12 percent to 11 percent) when women with MBAs are compared to business women with bachelor's degrees (statistics by Sylvia Ann Hewlett).
9. I advocated such a detour to both of my daughters—one of whom majored in communications and the other in theater arts. Both told me what I wanted to hear: they thought it a wise, indeed, splendid, idea. After that, they went back to normal routines, never taking a single course their father suggested. Now, seven and ten years later, respectively, both daughters express what I believe to be genuine remorse that they did not take the time in their educations to obtain some grounding in business.

10. Of course an MBA or other training is not foolproof either. Brenda Barnes, who does have an MBA, promised that under her leadership food company Sara Lee would achieve a 12 percent operating margin, a prediction the corporation has not come close to reaching. As a result, both she and Sara Lee have undergone significant reputational damage. See "High Costs Put Sara Lee CEO in a Bind," *Wall Street Journal*, July 23, 2008, at B-1.
11. Sheila Wellington, *Be Your Own Mentor* at 178 (New York, Random House, 2001).
12. See Chapter 11 in this volume.
13. Jim Collins, *Good to Great—Why Some Companies Make the Leap and Others Don't* at 195 (New York, Harper Business, 2001).
14. Barnard, *supra*, at 122.
15. Greg Burns, "Nobody's Business But Her Own: Brenda Barnes Was Accused of Betraying Working Women When She Quit to Be With Her Family; Now She's a CEO Again and Unapologetic About Her Personal and Career Choices," *Chicago Tribune* Sunday Magazine, Oct. 14, 2007, 12; Chapter 8 in this volume.
16. Address by Anne-Kathrin Deutrich, former Chairwoman of SICK AG and Chairwoman, University of Education, University of Freiburg, to Hengler & Mueller, Attorneys, Frankfurt am Main, July 2, 2007. See also Chapter 12 in this volume.
17. G.E. Clements, F.J. Lunding & D.S. Perkins, "Everyone Who Makes It Has a Mentor," *Harvard Business Review*, July–Aug., 1978, at 89.
18. *Be Your Own Mentor, supra*.
19. Idem at 3.
20. Rosabeth Moss Kanter, *Men and Women of the Corporation* at 188 (New York, Basic Books, rev. edn, 1993).
21. Idem at 182–83.
22. Idem at 184.
23. Some even give a sample list. See Pat Heim, *Hardball for Women—Winning at the Game of Business* at 262–63 (New York, Penguin Plume, rev. edn, 2005):

    > Your network needs to be wide and deep. Include those in the know, opinion leaders, and other heavy networkers. One of my employee's befriended the president's assistant. . . . Your network needs a little of everything:
    >
    > people inside the department
    > people outside the department
    > people inside the organization
    > people on other organizations
    > peers
    > subordinates
    > superiors
    > those whose opinions are valued by higher ups
    > those who control information
    > those who control budgets
    > administrative assistants
    > the receptionist (who probably knows more than anyone)
    > industry-wide organizations
    > people on boards where you may be serving

24. Wellington, *supra*, at 110.
25. Idem at 117.
26. Susan Abrams, *The New Success Books for Women* at 164 (Roseville, CA, Prima and Crown, 200) (quoting Marilyn Lederer).

27. Carol Gallagher, *Going to the Top* at 68–69 (New York, Viking, 2000).
28. See Chapter 11 in this volume.

20 Lessons Learned

1. Nina DiSesa, *Seducing the Boys' Club—Uncensored Tactics From a Woman at the Top* at 39 (New York, Ballantine, 2008).
2. Pat Heim & Susan Golant, *Smashing the Glass Ceiling—Tactics for Women Who Want to Win in Business* at 13 (New York, Fireside, 1995).
3. Kelly Love Johnson, *Skirt! Rules For the Workplace* (Guildford CT, Globe Pequot, 2008); Nina DiSesa, *Seducing the Boys' Club, supra.*
4. Pat Heim & Susan Golant, *Hardball for Women* (New York, Plume Penguin, 1992, rev. edn, 2005).
5. Gail Evans, *Play Like a Man, Win Like a Woman* (New York, Broadway, 2000).
6. Jean Hollands, *Same Game, Different Rules: How To Get Ahead Without Being a Bully Broad, Ice Queen, or "Ms. Understood"* (New York, McGraw Hill, 2002).
7. Betty Friedan, *The Feminine Mystique* (New York, Norton, 1963).
8. *Be Your Own Mentor, supra,* at 86.
9. Greg Mortenson & David Oliver Relin, *Three Cups of Tea* at 34 (New York, Penguin, 2006).
10. Idem at 191.
11. Idem at 88.
12. See Kara Scannell & Joanna Slater, "SEC Moves to Pull Plug on U.S. Accounting Standards," *Wall Street Journal*, Aug. 28, 2008, at A-1.

21 Conclusion: Evolving a New Paradigm for a New Century

1. Sheila Wellington, *Be Your Own Mentor* at 18 (New York, Random House, 2001).
2. Gail Evans, *Play Like a Man, Win Like a Woman* at 148–49 (New York, Broadway Books, 2000).
3. Idem at 19.
4. Idem at 113.
5. Idem at 71–2.
6. Attributed to the late Ann Richards, former governor of Texas.
7. Margaret Henning & Ann Jardim, *The Managerial Woman* at 188 (New York, Simon & Schuster, 1977).
8. Carol Gallagher, *Gong to the Top* at 127 (New York, Viking Penguin, 2000).
9. *Be Your Own Mentor* at 21.
10. Idem at 55.
11. Idem at 74, 77.
12. *Going to the Top* at 93.
13. *Play Like a Man, Win Like a Woman* at 129–30.
14. *Be Your Own Mentor* at 88–89.
15. Idem at 86.
16. *Play Like a Man, Win Like a Woman* at 39.
17. Idem at 86 (quoting Dorrit Bern, CEO of Charming Shoppes, Inc.).
18. Cf. Esther Wachs Book, *Why the Best Man for the Job is a Woman* at 2 (New York, Harper Bsuiness, 2000) (women interviewed fit *"the* paradigm").

Index